Science Fairs with Style

A Comprehensive, Step-by-Step Guide to Running a Successful Science Fair Program

by
Jerry DeBruin

illustrated by Charles Ortenblad

Cover by Jeff Van Kanegan

3/2004 JFund $27

Copyright © Good Apple, 1991

ISBN No. 0-86653-606-X

Printing No. 98

Good Apple, Inc.
A Division of Frank Schaffer Publications, Inc.
23740 Hawthorne Boulevard
Torrance, CA 90505-5927

SPECIAL THANKS

- The author thanks all the fifth-grade youngsters who participated in the Science Fair Mentorship Program. Your efforts made this book possible.
- The author thanks Mrs. Ruth Flaskamp, Mrs. Carolyn Boellner and Mrs. Karen Sigler, fifth-grade teachers at Stranahan Elementary School, Sylvania, Ohio, for their determination at seeing the Science Fair Mentorship Program become a reality.
- The author thanks Mr. George Offenburg, principal, Stranahan Elementary School, Sylvania, Ohio, for his support of the Science Fair Mentorship Program.
- The author thanks members of the community of Sylvania, Ohio, including parents, judges and members of the media, all of whom made the Science Fair Mentorship Program a huge success.
- The author thanks Mr. Zeny Pytlinski, retired skills tradesperson, who helped the students build science fair models and backdrop display boards from wood and triple wall for the Science Fair.
- The author thanks Dr. Frank P. Saul, Medical College of Ohio at Toledo for his assistance in the identification of members of the faculty who acted as mentors for the fifth-grade students.
- The author thanks members of the faculty at the Medical College of Ohio at Toledo who acted as mentors for the fifth-grade students.
- The author thanks his university students who acted as mentors for the fifth-grade students and for their suggestions, thoughtful ideas and comments.
- The author thanks Ms. Miriam Kassem who recorded significant events during the Science Fair Mentorship Program which subsequently formed the basis of her Master of Education Degree Project.
- The author thanks Mr. Thomas Gibbs, B.S.Ed., M.Ed., J.D., retired teacher, counselor, naval officer and locomotive engineer for his kind contributions, suggestions and assistance in making this book the best book that it could be.
- The author thanks Mrs. Zhiping Wang, doctoral student, who typed a rough draft of this book.
- The author thanks Mrs. Tina Hughes, secretary, who typed portions of the rough draft of this book.
- The author thanks Mrs. Michelle Hudson, secretary, who typed the final version of this book before it was submitted to the publisher.
- The author thanks members of the Martha Holden Jennings Foundation, Cleveland, Ohio, for their financial support of the Science Fair Mentorship Program.
- The author thanks Mr. David Link, earth science teacher, Port Clinton City Schools, Port Clinton, Ohio, for his visionary outlook and support.
- The author thanks the National Science Teachers Association, Ohio Academy of Science, Heldref Publications, Society for Personality Research, Inc., and the Institute of Laboratory Animal Resources for the use of selected materials in this book.

GA1325

DEDICATION

Of all the 4.5 billion people in the world, YOU, as a unique human being, have been chosen as one for whom this book is dedicated. Why? With the purchase of this book you have taken a risk, a risk that represents the first step towards a new and exciting chapter in your life. In the end, of all the people who *wonder* about the efforts of its contents, only one knows—YOU—and those who you choose to know.

PASTE an "I am special" photo of yourself here. THEN stare at yourself and just wonder . . .

GA1325

TABLE OF CONTENTS

GA1325

INTRODUCTION: A SPECIAL NOTE TO TEACHERS ON BEING SPECIAL

Dear Friends,

Thank you for the many kind comments about my previous twenty-one books—Touching & Teaching Metrics Series; *Cardboard Carpentry; Creative, Hands-On Science Experiences*; the Young Scientists Explore Series, Intermediate; *Scientists Around the World; Look to the Sky; School Yard-Backyard Cycles of Science* and *Creative Hands-On Science Cards & Activities*—all published by Good Apple from 1977-1990.

In conversations with people from all walks of life, I am always impressed with the number of positive comments made about teachers. "Other than parents, the teacher was the single most important influence in my child's life," parents often remark. Students frequently say, "Boy, I was really messed up, but my sixth-grade teacher really turned my life around." Thus YOU should know that YOU are special because YOU often determine whether a child succeeds or fails in life.

In conversations with YOU, I am always impressed with your genuine openness, thought-provoking questions, and insightful comments and suggestions. In fact, this book, *Science Fairs with Style*, is a result of listening to YOU, parents and members of various communities who often ask, "How can I get my kids interested in science?" *Science Fairs with Style* is an attempt to answer this question. Because of the interdisciplinary nature of the topic "science fairs," *Science Fairs with Style* is written for people of all ages and for those in any occupation. Classroom teachers, administrators and members of the community including parents; scientists; representatives from the media, business and industry; youth leaders and community volunteers such as retired people will hopefully find it useful. Based on our experience of directing a successful Science Fair Mentorship Program, *Science Fairs with Style* is designed first to prompt students to ask "why" and "what would happen if" type questions and then develop science fair projects based on these questions.

In an ever-changing society, there is a growing need for students to become actively involved in problem-solving science using science process skills with application of the knowledge gained in school directly to an everyday life setting. *Science Fairs with Style* meets this need with its unique format and contents. *Science Fairs with Style* is grounded in and supports current research findings in science education. Convenient, ready-to-use teacher and student materials support these findings in at least eight ways. First, the science fair activities are "hands-on" and reinforce the notion that people learn science best by becoming involved in concrete experiences, rather than by mere rote memorization of abstract, trivial and unrelated facts. Second, concepts mastered when doing the activities are appropriate for the developmental level of elementary, middle, junior and senior high school students. All students, teachers and parents who choose to become involved will find the activities challenging and useful. Third, the activities help teachers, students and parents reach the #1 goal of education which is to stimulate people to think, then take action. In addition, the activities feature an extensive utilization of higher order thinking and process skills. Memorization of irrelevant facts, at the knowledge level only, is kept to a minimum. Fourth, activities help teachers and parents involve students in experiences that will enable students to master concepts well beyond those found in the standard curriculum in commercially available textbook series. Fifth, the activities feature the integration of science with other academic disciplines. By participating in the activities, students, teachers and parents experience an interdisciplinary, integrated view of science with an emphasis on learning *holistic* science. Sixth, the activities enable students to apply knowledge gained in school directly to their home settings. Seventh, *Science Fairs with Style* is student centered. To accomplish this goal, the activities feature individual project work. Lastly, *Science Fairs with Style* provides the necessary background information in the form of teacher tips and specific content information on the teacher pages. Thus, it is hoped that teachers, youngsters and parents will benefit by the renewed emphasis on content and methodology found throughout the book.

My hope is that the contents of *Science Fairs with Style* will touch many minds, hearts and hands and that much personal growth will be experienced by all who use the book. Keep in touch. Let me know how YOU are doing. It is always good to hear from YOU because YOU are very special. Until then, best wishes for your continued growth as a scientist and as a complete human being.

Sincerely,

Jerry DeBruin

Jerry DeBruin

GA1325

OVERVIEW: HOW TO USE THIS BOOK

The major goal of *Science Fairs with Style* is to present a detailed guide on how to conduct a year-long Science Fair Mentorship Program that includes a culminating science fair day experience. Presented in a monthly format, *Science Fairs with Style* contains pages for the teacher, appropriately marked with this symbol (T) and five reproducible packets for you to make copies of and give to Students (S), Parents (P), Community Members (C), Judges (J) and Members of the Media (M).

Because of the interdisciplinary nature of the topic "science fairs," the pages are written for people of all ages and in any occupation. Based on previous experience in running a successful Science Fair Mentorship Program, it is recommended that *Science Fairs with Style* be used an *entire* year so students experience the long-term development of a science fair study. It is also recommended that you select the pages that fit your particular grade level and situation. A word of caution, however, is that you should aim *high* as students will often rise to meet your levels of expectation.

The pages in *Science Fairs with Style* are written in an easy-to-use format. Here is a reduced sample page that shows the major features found on each teacher page.

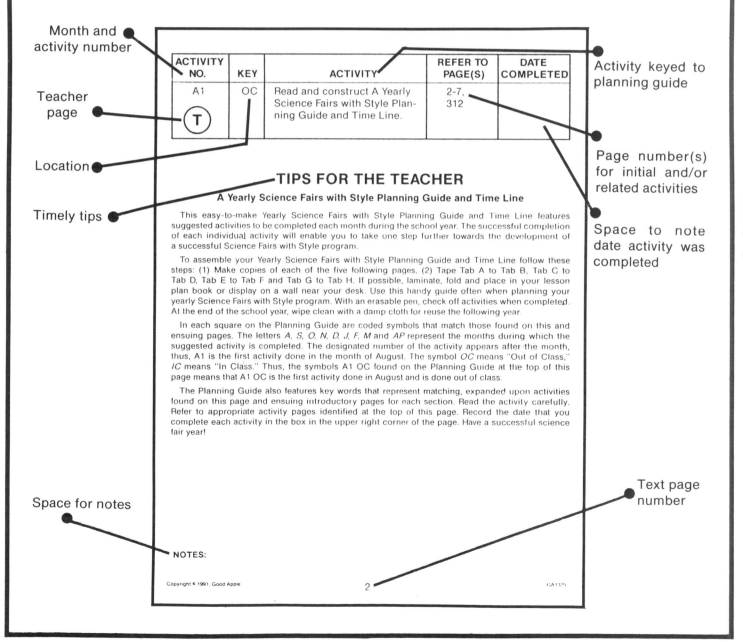

Month and activity number

Teacher page

Location

Timely tips

ACTIVITY NO.	KEY	ACTIVITY	REFER TO PAGE(S)	DATE COMPLETED
A1 (T)	OC	Read and construct A Yearly Science Fairs with Style Planning Guide and Time Line.	2-7, 312	

Activity keyed to planning guide

Page number(s) for initial and/or related activities

Space to note date activity was completed

TIPS FOR THE TEACHER
A Yearly Science Fairs with Style Planning Guide and Time Line

This easy-to-make Yearly Science Fairs with Style Planning Guide and Time Line features suggested activities to be completed each month during the school year. The successful completion of each individual activity will enable you to take one step further towards the development of a successful Science Fairs with Style program.

To assemble your Yearly Science Fairs with Style Planning Guide and Time Line follow these steps: (1) Make copies of each of the five following pages, (2) Tape Tab A to Tab B, Tab C to Tab D, Tab E to Tab F and Tab G to Tab H. If possible, laminate, fold and place in your lesson plan book or display on a wall near your desk. Use this handy guide often when planning your yearly Science Fairs with Style program. With an erasable pen, check off activities when completed. At the end of the school year, wipe clean with a damp cloth for reuse the following year.

In each square on the Planning Guide are coded symbols that match those found on this and ensuing pages. The letters A, S, O, N, D, J, F, M and AP represent the months during which the suggested activity is completed. The designated number of the activity appears after the month, thus, A1 is the first activity done in the month of August. The symbol OC means "Out of Class," IC means "In Class." Thus, the symbols A1 OC found on the Planning Guide at the top of this page means that A1 OC is the first activity done in August and is done out of class.

The Planning Guide also features key words that represent matching, expanded upon activities found on this page and ensuing introductory pages for each section. Read the activity carefully. Refer to appropriate activity pages identified at the top of this page. Record the date that you complete each activity in the box in the upper right corner of the page. Have a successful science fair year!

Space for notes

NOTES:

Text page number

2

GA1325

Each Teacher (T) page includes a planning guide in a rectangular box with smaller subdivisions that have coded symbols. Letters *A, S, O, N, D, J, F, M, AP* represent the months during which the suggested activity is completed. The designated number of the activity appears after the month, thus, A1 is the first activity done in the month of August. The symbol *OC* means "Out of Class," *IC* means "In Class." Thus, the symbols A1 OC found on the Planning Guide (page 3) and at the top of the sample (page 2) means that A1 OC is the first activity done in August and is done out of class.

The pages are easy to use. Merely read the activity at the top of the page and refer to the appropriate pages for the activity itself. In the box in the upper right corner, record the date that you complete the activity.

In addition to the planning guide at the top of each Teacher (T) page and a description of the activity, each page features a Notes section. Sometimes this section contains pertinent information but most often, the space is reserved for you to record personal reactions, pertinent information, additional tips and suggested changes. In addition to these, the space may be used for drawing your favorite scene, cartoon, doodle, mind bender, bumper sticker, T-shirt saying or postage stamp. Be sure to write about your fantasies, dreams, insights or other creative ideas because these reflections often lead to an even higher quality science fair program in the future.

If you choose to use Student (S) pages, it is recommended that you punch the pages for easy insertion into student three-ring binders. You may want to copy all student pages at the beginning of the year and have students insert the pages into three-ring binders. Review the pages so students develop a long-term perspective of the Science Fair Mentorship Program from beginning to end. Or you may choose to copy pertinent pages at selected times during the year. Once again you choose the method that best fits your style and situation.

Before you begin your Science Fair Mentorship Program, have your librarian purchase or collect some student books on science fairs. Perhaps a display or activity center could be set up in the library to generate further interest. In any event, enjoy *Science Fairs with Style*.

GA1325

INTRODUCING THE MAJOR CHARACTERS WHO APPEAR MONTHLY IN THIS BOOK

AUGUST

SEPTEMBER

OCTOBER

NOVEMBER

DECEMBER

JANUARY

FEBRUARY

MARCH

APRIL

GA1325

THEIR MONTHLY KEYS ARE . . .

Month	Key	Activity	Audience	Page(s)
August (A)	APTF	= Planning (P)	Teacher Focus (TF)	1–24
September (S)	SPSF	= Planning (P)	Student Focus (SF)	25–90
October (O)	OPPF	= Planning (P)	Parent Focus (PF)	91–130
November (N)	NPCF	= Planning (P)	Community Focus (CF)	131–162
December (D)	DPJF	= Planning (P)	Judges Focus (JF)	163–186
January (J)	JPMF	= Planning (P)	Media Focus (MF)	187–232
February (F)	FISFMF	= Implementation (I)	Science Fair Month Focus (SFM)	233–262
March (M)	METF	= Evaluation (E)	Teacher Focus (TF)	263–274
April (AP)	APRTF	= Reflections (R)	Teacher Focus (TF)	275–317

THEIR CHAPTER TITLES ARE . . .

GA1325

♍   A   P   T   F   =   **August**

Planning

Teacher

Focus

THE SCIENCE FAIR TEACHER COMMUNICATES WITH THE SELF BY LOOKING INWARD AND FORWARD

Going in Ness, Going out Ness, Ever There Ness

ACTIVITY NO.	KEY	ACTIVITY	REFER TO PAGE(S)	DATE COMPLETED
A1 Ⓣ	OC	Read and construct A Yearly Science Fairs with Style Planning Guide and Time Line.	2-7, 312	

TIPS FOR THE TEACHER

A Yearly Science Fairs with Style Planning Guide and Time Line

This easy-to-make Yearly Science Fairs with Style Planning Guide and Time Line features suggested activities to be completed each month during the school year. The successful completion of each individual activity will enable you to take one step further towards the development of a successful Science Fairs with Style program.

To assemble your Yearly Science Fairs with Style Planning Guide and Time Line follow these steps: (1) Make copies of each of the five following pages, (2) Tape Tab A to Tab B, Tab C to Tab D, Tab E to Tab F and Tab G to Tab H. If possible, laminate, fold and place in your lesson plan book or display on a wall near your desk. Use this handy guide often when planning your yearly Science Fairs with Style program. With an erasable pen, check off activities when completed. At the end of the school year, wipe clean with a damp cloth for reuse the following year.

In each square on the Planning Guide are coded symbols that match those found on this and ensuing pages. The letters *A, S, O, N, D, J, F, M* and *AP* represent the months during which the suggested activity is completed. The designated number of the activity appears after the month, thus, A1 is the first activity done in the month of August. The symbol *OC* means "Out of Class," *IC* means "In Class." Thus, the symbols A1 OC found on the Planning Guide at the top of this page means that A1 OC is the first activity done in August and is done out of class.

The Planning Guide also features key words that represent matching, expanded upon activities found on this page and ensuing introductory pages for each section. Read the activity carefully. Refer to appropriate activity pages identified at the top of this page. Record the date that you complete each activity in the box in the upper right corner of the page. Have a successful science fair year!

Meanings of Symbols on Pages 4-7: AUGUST: (1) autumn, (2) the world spirit, (3) the spirit of silver, (4) the spirit of mercury, (5) the spirit of copper, (6) the spirit of tin, (7) one pound, (8) equal quantity, (9) one dram, (10) one ounce, (11) one scruple, (12) one pinch, (13) one pint, (14) crucible, (15) still, (16) retort, (17) grille **SEPTEMBER:** none **OCTOBER:** (1) receiver, (2) skull, (3) glass dropper, (4) wick, (5-11) gold, (12) silver **NOVEMBER:** (1) silver, (2) silver, (3) copper, (4) lead, (5) antimony, (6) mercury, (7) tin, (8) nickel, (9) iron, (10) magnesia, (11) zinc, (12) steel, (13) bismuth, (14) iron filings, (15) copper splints, (16) brass, (17) glass, (18) sulphur, (19) nitre flowers, (20) red arsenic **DECEMBER:** (1) winter, (2) white arsenic, (3) arsenic sulphur, (4) yellow arsenic, (5) nitric acid, (6) aqua vitae, (7) cinder, (8) wood, (9) soot, (10) vitriol, (11) caustic lime, (12) lime, (13) cribbled ashes, (14) crystal, (15) clay, (16) borax, (17) alum, (18) soapstone **JANUARY:** (1) burned pebbles, (2) gravel, (3) burned alum, (4) chalc, (5) stone, (6) potash **FEBRUARY:** (1) nitre oil, (2) vinegar, (3) burned hartshorn, (4) urine (5) verdigris **MARCH:** (1) spring, (2) ginger, (3) manure, (4) eggshells, (5) sugar, (6) wine spirit, (7) yellow wax, (8) honey, (9) rock salt, (10) sea salt, (11) cinnabar, (12) torrefaction of gold, (13) torrefaction of silver, (14) amalgamation, (15) to mix, (16) to boil, (17) to purify, (18) to pulverize, (19) to filter, (20) to rot **APRIL:** (1) summer, (2) amalgam, (3) fumes, (4) powder, (5) to distill, (6) to sublime, (7) essence, (8) to take, (9) to compose, (10) to solve

Activity Month	**A**	**Y**	**E**	**A**	**R**	**L**
August Teacher	A1 OC Read and construct A Yearly Planning Guide and Time Line.	A2 OC Read Why Have a Science Fair?	A3 OC Read Science Fair Goals for the Teacher.	A4 OC Read and study The Science Fairs with Style Interdisciplinary Web.	A5 OC Read Science Fair Projects Should Go Beyond	A6 OC Read Science Fair Projects Should Be . . . .
September Students	S1 OC Meet with Science Fair Committee to draft guidelines.	S2 OC Follow up on Letter of Appeal for Funding.	S3 OC Meet with principal, et al., to insure February date for Science Fair.	S4 OC Set date of the Science Fair.	S5 OC Reserve location for Science Fair.	S6 OC Draft a written building request.
October Parents	O1 OC Design parents' packet. Draft cover letter to parents that explains packet.	O2 OC Include parents' volunteer and scrounge and save letters.	O3 OC Include letter of requirements, criteria and time line.	O4 OC Include article on "How Parents Can Help Their Child with a Science Fair Project."	O5 OC Include Guidelines for a Science Fair Display.	O6 OC Include parent evaluation form in packet.
November Community	N1 OC Make copies of packet for community members.	N2 OC Follow up on packets. Match mentors with students.	N3 OC Prepare spread sheet of mentor, student and teacher names.	N4 OC Prepare ten-week mentor attendance form.	N5 IC Review week-to-week schedule for October.	N6 IC Restate science topic in question or statement form.
December Judges	D1 OC Identify and contact judges.	D2 OC Make copies of packet for judges.	D3 OC Prepare a spread sheet with names of judges.	D4 OC Invite a judge to class.	D5 OC Design a student entry form.	D6 OC Design a final report form.
January Media	J1 OC Contact members of the media.	J2 OC Make copies of packet for members of the media.	J3 OC Prepare spread sheet of names of members of the media.	J4 OC Invite a member of the media to class.	J5 OC Publicize the Science Fair.	J6 OC Place science fair message on school marque.
February Science Fair Month	F1 OC Develop final schedule for judges.	F2 OC Send final letter with abstracts to judges.	F3 OC Prepare judges' folders.	F4 OC Identify hosts to greet all who attend.	F5 OC Assign exhibit numbers.	F6 OC Set up tables and microphones.
March Teacher	M1 OC Print names on award certificates.	M2 OC Send thank-you notes and letters.	M3 OC Tally results of final evaluation surveys.	M4 OC Publicize results of Science Fair.	M5 OC Develop data bank of science fair topics.	M6 OC Place photographs in photo albums.
April Teacher	AP1 OC Plan an article for publication.	AP2 OC Read "Teach, Reflect and Write." Write, submit article for publication.	AP3 OC Assist students in writing articles for publication.	AP4 OC Gather data for support of grant proposal activity.	AP5 OC Write and submit grant proposal.	AP6 OC Write, submit and present a paper at a professional conference.

TAB A

GA1325

Y	S	C	I	E	N	C
A7 OC Read Student's Guide to Science Fair Safety.	A8 OC Read Student's Guidelines on Working with Animals.	A9 OC Read Science Fair Guidelines on Human Subjects.	A10 OC Read Student's Science Fair Glossary.	A11 OC Read Science Fair Symbols and Abbreviations.	A12 OC Draft a Parents' Volunteer Letter.	A13 OC Contact funding agencies with a letter of appeal for funding.
S7 OC Meet with food service personnel for science fair location.	S8 OC Introduce Science Fair at first staff meeting.	S9 OC Explore cross-grade level science fair programs.	S10 OC Explore inter-disciplinary Science Fair.	S11 OC Encourage inter and cross-departmental science fair projects.	S12 OC Visits to recruit science fair students.	S13 OC Data based listing of science fair projects.
O7 OC Copy science fair packet and distribute to parents.	O8 OC Meet with parents to discuss weekly time line.	O9 OC Save other teachers' students' work for science fair projects.	O10 OC Meet with public library personnel on availability of science fair materials.	O11 OC Meet with school librarian on availability of science fair materials.	O12 OC Reserve vacant school room for science fair projects.	O13 OC Give students week-to-week schedule of science fair activity.
N7 IC Student oral report of initial observations.	N8 IC Outline and rough draft of paper reviewed.	N9 IC Record of observations in diary or logbook.	N10 IC Graphing of simulated results. Review variables.	 (1)	 (2)	 (3)
D7 IC Week-to-week December schedule.	D8 IC Statistical analyses.	D9 IC Meeting the mentors.	D10 IC Oral and written progress reports.	D11 IC Reporting changes in project activities.	D12 IC Rough draft of paper due.	 (1)
J7 OC Operation Science Fair Breakdown.	J8 OC Hold a program cover design contest.	J9 OC Identify winner of program design contest.	J10 OC School media director to make videotape and take photos.	J11 OC Arrange for refreshments.	J12 OC Publicize the Science Fair.	J13 OC Science Fair awards and certificates.
F7 OC Form Tabulation Committee.	F8 IC Conduct classroom Science Fair.	F9 IC Have students revise presentations.	F10 IC Review final schedule for Science Fair.	F11 IC Distribute final checklist to students.	F12 IC Post lists of projects and maps at various locations.	F13 IC Projects set up by students.
M7 OC Give results to all who participated.	M8 IC Parents and students revise projects.	M9 IC Students enter district, state and national science fairs.	M10 IC Tally results of final evaluation surveys.	 (1)	 (2)	 (3)
AP7 OC Use student recruiters for next year's Science Fair.	AP8 OC Publicize next year's science fair date and entry deadline.	AP9 OC Encourage summer science for students.	AP10 OC Relax, enjoy the summer feeling of accomplishment and contentment.	 (1)	 (2)	 (3)

TAB B

TAB C

GA1325

E	F	A	I	R	P	L
(1)	(2)	(3)	(4)	(5)	(6)	(7)

S14 IC	S15 IC	S16 IC	S17 IC	S18 IC	S19 IC	S20 IC
Introduce Science Fair to students.	Introduce science fair goals for student.	Student Science Fair Project Should Go Beyond	A Student's Science Fair Project Is	What Is the Scientific Method?	A Student's Guide to Science Fair Safety	Student's Safety Contract

O14 IC	O15 IC	O16 IC	O17 IC	O18 IC		
Review scientific method.	Do controlled experiment using the scientific method.	Require students to write summaries of their controlled experiments.	Help students narrow down science fair topic.	Require students to choose final science fair topics and begin work promptly.	(1)	(2)

(4)	(5)	(6)	(7)	(8)	(9)	(10)
(2)	(3)	(4)	(5)	(6)	(7)	(8)

J14 OC	J15 OC	J16 OC	J17 IC	J18 IC	J19 IC	J20 IC
Plan final science fair schedule.	Send invitations to support groups.	Send invitations to mentors and resource personnel.	Have students write press releases.	Have students draw final conclusions from data collected.	Have students type final written papers.	Have students construct backdrop display.

F14 IC	F15 IC	F16 IC	F17 IC	F18 IC	F19 IC	F20 IC
Reminder to dress appropriately.	Hold school Science Fair.	Media Director makes videotape.	Media Director takes photographs.	Have student hosts greet all who attend.	Hold meeting with judges before judging.	Reminder: only students and judges in judging area.

(4)	(5)	(6)	(7)	(8)	(9)	(10)
(4)	(5)	(6)	(7)	(8)	(9)	(10)

TAB D

TAB E

GA1325

A	N	A	N	D	T	I
(8)	(9)	(10)	(11)	(12)	(13)	(14)
S21 IC Student's Guidelines on Working with Animals	**S22** IC Student Vertebrate Animal Certificate	**S23** IC Student's Science Fair Glossary	**S24** IC Student's Guide to Symbols and Abbreviations	**S25** IC Student's Science Fair Contract	**S26** IC Student's Monthly Project Completion Schedule	**S27** IC Judging Criteria for Science Fair Projects
(3)	(4)	(5)	(6)	(7)	(8)	(9)
(11)	(12)	(13)	(14)	(15)	(16)	(17)
(9)	(10)	(11)	(12)	(13)	(14)	(15)
J21 IC Student audio and/or videotape presentations	**J22** IC Students present results to various classes.	**J23** IC Students write abstracts for judges.	**J24** IC Students complete entry forms.	(1)	(2)	(3)
F21 IC Tabulation of results.	**F22** IC Hold awards ceremony.	**F23** IC Judges complete next year's volunteer form.	**F24** IC Distribute final evaluation surveys to be completed by all attending.	**F25** OC Post thank-you notice on school marque.	(1)	(2)
(11)	(12)	(13)	(14)	(15)	(16)	(17)

TAB F

TAB G

GA1325

M	E	L	I N E . . .

(15)	(16)	(17)
S28 IC High-Quality Research Project	S29 IC How to Write Science Fair Reports	S30 IC Possible Science Fair Topics and Ideas
(10)	(11)	(12)
(18)	(19)	(20)
(16)	(17)	(18)
(4)	(5)	(6)
(3)	(4)	(5)
(18)	(19)	(20)

TAB H

HOW TO USE A YEARLY SCIENCE FAIR PLAN AND TIME LINE

When assembled, pages 3-7 make up this time line. For easy reference each cell on the time line is coded to the corresponding page in the text itself. Symbol A1 OC is found both on the time line and in the text.

It is recommended that you laminate the time line after it is assembled. Some teachers post the time line in the classroom, others prefer to keep it in their lesson plan books or taped to their desks. Make an X through the cell on the time line as you complete each activity. Record the date on the corresponding text page. At the end of the school year, observe the number of completed cells in the completion of a successful science fair. To reuse the time line in the future, merely wipe it clean with a damp cloth. Then the time line will be ready for use next year.

Planning a successful science fair is similar to the process used by ancient astronomers and alchemists in perfecting their methods that led to many modern day advancements in science. Some of their symbols, along with others, are noted on this time line. The names of the symbols are found on page 2 of the text if you and your students are curious to find out what they mean. Of course, there are some blank squares to fill in extra activities and symbols.

Good luck.

GA1325

ACTIVITY NO.	KEY	ACTIVITY	REFER TO PAGE(S)	DATE COMPLETED
A2 ⓣ	OC	Read Why Have a Science Fair?	8-9, 313	

TIPS FOR THE TEACHER
Why Have a Science Fair?

There are many reasons why you may want to involve your students in the development of science fair projects. Generally, for many teachers, planning and carrying out a successful science fair represents the ultimate challenge in teaching. Throughout the experience, many teachers find that their total science program is enriched. Consequently, the school's commitment to science education is solidified as students, when doing science fair projects, gain knowledge and skills that are applied directly to real-life settings.

Science fair projects have the potential for building a student's self-esteem by allowing for individualized attention and thus the expression of individual differences. Students who never achieve the highest grades on any test may shine while doing science fair projects. This success builds morale which carries over to other areas in the regular classroom.

Specifically, when you conduct a science fair, you will find that science fair projects provide students with hands-on purposeful inquiry. Science fair projects provide students with an excellent opportunity to understand the scientific method and learn that science is a human endeavor which does not have all the answers but does provide a method for asking questions.

When involved in science fairs, you will find that students understand that science is an integral part of life. For some, science *is* life. Students first learn how to develop and then master the process skills of science such as observing, inferring, measuring, collecting data, communicating and forming conclusions. Students use the process skills inherent in the scientific method in an effort to identify and interpret interactions between experimental variables and controls. The scientific method used in problem solving is unique to science and has valuable carryover to life in general. Thus, involving students in a science fair is a superb way to promote student learning about scientists and how they actually work.

While using science process skills, you will notice that some of your students learn a great deal by observing and communicating with others who are doing science fair experiments. An added advantage when helping students with their science fair projects is that it provides an excellent opportunity for you to get to know them and their interests.

You will also find that science fair projects help students view the world with a holistic perspective. Science is viewed as being interdisciplinary and cyclic in nature with a vast potential for being an interest generator and motivator. By nature, science fair projects are interdisciplinary and can be used to stimulate student interest in other areas of the curriculum and life in general. Thus, working on science projects can be a profitable interdisciplinary activity that permeates many other academic disciplines in the curriculum.

If your school subject matter areas are taught by specialists, science fairs allow for the inclusion of these teachers as part of your science fair program. English teachers and librarians can assist in reading and writing related to science fair projects. Working on the projects can, and should, include periodic progress reports in logbooks. This gives students practical opportunities in other subject matter areas to develop and apply reading and writing skills in a lifelong setting. By doing this, students become aware of the interdisciplinary nature of science and can view the world in a holistic perspective.

GA1325

In the presentation of a science fair project, there are also opportunities for correlation of science with art, industrial arts and mathematics. This correlation is strongly recommended. You must be careful, however, not to let a science fair project become an art project which is only science related. The display must not become an end in itself, but rather a means of communicating what the student has achieved in the science fair study.

In essence, science fair projects help students develop reading and writing skills that enable them to master a sequence of science fair concepts appropriate for their developmental level of maturity. An understanding of these concepts helps students develop their own innate abilities to the fullest extent possible.

You will also note that science fairs supply a welcome opportunity for students to use higher order thinking skills such as critical thinking. Science projects are an effective means to stimulate a student's imagination by encouraging this independent thinking. In addition, science fair projects also provide students with an opportunity to critically examine the possible sociological implications of technological decision making. As citizens in a democratic society, students have the responsibility to make informed decisions about present and future scientific fields of study and understand what effects such studies have on a global society. Science fair projects also help students make decisions in related areas and thus promote lifelong learning on the part of the students.

Science fair projects are often the means by which students discover scientific interests. These interests may lead to vocational choices or hobbies in science. Thus, beyond preparation for citizenship, students need high level experiences that demonstrate the value of science as a viable career choice. Many vocations in existence today will cease to exist tomorrow. The number of vocations that require a hands-on, problem solving, challenging, holistic, creative, interdisciplinary and ever-changing view of the world will show a marked increase in the future. Teachers and parents who involve students in science fair projects provide opportunities for students to identify science as a viable career choice to meet the needs of an ever-changing world.

For advanced students, superior work on science fair projects can also be an important consideration for college admissions and scholarships. There are some monetary awards. Others come in the form of trips to science functions for students with outstanding research projects. The time to provide science fair experience is *early* in a student's life so long-term planning for the achievement of future long-range goals can be done.

Science fairs also promote superior public relations and extend the role of the school into the community. Science fairs are an excellent way to familiarize adults with the school. A PTA meeting, Parents' Night, or a special Science Fair Night that is centered around student science projects can bring out large numbers of parents, grandparents and other family members. Science fair projects provide an opportunity for parents to see something tangible that indicates their children are learning science concepts and processes in school.

You will find that science fairs can create a partnership between parents, business leaders, members of the media and schools. For example, when parents help guide student projects, they become more actively involved in their child's education. When business leaders judge science fair projects or offer financial support for a science fair, stronger ties are established between the school and the community. Science fairs are an excellent way to help your community become aware of various academic programs and opportunities offered in your school. Thus, you will find that members of your community will support you in your efforts. Working on science fair projects will enable you to grow personally and professionally. You will often be called upon to speak to various community groups about your program. You will also have opportunities to write for publication and give presentations at conferences for educators in an effort to spread the word that involvement in science fairs can help people become the best people they can be and, in essence, make the world a better place in which to live. That's what teaching is all about.

NOTES:

ACTIVITY NO.	KEY	ACTIVITY	REFER TO PAGE(S)	DATE COMPLETED
A3 (T)	OC	Read Science Fair Goals for the Teacher. Make a copy of yearly goals. Place in a sealed envelope. In April, open the envelope to learn whether you have reached your goals. Then set new goals for the second year.	10, 40, 303-307	

TIPS FOR THE TEACHER

Science Fair Goals for the Teacher

Science fairs have become an American tradition that often reflects the specific needs of your students, school and community. The following goals are generic in nature and are designed to stimulate your thinking on how your science fair can meet the needs of your students, school and community. Feel free to modify, delete or add further goals to meet the needs of your particular situation.

My goals in the development of a science fair program are

1. To motivate students and give them an opportunity to conduct scientific research using available resources.

2. To provide students with an opportunity to gain self-esteem and confidence in setting and accomplishing realistic, individual goals.

3. To provide students an opportunity to develop science research skills using the scientific method. These skills are valuable in later schooling and life.

4. To provide students with an opportunity to develop higher order, critical thinking skills.

5. To provide students with an opportunity to develop skills in the use of technological innovations and equipment.

6. To provide students with an opportunity to enhance library skills and access information by using basic retrieval systems and data bases.

7. To provide students with an opportunity to exchange, both orally and in writing, scientific ideas with other students, teachers, parents and the members of the general public.

8. To give students an opportunity to display their scientific talent and receive recognition for their talent.

9. To motivate students to pursue a career in science, mathematics, engineering and the social sciences.

10. To involve teachers who teach other academic disciplines in learning the value of interdisciplinary planning and learning in the development of science fair projects.

11. To increase parental involvement and involve them and their youngsters in the process of gaining knowledge of themselves, others and the world around them.

12. To increase community involvement in the process of carrying out a successful community Science Fair Mentorship Program.

Extension: Use these goals when writing a grant proposal (page 303) to obtain funding for your Science Fair Mentorship Program.

NOTES:

GA1325

ACTIVITY NO.	KEY	ACTIVITY	REFER TO PAGE(S)	DATE COMPLETED
A4 (T)	OC	Read and study The Yearly Science Fairs with Style Interdisciplinary Web.	11, 35	

THE YEARLY SCIENCE FAIRS WITH STYLE INTERDISCIPLINARY WEB

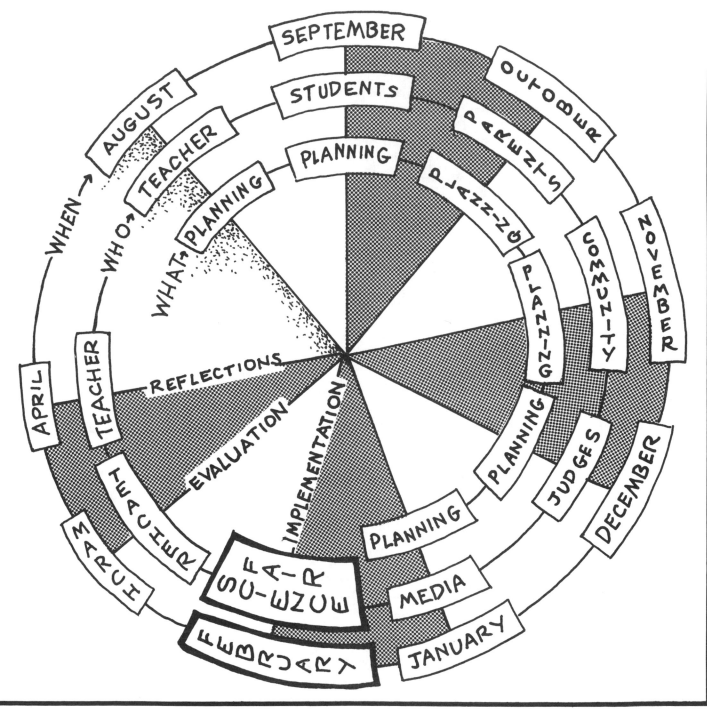

ACTIVITY NO.	KEY	ACTIVITY	REFER TO PAGE(S)	DATE COMPLETED
A5 Ⓣ	OC	Read Science Fair Projects Should Go Beyond	12-13, 41-42	

TIPS FOR THE TEACHER
Science Fair Projects Should Go Beyond . . . .

Science teachers need to examine objectively and critically the types of science fair projects exhibited over time and ask themselves a basic question, "Are the projects done for science fairs really 'science'?"

The major criterion emphasized throughout this book in the development of a science fair project is the use of the scientific method. Frequently, however, an examination of science fair projects often reveals a widespread emphasis on "nonscientific" projects which are often rewarded with "superior" or "excellent" ratings by judges. The following includes an examination of a few of these "nonscientific" projects. These include book reports, art projects, models/mock-ups, hobbies/collections, technological innovations and research studies. Should these "nonscientific" projects be eliminated from science fairs? Certainly not! Teachers can use these projects especially at the early elementary school level, as a starting point to encourage students to incorporate and extend these activities into projects that are genuinely "scientific," that is, if they employ the scientific method.

BOOK REPORTS
A book report is a project in which the student identifies a topic of interest and obtains a book about such a topic. The book is read and a written and/or an oral report of its contents is usually done. A book report can be extended into a genuine science fair project by asking a question about a specific study or principle described in the book, designing a study and testing a hypothesis about such study or principle.

ART PROJECTS
Art projects that feature drawings or paintings of various pieces of scientific equipment or principles are often displayed at science fairs. Although not a genuine science fair project, a drawing or painting can be extended into a genuine science fair project with the actual testing of the scientific apparatus or principle drawn in an effort to actually solve a problem related to such phenomena.

MODELS/MOCK-UPS
Students often obtain a commercial model/mock-up or construct such a model/mock-up for a science fair project. They are often able to demonstrate or explain a scientific principle about something or how something works. Students usually do library reading about their topics. They then collect and assemble materials to demonstrate various scientific principles.

HOBBIES/COLLECTIONS
Hobbies and collections are often exhibited by students at science fairs. Rock and leaf collections are examples of this activity. You can extend these collections easily into science fair projects by posing questions, testing genuine experimental hypotheses and drawing conclusions about such collections.

GA1325

TECHNOLOGICAL INNOVATIONS

Many times students invent things that feature unique ways to accomplish a task. Although these inventions are not genuine science fair projects, they are useful because they do require students to think about and manipulate actual materials. Science principles are demonstrated in the process as students often start with an object and make it better, or design a complicated procedure to follow or accomplish a simple task.

RESEARCH STUDIES

A research study is one in which the student identifies a topic of interest and conducts a library investigation to obtain as much information about the topic as possible. Encyclopedias, books, almanacs and interviews with knowledgeable people who have expertise in an area are used. After the information is collected, the student writes a research paper or gives an oral presentation on the research study.

It should be emphasized that the "nonscientific" projects outlined above such as book reports, art projects, models/mock-ups, hobbies/collections, technological innovations and research studies *can* be used as introductory investigations that, when pursued and extended, can lead to superior "scientific" science fair projects that employ the scientific method.

Extension: You may want to set up a separate judging category for the scientific investigations described above or have "A Science Investigation Fair" especially for younger students. This would motivate students and teachers to investigate "true" science fair projects as the separate judging category or a special science fair would guarantee recognition for such projects. Over the years, the scientific investigation projects would evolve into "true" science fair projects based on the use of the scientific method. In addition, you may want to remind students that science fair projects do not necessarily feature a new discovery or an original piece of research; they can be a different way of looking at something already done. Emphasize, however, that true science fair projects are not enlarged models or drawings, reports, constructing a model from a kit or a weekend task often done by parents to help the student meet a deadline for the Science Fair. Emphasize that a true science fair project involves the use of the scientific method in gathering data to solve a problem of interest to the student over a long period of time.

NOTES:

ACTIVITY NO.	KEY	ACTIVITY	REFER TO PAGE(S)	DATE COMPLETED
A6 ⓉT	OC	Read Science Fair Projects Should Be	14, 43, 63	

TIPS FOR THE TEACHER

Science Fair Projects Should Be . . . .

This book is based on the belief that students should DO science fair projects that involve use of the scientific method. The scientific method involves using the processes of science to actually solve a particular problem. Some processes inherent in the scientific method include imagining, creating, observing, predicting, experimenting, classifying, measuring, inferring, collecting and interpreting data, evaluating and communicating. When involved in science fair projects, students master the processes of science and learn about what scientists actually do. Based on their experiences, basic beliefs held by students and their teachers are often modified to include the following beliefs:

1. Students best learn how to do science fair projects when they are active learners engaged in hands-on studies rather than passive learners involved in activities that require mere writing about some topic. In other words, students *learn first by doing* and then by thinking about what they have done.

2. Students best learn how to do science fair projects when they attack problems that are directly related to their everyday lives. This allows students to critically examine the sociological implications of technology-based decision making. In essence, students need to know how to access and retrieve information in an effort to develop the best science fair projects they can produce.

3. Students best learn how to do science fair projects when they are engaged in hands-on activities that develop sequential science concepts appropriate for their developmental age level of maturity. Many hands-on activities require the mastery of reading and writing skills. Students master sequential science concepts appropriate for their developmental level by using these skills.

4. Students best learn how to do science fair projects when they develop an understanding of the interdisciplinary nature of science and recognize how science is an integral part of *all* other academic disciplines both in and out of school. Teachers can do the same.

5. Students best learn how to do science fair projects when they are engaged in scientific activities that provide experiences and information on career opportunities in science. Hopefully, careers in science, engineering or related areas will be the choices of your students as they master the processes of science inherent in the scientific method.

NOTES:

GA1325

ACTIVITY NO.	KEY	ACTIVITY	REFER TO PAGE(S)	DATE COMPLETED
A7 (T)	OC	Read Student's Guide to Science Fair Safety.	15, 44-45, 64	

TIPS FOR THE TEACHER
Student's Guide to Science Fair Safety

Following proper safety precautions is essential when having students do science fair projects both in and out of school. The following includes some general safety precautions to follow. Careful planning preparation can prevent many accidents. For further information on safety, contact Flinn Scientific Inc., P.O. Box 219, Batavia, IL 60510 and the National Science Teachers Association, 1742 Connecticut Avenue, N.W., Washington, D.C. 20009.

As a teacher, be aware of the importance of following safety rules to ensure your own safety and the safety of others.

1. Be aware of safety hazards inherent in projects suggested by students.
2. Encourage parents to be on the lookout for hazards. Encourage students to have ample space in which to do their projects. Arrange equipment and supplies so they are easily accessible.
3. If your classroom is used for projects, familiarize yourself with the location of all safety equipment.
4. Have students use only the equipment and materials necessary to do the science fair projects.
5. Inform students of the proper safety procedures to follow if an accident should occur.
6. Encourage students to work with someone when they are handling equipment and materials while doing their projects.
7. Stress that students should wear proper clothing including safety goggles and aprons when doing science fair projects. Also tie back long hair and push up long sleeves.
8. Be certain that students dispose of (recycle) all broken equipment and materials properly.
9. Stress that students should keep their work area clean after completing each day's work on their projects.
10. Introduce students to the international safety symbols used in science. (See page 64 for these symbols.)

Extension: Have students and parents read and sign the Student's Safety Contract on page 65. Keep the contract on file. See *Creative Hands-On Science Cards & Activities* by Jerry DeBruin, (Good Apple, Inc., 1990, pp. 12-18) for a complete Learning Activity Packet on science safety that features handy cards and activities for student use.

NOTES:

GA1325

ACTIVITY NO.	KEY	ACTIVITY	REFER TO PAGE(S)	DATE COMPLETED
A8 (T)	OC	Read Student's Guidelines on Working with Animals.	16–17, 46–47	

TIPS FOR THE TEACHER
Student's Guidelines on Working with Animals

The purpose of this section is to identify basic principles involved in the humane care and use of laboratory animals in science fair projects. The following principles were prepared by The Council, Institute of Laboratory Animal Resources National Research Council, and are recommended whenever animals are used in precollege education or in science fair projects.

PRINCIPLES AND GUIDELINES
FOR THE USE OF ANIMALS IN PRECOLLEGE EDUCATION

The humane study of animals in precollege education can provide important learning experiences in science and ethics and should be encouraged. Maintaining classroom pets in preschool and grade school can teach respect for other species, as well as proper animal husbandry practices. Introduction of secondary school students to animal studies in closely supervised settings can reinforce those early lessons and teach the principles of humane care and use of animals in scientific inquiry. The National Research Council recommends compliance with the following principles whenever animals are used in precollege education or in science fair projects.

Principle 1. Observational and natural history studies that are not intrusive (that is, do not interfere with an animal's health or well-being or cause it discomfort) are encouraged for all classes of organisms. When an intrusive study of a living organism is deemed appropriate, consideration should be given first to using plants (including lower plants such as yeast and fungi) and invertebrates with no nervous systems or with primitive ones (including protozoa, planaria and insects). Intrusive studies of invertebrates with advanced nervous systems (such as octopi) and vertebrates should be used only when lower invertebrates are not suitable and only under the conditions stated below in Principle 10.

Principle 2. Supervision shall be provided by individuals who are knowledgeable about and experienced with the health, husbandry, care and handling of the animal species used and who understand applicable laws, regulations and policies.

Principle 3. Appropriate care for animals must be provided daily, including weekends, holidays and other times when school is not in session. This care must include:

a. nutritious food and clean, fresh water
b. clean housing with space and enrichment suitable for normal species behaviors
c. temperature and lighting appropriate for the species

Principle 4. Animals should be healthy and free of diseases that can be transmitted to humans or other animals. Veterinary care must be provided as needed.

Principle 5. Students and teachers should report immediately to the school health authority all scratches, bites and other injuries; allergies; or illnesses.

GA1325

T

Principle 6. Prior to obtaining animals for educational purposes, it is imperative that the school develop a plan for their procurement and ultimate disposition. Animals must not be captured from or released into the wild without the approval of the responsible wildlife and public health officials. When euthanasia is necessary, it should be performed in accordance with the most recent recommendations of the American Veterinary Medical Association's "Panel Report on Euthanasia" (*Journal of the American Veterinary Medical Association* 188[3]: 252-268, 1986, et seq.). It should be performed only by someone trained in the appropriate technique.

Principle 7. Students should not conduct experimental procedures on animals that:
a. are likely to cause pain or discomfort or interfere with an animal's health or well being
b. induce nutritional deficiencies or toxicities
c. expose animals to microorganisms, ionizing radiation, cancer-producing agents or any other harmful drugs or chemicals capable of causing disease, injury or birth defects in humans or animals

In general, procedures that cause pain in humans are considered to cause pain in other vertebrates.

Principle 8. Experiments on avian embryos that might result in abnormal chicks or in chicks that might experience pain or discomfort shall be terminated seventy-two hours prior to the expected date of hatching. The eggs shall be destroyed to prevent inadvertent hatching.

Principle 9. Behavioral conditioning studies shall not involve aversive stimuli. In studies using positive reinforcement, animals should not be deprived of water; food deprivation intervals should be appropriate for the species but should not continue longer than twenty-four hours.

Principle 10. A plan for conducting an experiment with living animals must be prepared in writing and approved prior to initiating the experiment or to obtaining the animals. Proper experimental design of projects and concern for animal welfare are important learning experiences and contribute to respect for and appropriate care of animals. The plan shall be reviewed by a committee composed of individuals who have the knowledge to understand and evaluate it and who have the authority to approve or disapprove it. The written plan should include the following:
a. a statement of the specific hypotheses or principles to be tested, illustrated or taught
b. a summary of what is known about the subject under study, including references
c. a justification for the use of the species selected and consideration of why a lower vertebrate or invertebrate cannot be used
d. a detailed description of the methods and procedures to be used, including experimental design; data analysis; and all aspects of animal procurement, care, housing, use and disposal

Exceptions: Exceptions to Principles 7-10 may be granted under special circumstances by a panel appointed by the school principal or his/her designee. This panel should consist of at least three individuals including a science teacher, a teacher of a nonscience subject and a scientist or veterinarian who has expertise in the subject matter involved.[1] At least one panel member should be affiliated with the school or Science Fair, and none should be a member of the student's family.

---

[1]In situations where an appropriate scientist is not available to assist the student, ILAR might be able to provide referrals. Contact ILAR, National Research Council, 2101 Constitution Avenue, N.W., Washington, D.C. 20418 (202/334-2590).

Reprinted from the *Institute of Laboratory Animal Resources News*, Volume 31, Number 3, Summer, 1989. Copyright © 1989 National Academy Press, National Academy of Science, Institute of Laboratory Animal Resources. Used with permission. Reprints of these principles in brochure form are available from Institute of Laboratory Animal Resources, National Research Council, 2101 Constitution Avenue, N.W., Washington, D.C. 20418.

GA1325

SPECIFIC TIPS FOR THE TEACHER ON HOW TO CARE FOR AND HANDLE ANIMALS IN THE CLASSROOM

1. Do your homework. Have a special purpose in mind. Plan and prepare *before* bringing any animal into the classroom.

2. Contact the state agency responsible for the development of humane laws and procedures for animals. Some states prohibit the caging of certain animals, so it is important to become familiar with your state's animal laws and regulations.

3. Know specific requirements for each animal such as food, water, exercise, environmental temperature, living space, sanitation and rest. Check school board policy on the use of animals.

4. Inform principal and janitorial staff about animal needs. Find out temperature of school on weekends or during vacations.

5. Have only responsible students, under the direct supervision of the teacher, care for the animals. Set up a daily schedule for feeding and cleaning.

6. Know and use scientific terms when discussing the features, characteristics and behavior of any animal. Find out if veterinary care is available. Ask a veterinarian to come to the class to share information.

7. Tell students to leave native wild animals in their natural habitats. These animals do *not* adapt well to a classroom setting, plus they may carry diseases that produce germs, viruses and parasites.

8. Exotic animals such as snakes and monkeys should be brought into the classroom only by experienced people from an agency such as a zoo.

9. All animals in the classroom must be caged, on a leash or confined by other means in appropriate containers.

10. Use a variety of locally acquired organisms in your classroom. Students obtain additional knowledge about organisms found in their everyday environment.

11. Try to keep a stock supply of organisms to replenish organisms for individual projects. However, avoid overcrowding of organisms.

12. All animals should be handled gently by the teacher and should have ample time for eating, exercise and rest.

13. Avoid teasing, abusing or frightening the animals. If loose, animals are potentially harmful to students and themselves.

14. Make special provisions (food, water, comfort, safety) if animals are to be left in the classroom.

15. Treat classroom animals as classroom pets with rights and privileges.

16. Think about what will be done to the animals after the Science Fair is over.

17. Return animals to their natural homes or habitats, being sure that they will survive.

NOTES:

AT THE SCIENCE FAIR... I HAVE A WELL-KEPT, CLEAN CAGE AND GOOD FOOD!

GA1325

ACTIVITY NO.	KEY	ACTIVITY	REFER TO PAGE(S)	DATE COMPLETED
A9 Ⓣ	OC	Read Science Fair Guidelines on the Use of Human Subjects in Scientific Research.	19, 298-300	

TIPS FOR THE TEACHER
Science Fair Guidelines on the Use of Human Subjects in Scientific Research

The teacher who has students who want to use human subjects in science fair projects should contact the principal for clarification of school district policy. The following *general* guidelines are used to assist your students in writing a proposal for the use of human subjects in science fair projects.

PROJECT DESCRIPTION

Briefly describe the objectives of your research, data collection procedures, the need for human subjects and any special conditions or procedures for their involvement. Provide enough information so the teacher can assess the risks to which your subjects may be exposed and the benefits likely to result from your proposed experiments.

CHARACTERISTICS OF THE SUBJECTS

Describe the following characteristics of the individuals used in the study: (1) sex, race or ethnic group, age range; (2) affiliation of subjects (e.g., high school students, elementary school youngsters, general public, hospital patients); (3) subject's general state of health; (4) necessity for using these subjects; (5) explanation of how subjects will be recruited and procedures for gaining their consent; (6) describe what the subject will be asked to do in the study.

RISKS TO SUBJECTS

Describe in detail any physical, psychological, social, legal, economic or other risks you can foresee, both immediate and long range on the part of the subjects in the study. Explain how you feel the knowledge gained will outweigh the risk.

CONFIDENTIALITY OF DATA

What precautions will be taken to safeguard identifiable records of individuals? This question also applies if you use secondary sources of data. Be specific about the long range and immediate use of data by both you and others.

CONSENT PROCEDURES

Federal regulations require precautionary measures to be taken to insure the protection of human subjects on physical, psychological, social and other issues. This includes the use of "informed consent" procedures, such as parental consent for use of minors in research studies.

NOTES:

GA1325

ACTIVITY NO.	KEY	ACTIVITY	REFER TO PAGE(S)	DATE COMPLETED
A10 (T)	OC	Read Student's Science Fair Glossary.	20, 70-75	

TIPS FOR THE TEACHER

Student's Science Fair Glossary

Student's Science Fair Glossary found in the Science Fairs with Style Student's Packet (pp. 70-75) is a convenient reproducible booklet of over 130 scientific terms most frequently encountered in science fair activities. Review each entry carefully. Add new entries. In September, make punched copies for each student and have them place the glossary in three-ring binders. Have students add new entries as they occur throughout the year.

NOTES:

GA1325

ACTIVITY NO.	KEY	ACTIVITY	REFER TO PAGE(S)	DATE COMPLETED
A11 (T)	OC	Read Student's Guide to Science Fair Symbols and Abbreviations. Begin to make matching cards for each. Match the symbol with the correct word.	21, 76-77	

TIPS FOR THE TEACHER

Student's Guide to Science Fair Symbols and Abbreviations

Student's Guide to Science Fair Symbols and Abbreviations found in the Science Fairs with Style Student's Packet (pp. 76-77) is a convenient list of over sixty scientific terms and their matching symbols encountered in science fair activities. Review each entry carefully. Print terms on one set of cards, symbols on another set. If possible, laminate the cards. When school begins, have the students match the symbol cards with their correct terms.

NOTES:

ACTIVITY NO.	KEY	ACTIVITY	REFER TO PAGE(S)	DATE COMPLETED
A12 (T)	OC	Draft a Parents' Volunteer Letter.	22, 93, 220	

TIPS FOR THE TEACHER
Parents' Volunteer Letter

Date _____

Dear Parents:

In your child's study of science this year, we will be involved in a unique Science Fair Mentorship Program. As avid teachers of science, our major goal is to offer your child an opportunity to conduct a scientific research study under the careful guidance of a mentor, a person experienced in a subject area. Last year, some students worked with physicians, veterinarians and engineers. The results of their efforts were displayed at our annual Science Fair in February.

In order to reach our goal of having a successful Science Fair Mentorship Program, we need your help. Below is a Science Fair Volunteer Form. Please check the tasks that you could do to help us reach our goal. Clip the form and return it to us by the date shown on the form. We will organize volunteers in groups by tasks. You will receive further information throughout the year on our progress.

Thank you for your support.

Sincerely,

_____

SCIENCE FAIR VOLUNTEER FORM

I would like to volunteer for the following activity(ies) involved in the Science Fair Mentorship Program:

_____ Be a member of the Science Fair Committee
_____ Contact librarians
_____ Contact judges
_____ Contact community mentors
_____ Help set up gym for Science Fair
_____ Help supply and dispense refreshments
_____ Be a classroom helper
_____ Develop science fair program
_____ Help construct display boards
_____ Contact retired people for assistance
_____ Other

_____ Organize field trips to research sites
_____ Be a science fair mentor
_____ Donate science periodicals and books
_____ Contact members of the media
_____ Supervise students setting up projects
_____ Donate science equipment
_____ Supervise students during judging
_____ Contact guest speakers
_____ Help in fund-raising
_____ Distribute copy of this form to anyone who would be of help

Name _____ Address _____

Telephone (work) _____ (home) _____ Please return by _____

GA1325

ACTIVITY NO.	KEY	ACTIVITY	REFER TO PAGE(S)	DATE COMPLETED
A13 (T)	OC	Contact president of PTA, Mother's Club and/or community agencies for funds needed to run the program. Inventory each item needed and prioritize your list.	23-24, 27, 303-307	

TIPS FOR THE TEACHER

Letter of Appeal for Funding
for a Unique Science Fair Mentorship Program for Students

Date _____

Dear _____ :

This school year we are involved in a unique Science Fair Mentorship Program for students. As avid teachers of science, our major goal in the program is to provide students an opportunity to conduct a scientific research study under the careful guidance of a mentor in the community, a person knowledgeable in a subject area such as a physician, veterinarian or engineer. The results of the students' research efforts will be displayed at our annual Science Fair in February.

In order to reach our goal of having a successful Science Fair Mentorship Program, we need your help. Enclosed is a prioritized listing of materials that we will need. We hope that you will support our program and thus give our students an opportunity to participate in this unique experience.

Our first annual Science Fair will be held on _____ at _____ . Please join us to view the accomplishments of these students all of which are a result of being placed in an environment in which they could be the very best that they could be. Thank you.

Sincerely,

Please return by _____

NOTES:

GA1325

PRIORITIZED LISTING OF MATERIALS NEEDED FOR THE SCIENCE FAIR MENTORSHIP PROGRAM PER CLASS (30)

Item	Number Needed	Cost Per	Total	Priority No.
Triple-wall backboards	30	$ 4.00	$120.00	1
Stencils	8 sets	5.00	40.00	1
Paint	10 pints	4.00	40.00	1
Rubber cement	10 bottles	3.00	30.00	1
Markers	10 sets of 12	11.00	110.00	1
Construction paper	20 packs	2.50	50.00	1
Poster board	30	1.50	45.00	1
Note cards	10 packs	3.00	30.00	1
Judges' packets	6	6.00	36.00	1
Masking tape	30 rolls	2.00	60.00	1
Film (35mm)	10 rolls	6.00	60.00	1
Film developing	10 rolls	6.00	60.00	1
Videotapes	10	6.00	60.00	1
Audio cassette tapes	10	4.00	40.00	1
Slide trays	2	15.00	30.00	1
Computer discs	30	3.00	90.00	1
Computer paper	2 cartons	40.00	80.00	1
Exhibit paper	5 packets	9.00	45.00	2
Duplicating paper	5 reams	7.00	35.00	1
Stationery and thank-you notes	Asstd.	30.00	30.00	1
Ribbons and awards	30	5.00	150.00	1
Certificates of appreciation	30 (5 per pack)	3.00	15.00	1
Electrical cords	10	8.00	80.00	1
Photo albums	2	12.00	24.00	1
Reference books	20	10.00	200.00	1
Postage	—	—	150.00	1
Transportation to labs	3 trips	Variable	100.00	2
Miscellaneous science supplies	Asstd.	Variable	280.00	1
Refreshments	Variety for 100 people	1.50 per person	250.00	1
			$2340.00*	

*Prices are approximate and subject to change based on time, location and number of items requested.

NOTES:

S P S F = **September**

Planning

Student

Focus

THE SCIENCE FAIR TEACHER COMMUNICATES WITH STUDENTS

25

GA1325

ACTIVITY NO.	KEY	ACTIVITY	REFER TO PAGE(S)	DATE COMPLETED
S1 (T)	OC	Meet with Science Fair Committee to draft guidelines for science fair program.	22, 26	

TIPS FOR THE TEACHER

Science Fair Committee Guidelines for the Science Fair

Analyze results obtained from the Parents' Volunteer Letter to form your Science Fair Committee. Members may include your teaching colleagues, parents, mentors, community representatives, students, science fair judges, members of the media and librarians. Meet with the Science Fair Committee early this month. Elect a chairperson. Elicit guidelines from the committee members on what they feel are important components of a successful Science Fair Mentorship Program. Use the following NSTA Position Statement on Science Fairs as the basis for your discussion. Then draft guidelines to meet your particular science fair situation.

NSTA POSITION STATEMENT ON SCIENCE FAIRS

The National Science Teachers Association recognizes that many kinds of learning experiences, both in and beyond the classroom and laboratory, can contribute significantly to the education of students of science. With respect to science fair activities, the Association takes the position that participation should be guided by the following principles: (1) student participation in science fairs should be voluntary; (2) emphasis should be placed on the learning experience rather than on competition; (3) participation in science fairs should not be made the basis for a course grade; (4) science fair activities should supplement other educational experiences and not jeopardize them; (5) the emphasis should be on scientific content and method; (6) the scientific part of the project must be the work of the student; (7) teacher involvement in science fairs should be based upon teacher interest rather than on external pressures or administrative directives; (8) if a science fair is to be undertaken, such an assignment should be a replacement for one of the teacher's current responsibilities and not an additional duty. The National Science Teachers Association's Position Statement on Science Fairs was approved by the NSTA Board of Directors in 1968. This position statement is intended as a guide and does not reflect the whole range of interest of our members.

NOTES:

ACTIVITY NO.	KEY	ACTIVITY	REFER TO PAGE(S)	DATE COMPLETED
S2 ⓣ	OC	Follow up on Letter of Appeal for Funding from PTA, Mother's Club and/or community agencies.	23-24, 27, 303-307	

TIPS FOR THE TEACHER

Follow-Up Letter of Appeal for Funding

Date _____

Dear _____ :

A special thanks to all who have contributed funds, equipment and services to help us run our Science Fair Mentorship Program. You may recall that our major goal in the program is to offer students an opportunity to conduct a scientific research study under the guidance of a person knowledgeable in the subject area such as a physician, veterinarian or engineer. Your support in helping us reach this goal is appreciated.

Enclosed is a prioritized listing of materials that we will need to run this unique program. We are making progress toward our goal. If you have not done so already, we hope that you will consider supporting our program. Your assistance will help students become the best students that they can be.

Please come and join us on _____ , 19 _____ , at _____ School, to view the accomplishments of these students. Thank you.

Sincerely,

Please return by _____ .

NOTES:

GA1325

ACTIVITY NO.	KEY	ACTIVITY	REFER TO PAGE(S)	DATE COMPLETED
S3 (T)	OC	Meet with principal, athletic director, coaches, physical education teacher, et al., to be sure dates for Science Fair are open and scheduling conflicts will be kept to a minimum.	28, 33-35	

TIPS FOR THE TEACHER

Meet Others to Avoid Scheduling Conflicts

Before you set the date for the Science Fair, check with these people in your school on possible dates for a science fair. Have a number of alternative dates in mind before you see these people.

NOTES:

GA1325

ACTIVITY NO.	KEY	ACTIVITY	REFER TO PAGE(S)	DATE COMPLETED
S4 (T)	OC	Set date of Science Fair for late February.	28-29	

TIPS FOR THE TEACHER

Setting the Date

After consulting support personnel in early September, set the final science fair date for late February.

GA1325

ACTIVITY NO.	KEY	ACTIVITY	REFER TO PAGE(S)	DATE COMPLETED
S5 Ⓣ	OC	Reserve location for Science Fair. Meet with physical education teacher, media center director and/or librarian to insure that rooms are available for setups, displays and takedowns. Offer to trade rooms with others on science fair day.	28, 30, 117	

TIPS FOR THE TEACHER

Reserve Location

After consulting various support personnel in early September, reserve the location for the Science Fair for late February.

NOTES:

GA1325

ACTIVITY NO.	KEY	ACTIVITY	REFER TO PAGE(S)	DATE COMPLETED
S6 (T)	OC	Meet with principal and draft a written building request, if needed, for Science Fair in February.	31 241	

TIPS FOR THE TEACHER

Building Request

Here is a sample building request, if it is required that you fill one out in your school system. This will insure building arrangements have been made for the Science Fair.

Use of School Facilities Building Permit

School facility _____ Permit no. _____

Space required _____

Organization _____

Number in organization_____ Number to attend event _____

Purpose _____

Free day admission_____ Admission charge_____ By solicitation_____

Day date_____ Hours_____ Heat_____ A/C or Ventilation_____

_____

_____

_____

Equipment needed: No. of chairs_____ No. of tables_____ Projectionist_____ Piano_____

P.A. system_____ Movie screen_____ Lectern_____ Lighting_____ Risers_____

Other_____

I have read the rules governing the Use of School Facilities, and I hereby agree to all terms and conditions.

Applicant's signature_____ Date applied_____

Address_____ Telephone_____

_____

Date cleared_____ Rental fee_____
        Principal

Approval_____ Remarks:_____
    Director, Building Services

NOTES:

ACTIVITY NO.	KEY	ACTIVITY	REFER TO PAGE(S)	DATE COMPLETED
S7 (T)	OC	Meet with food service personnel to insure that the cafeteria will be open so parents, community members, mentors and guests will have a place to meet while judging is taking place.	32, 215, 237	

TIPS FOR THE TEACHER

Meet Food Service Personnel

In early September, meet with the food service personnel on the availability of the cafeteria for the Science Fair. Discuss setups and the availability of health foods, perhaps prepared by students in home economics.

NOTES:

ACTIVITY NO.	KEY	ACTIVITY	REFER TO PAGE(S)	DATE COMPLETED
S8 (T)	OC	Ask the principal for ten minutes to introduce the Science Fair Mentorship Program at the first staff meeting. Display pictures and newspaper clippings. Show short videotape of previous science fairs to enlist the support of others.	28, 33	

TIPS FOR THE TEACHER

Meet the Principal to Spread the Word

The principal often holds the key in the development of a successful Science Fair Mentorship Program. Explore various possibilities with the principal on how other staff members may become involved in your science fair program. For information on commercial science fair videos, write to Insights Visual Productions, P.O. Box 644, Encinitas, CA 92024.

NOTES:

ACTIVITY NO.	KEY	ACTIVITY	REFER TO PAGE(S)	DATE COMPLETED
S9 (T)	OC	Talk with teachers of different grade levels to explore possibility of cross-grade level Science Fair Mentorship Programs, sixth-grade students acting as mentors for fourth-grade students.	34, 37	

TIPS FOR THE TEACHER

Cross-Grade Level Science Fair Programs

For an excellent description of an actual cross-grade level mentorship program, see "A Sixth Grade-Kindergarten Mentorship Program," unpublished Master's Degree Project, The University of Toledo, Toledo, OH 43606, Summer, 1986, written by Karen Shelt.

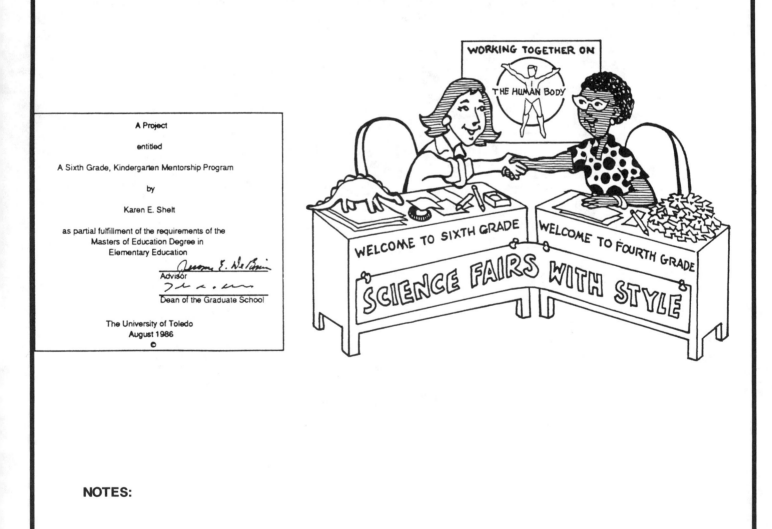

A Project

entitled

A Sixth Grade, Kindergarten Mentorship Program

by

Karen E. Shelt

as partial fulfillment of the requirements of the
Masters of Education Degree in
Elementary Education

Advisor

Dean of the Graduate School

The University of Toledo
August 1986
©

NOTES:

GA1325

ACTIVITY NO.	KEY	ACTIVITY	REFER TO PAGE(S)	DATE COMPLETED
S10 (T)	OC	Talk with teachers of other subjects to seek their help, e.g., English (writing of science fair reports), math (charts, graphs and statistics), social studies (library research), art (displays, programs, announcements and publicity) and home economics (goodies).	11, 35-36	

TIPS FOR THE TEACHER
An Interdisciplinary Science Fair Program

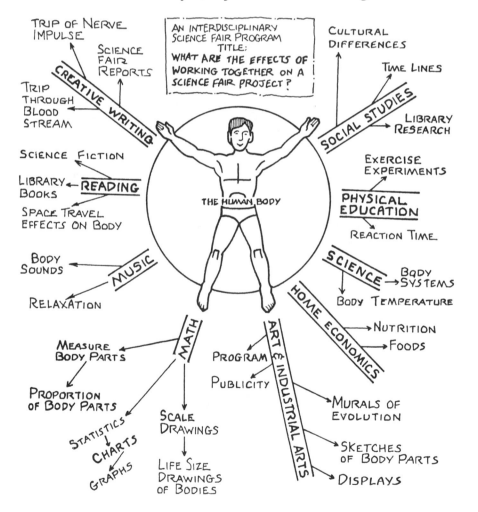

NOTES:

GA1325

ACTIVITY NO.	KEY	ACTIVITY	REFER TO PAGE(S)	DATE COMPLETED
S11 ⓣ	OC	If in a departmentalized set-up, urge fellow teachers to assign science fair students a research report to support their science fair activities.	35-36, 116	

TIPS FOR THE TEACHER

Interdisciplinary Science Fair Activity

Here is a sample chart that features the integration of various disciplines into the Science Fair Mentorship Program.

DISCIPLINE	TITLE OF RESEARCH REPORT
Science	"Which Takes More Water, a Shower or a Bath?"
Social Studies	"Characteristics of Stonehenge as a Time-Telling Device"
Art	"Factors That Affect the Perception of Horizontal and Vertical Lines"
Music	"What Factors Affect the Performance of Woodwinds in the Production of Sound?"
Math	"Factors That Affect the Specific Gravity of a Rock"
Reading and Language Arts	"The Effects of Contact Lenses on Reading Ability"
Creative Writing	"The Effects of Living in Future Underwater Cities"
Health Education	"The Effects of Steroid Use in Adolescents"
Home Economics	"The Effects of Food Additives and Dyes in Prepared Foods"
Physical Education	"A Study of the Factors That Cause Muscle Fatigue"
Career Education	"Decision Making Factors That Affect Choosing Science as a Career"
Vocational Education	"Which Type of Glue Holds Two Boards Together the Best?"

NOTES:

GA1325

ACTIVITY NO.	KEY	ACTIVITY	REFER TO PAGE(S)	DATE COMPLETED
S12 ⓣ	OC	Talk with teachers about a visit to their classes to inform all prospective students of the Science Fair. Recruit past science fair participants to go with you on these visits.	34, 37, 254	

TIPS FOR THE TEACHER

Recruitment

If time permits, have previous science fair students show a short videotape to students in different classes in an attempt to recruit more students to become involved in science fair activities. The short videotape may be the one shown at the initial faculty meeting.

NOTES:

GA1325

ACTIVITY NO.	KEY	ACTIVITY	REFER TO PAGE(S)	DATE COMPLETED
S13 (T)	OC	Using a computer, develop a data base listing of suggested science fair topics. Use papers and photos of past projects for this list. Write a letter like the one below, for up-to-date information on science project data bases.	36, 38, 89-90	

TIPS FOR THE TEACHER
Data Base of Science Fair Topics

On school stationery write the following letter for up-to-date information on Science Project Data Bases and other pertinent information on how to run a science fair program.

Date _____

Applied Educational Technology
P.O. Box 193
Tigerville, SC 29688

Dear Sir:

Please send current information on how to order your publications related to science fairs, including the book *Science Project Data Bases*, which I plan to use in my science fair activity this year.

Thank you for your assistance.

Sincerely,

NOTES:

GA1325

ACTIVITY NO.	KEY	ACTIVITY	REFER TO PAGE(S)	DATE COMPLETED
S14 (T)	IC	Introduce Science Fair Mentorship Program to students. Make copies of the Science Fairs with Style Student's Packet. Punch and place in three-ring binders. Review Table of Contents.	39, 56-90, 58-59	

TIPS FOR THE TEACHER

Science Fairs with Style Student's Packet

Pages 56 to 90 represent the first of five reproducible packets in this book: (1) student, (2) parents, (3) community members, (4) judges, (5) media. Select and make copies of the pages that fit your situation. The first two pages are the front and back covers of the Science Fairs with Style Student's Packet. Add name of student and school. Have students place punched pages between the covers of the packet and insert in three-ring binder for safekeeping. Review Table of Contents to introduce Science Fair Mentorship Program to students. Outline yearly expectations for the program.

NOTES:

GA1325

ACTIVITY NO.	KEY	ACTIVITY	REFER TO PAGE(S)	DATE COMPLETED
S15 (T)	IC	Review and discuss Science Fair Goals for the Student.	10, 40, 53, 60	

TIPS FOR THE TEACHER

Science Fair Goals for the Student

Emphasize how setting goals is an important exercise for both the teacher and students in science fair activity. Review Science Fair Goals for the Teacher on page 10. Point out to students that the teacher sets goals too in an effort to develop a successful science fair program. Introduce Science Fair Goals for the Student (p. 60). Read each goal carefully. Explain what the students will do to achieve each goal. By doing this, the Science Fair Mentorship Program will be introduced to the students in a well-planned manner.

NOTES:

GA1325

ACTIVITY NO.	KEY	ACTIVITY	REFER TO PAGE(S)	DATE COMPLETED
S16 (T)	IC	Review Science Fair Projects May Begin with These but Should Go Beyond . . . . Discuss various types of science fair projects.	12-13, 61	

TIPS FOR THE TEACHER

Science Fair Projects May Begin with These but Should Go Beyond . . . .

Before class, reread pages 12-13. In class, introduce various types of science fair projects to the students. Point out that science fair projects that feature book reports, art projects, models/ mock-ups, hobbies/collections, technological innovations and research studies are excellent starting points for science fair activity. Emphasize, however, that true science fair projects go beyond these and involve the use of the scientific method in solving actual problems.

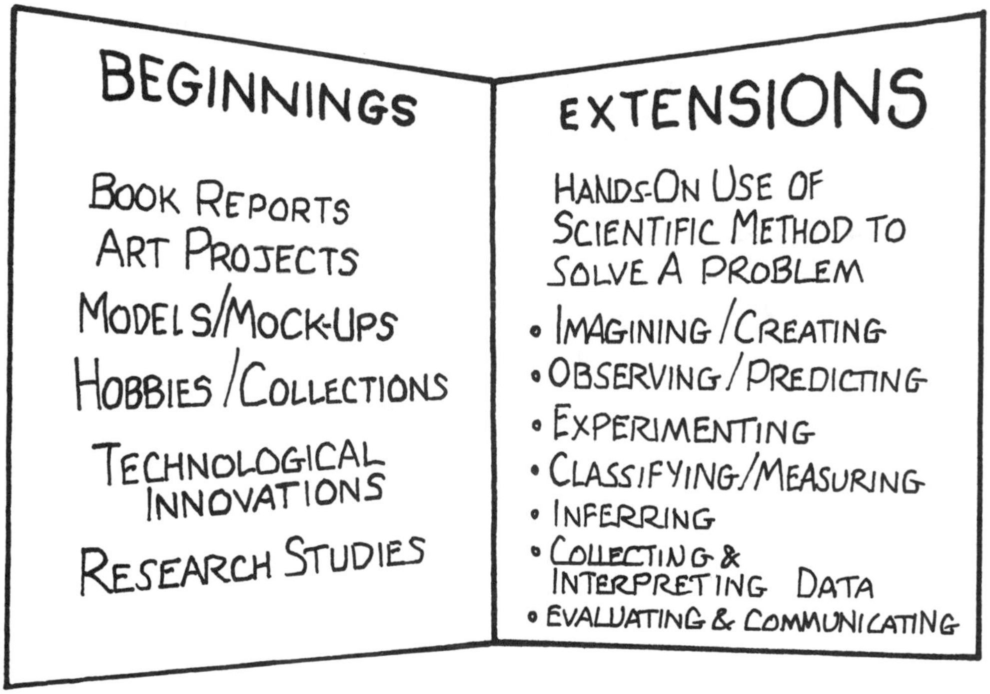

BEGINNINGS

BOOK REPORTS
ART PROJECTS
MODELS/MOCK-UPS
HOBBIES/COLLECTIONS
TECHNOLOGICAL INNOVATIONS
RESEARCH STUDIES

EXTENSIONS

HANDS-ON USE OF SCIENTIFIC METHOD TO SOLVE A PROBLEM
• IMAGINING/CREATING
• OBSERVING/PREDICTING
• EXPERIMENTING
• CLASSIFYING/MEASURING
• INFERRING
• COLLECTING & INTERPRETING DATA
• EVALUATING & COMMUNICATING

NOTES:

GA1325

ACTIVITY NO.	KEY	ACTIVITY	REFER TO PAGE(S)	DATE COMPLETED
S17 (T)	IC	Review A Student's Science Fair Project Is . . . . Have students check each item as it is discussed.	42, 62	

TIPS FOR THE TEACHER

A Student's Science Fair Project Is . . . .

This activity is designed to reinforce the concept that a true science fair project is based on the scientific method which is a method used to solve a real-life problem. Review A Student's Science Fair Project Is . . . (p. 62). Discuss each point carefully. Elicit answers to questions such as "What does it mean to set a goal?" or "What does *hands-on science* mean?" Have students check each point when they feel they understand the concept thoroughly.

Reference Book: Beveridge, W.I.B. (1968). *The Art of Scientific Investigation*. London: Heinemann.

NOTES:

GA1325

ACTIVITY NO.	KEY	ACTIVITY	REFER TO PAGE(S)	DATE COMPLETED
S18 ⓣ	IC	Discuss with students how a science fair project is based on the scientific method. Review What Is the Scientific Method? Discuss style.	14, 43, 63	

TIPS FOR THE TEACHER

What Is the Scientific Method?

Students need to know that science is an integral part of life. They also need to master the process skills inherent in the scientific method. Some of these process skills include imagining, creating, observing, classifying, measuring, predicting, experimenting, inferring, collecting, organizing and interpreting data, evaluating and communicating. Introduce What Is the Scientific Method? by giving each of seven students an enlarged card found on page 63. Inform students that the scientific method is unique to science and is used to solve a real-life problem. Have the seven students line up in correct order to show the seven steps in the scientific method. Discuss each step. Stress how the scientific method also has valuable carryover to life in general. When students return to their seats, have them review their copy and insert into three-ring binders.

Special Tip: Laminate cards. Attach magnetic tape to the back of each card. Place cards in correct order on magnetic chalkboard in the classroom to illustrate steps followed when using the scientific method.

NOTES:

GA1325

ACTIVITY NO.	KEY	ACTIVITY	REFER TO PAGE(S)	DATE COMPLETED
S19 (T)	IC	Introduce Student's Guide to Science Fair Safety. Review and discuss each item carefully.	15, 44, 64	

TIPS FOR THE TEACHER

Student's Guide to Science Fair Safety

Students need to become aware of safety hazards, avoid unnecessary dangers, exercise reasonable safety precautions and be prompt in case an emergency occurs while doing science fair projects. Review page 64, Student's Guide to Science Fair Safety. Review each item carefully. Emphasize *student* responsibility when conducting science fair projects. Review international safety symbols at bottom of page. Discuss what each symbol means. Each day provide examples of each. Have students review these safety procedures often while doing science fair experiments.

NOTES:

GA1325

ACTIVITY NO.	KEY	ACTIVITY	REFER TO PAGE(S)	DATE COMPLETED
S20 (T)	IC	Introduce Student's Safety Contract. Review contract carefully. Have students and parents sign and return contract. Be sure the teacher, parents and students have signed copies of the contract.	15, 45, 65	

TIPS FOR THE TEACHER

Student's Safety Contract

The Student's Safety Contract is designed to have each student accept responsibility for personal safety when conducting science fair projects. The contract also promotes a feeling of sincerity that may yield a positive attitude toward science. After a thorough discussion of Student's Guide to Science Fair Safety (page 64), introduce the Student's Safety Contract (page 65). Carefully read the contract to the students. Have students sign and date the contract. To promote further responsibility, have students obtain signatures from parents and mentors. When properly signed, contracts are returned to school and signed by the teacher. Then students are permitted to conduct science fair projects. Make copies of the signed contracts for students, parents and mentors. Keep original copy in a file for future consultation if needed.

NOTES:

GA1325

ACTIVITY NO.	KEY	ACTIVITY	REFER TO PAGE(S)	DATE COMPLETED
S21 (T)	IC	Introduce Student's Guidelines on Working with Animals. Discuss. Do activity Mealworm Mania. Discuss safety factors and results.	46, 66-68	

TIPS FOR THE TEACHER

Student's Guidelines on Working with Animals

The care and use of animals in science fair projects is an important consideration. Teachers often ask "Should live animals be used in the study of science?" One answer is "Yes," but with the use of animals comes the responsibility for their care and safety.

Teachers who recognize the value in using animals must be aware of the special precautions, problems and responsibilities that animals create. Students must be taught how to care for animals so they can develop a deep appreciation for all living things. In addition, students will develop positive attitudes specifically towards animals and science in general by how they respond to animals.

Introduce Mealworm Mania (page 67) to promote positive attitudes in students towards animals. Mealworms are ideal creatures to use with students to gain an understanding of the care for and use of animals in the classroom. Purchase 100 mealworms at a pet shop. Place in clear plastic shoe box with cover. Add cornmeal, cereal flakes and other suitable materials such as a piece of apple so the mealworms have "water" to drink. Observe the four stages of the mealworm: egg, larva, pupa and adult. Give each student a mealworm in a small, clear plastic container with small holes in the lid for air passage. Have students feed and care for the mealworms. Discuss proper ways to care for the mealworms and how animals are used in the study of science. Do the activities. Teach students that they are responsible for the care and feeding of their mealworms. Discuss ways to insure the health and safety of the mealworm, e.g., a safe and happy environment in the classroom. Emphasize the development of a deep appreciation for the mealworms and life in general. For additional activities on animals, see *Young Scientists Explore Animals* (Good Apple, Inc., 1982) and *Creative Hands-On Science Cards & Activities* (Good Apple, Inc., 1990), both books written by Jerry DeBruin.

NOTES:

GA1325

ACTIVITY NO.	KEY	ACTIVITY	REFER TO PAGE(S)	DATE COMPLETED
S22 ⓣ	IC	Introduce Student Vertebrate Animal Certificate. Emphasize that this certificate must be completed before the project begins and must be displayed with the project on science fair day.	47, 69	

TIPS FOR THE TEACHER
Student Vertebrate Animal Certificate

The proper use and care of animals is an important consideration when planning science fair projects. Some states require committees in schools to approve all projects on vertebrate animals *prior* to research. This is a sample teacher/mentor/supervisor certification form that insures the *prior* approval for such projects.

TEACHER/MENTOR/SUPERVISOR CERTIFICATION

(Must be completed for *all* research involving vertebrate animals *prior* to the research.)

Student's name _____

I agree to sponsor the student named above and assume responsibility for compliance with existing Rules for Research Involving Live Vertebrate Animals.

Date _____

Signature:

| Teacher | Supervisor | Mentor |

Name:

| Teacher | Supervisor | Mentor |

Position:

| Teacher | Supervisor | Mentor |

Institution:

| Teacher | Supervisor | Mentor |

Address:

| Teacher | Supervisor | Mentor |

Office Phone:

| Teacher | Supervisor | Mentor |

Home Address:

| Teacher | Supervisor | Mentor |

Home Phone:

| Teacher | Supervisor | Mentor |

NOTES:

GA1325

ACTIVITY NO.	KEY	ACTIVITY	REFER TO PAGE(S)	DATE COMPLETED
S23 (T)	IC	Introduce Student's Science Fair Glossary. Discuss terms with students.	48, 70-75	

TIPS FOR THE TEACHER
Student's Science Fair Glossary

This glossary of over 130 scientific terms most frequently encountered in science fair activity may be duplicated for student use. Make an extra copy of the glossary to be kept as a classroom glossary. Encourage students to add new entries to both their own personal glossary and the classroom glossary as new scientific terms are encountered. Terms and matching definitions can be typed on index cards and laminated. Have the students match the cards of terms with the appropriate cards of definitions. Concentration and quiz bowl games can be played. Be sure to have students add new terms to their glossaries as new words are encountered.

NOTES:

GA1325

ACTIVITY NO.	KEY	ACTIVITY	REFER TO PAGE(S)	DATE COMPLETED
S24 ⓣ	IC	Introduce Student's Guide to Science Fair Symbols and Abbreviations. Review each term, symbol and note.	49, 76-77	

TIPS FOR THE TEACHER

Student's Guide to Science Fair Symbols and Abbreviations

Reread teacher page 21, Student's Guide to Science Fair Symbols and Abbreviations, that was read previously in August. If you made your matching cards in August, you are ready to have your students match the terms with their correct symbols. If not, that's okay too. Merely print terms on one set of cards, their matching symbols on another set of cards. A computer can help you do this easily. If possible, laminate the cards. After reviewing each term, have student match the symbol with the correct term. Cards of terms and symbols can be displayed on a bulletin board. If magnetic tape is used, the cards can be displayed on a magnetic chalkboard.

NOTES:

GA1325

ACTIVITY NO.	KEY	ACTIVITY	REFER TO PAGE(S)	DATE COMPLETED
S25 (T)	IC	Introduce Student's Science Fair Contract. Review contract carefully. Have students' parent/guardian and mentor sign contract. Give signed copies to all parties.	50, 78	

TIPS FOR THE TEACHER

Student's Science Fair Contract

The Student's Science Fair Contract is designed to obtain a commitment from students that insures the successful completion of a science fair project. The contract gives students, their parents and mentors a broad overview of the science fair program and related responsibilities. Make copies of page 78. Give a copy to each student. Have students sign and date the contract. Have students obtain signatures of parents and mentors if applicable. When properly signed contracts are returned to school and signed by the teacher, students are permitted to conduct science fair studies. Make copies of the signed contracts for students, parents and mentors. Keep original in a file for future consultation if needed.

NOTES:

GA1325

ACTIVITY NO.	KEY	ACTIVITY	REFER TO PAGE(S)	DATE COMPLETED
S26 ⓣ	IC	Develop a monthly schedule for the year with due dates of major science fair activities done by students. Review the schedule each month through-out the year.	51, 79	

TIPS FOR THE TEACHER

Student's Monthly Science Fair Project Completion Schedule

The Student's Monthly Science Fair Project Completion Schedule gives students, parents and mentors a broad overview of monthly activities over the course of a year in the Science Fair Mentorship Program. After a thorough review of the signed Student's Science Fair Contract, introduce the schedule with due dates. Have students write in the month and date for each completed activity. Add pertinent written comments. By so doing, students will have a long-range plan for the Science Fair Mentorship Program from its inception to its end. Have students refer to schedule frequently while doing their investigations.

NOTES:

GA1325

ACTIVITY NO.	KEY	ACTIVITY	REFER TO PAGE(S)	DATE COMPLETED
S27 (T)	IC	Introduce Criteria for Judging Science Fair Projects. Discuss each criterion item and levels of performance.	52, 80	

TIPS FOR THE TEACHER
Criteria for Judging Science Fair Projects

There are many methods to choose from when judging science fair projects. It is important that students, parents and judges be involved in the determination of criteria on which science fair projects will be judged. Invite a parent representative from the PTA, mentor and a science fair judge from the community to visit your classroom to cooperatively develop criteria for judging. Make and distribute copies of Criteria for Judging Science Fair Projects to all who attend. You may use the copy as a guide to establish criteria for judging. Have students review the criteria for judging often during their science fair activities.

NOTES:

GA1325

ACTIVITY NO.	KEY	ACTIVITY	REFER TO PAGE(S)	DATE COMPLETED
S28 (T)	IC	Introduce Student's Guide on How to Do a High-Quality Science Fair Project. Discuss, assign to be read as homework and countersigned by parents/guardian.	53, 81-85	

TIPS FOR THE TEACHER

Student's Guide on How to Do a High-Quality Science Fair Project

The letter on pages 81-85 can be personalized by you with appropriate signature and add best wishes to students in an attempt to develop a high-quality science fair project. You are invited to add, change or delete items from the letter to make it appropriate for your age group. Make copies of your final letter or the one on pages 81-85, for both students and parents to read. In class, have the students read the letter carefully. Instruct students to take the letter home to have parents read and sign indicating acknowledgement of receipt of the letter. Have students "file" the letter in their Science Fairs with Style Student's Packet for future use.

SEE PAGES 81-85...

STUDENT'S GUIDE ON HOW TO DO A HIGH-QUALITY SCIENCE FAIR PROJECT...

NOTES:

GA1325

ACTIVITY NO.	KEY	ACTIVITY	REFER TO PAGE(S)	DATE COMPLETED
S29 (T)	IC	Introduce Student's Guide on How to Write a Science Fair Report. Discuss cards A-P and how the topics on cards A-P make up the final written paper.	54, 86-88	

TIPS FOR THE TEACHER

Student's Guide on How to Write a Science Fair Report

This activity involves students in the steps followed in conducting and the subsequent reporting of results when doing a science fair project. Make copies of the sixteen cards for each student or enlarge each card for a classroom set. Have students place cards in order. If one set of cards is used, have sixteen students, with one card per person, line up in the correct order that shows the steps followed when doing a science fair study. Use as a preliminary activity before involving student in actual science fair projects. Make copies of the student activity on page 88. Have the student write the letter of the card in the correct space, then rewrite steps in order. As a group, involve students by doing research on a science fair topic. Emphasize the idea that a science fair project is a research study in which a solution to a particular problem is attempted to be found.

Student Activity Page Answers: Column A: A, C, E, G, H, F, D, B, P, I, N, K, L, M, J, O. Column B: title page, table of contents, abstract, background research, background bibliography, statement of the problem, statement of the hypothesis, procedures and methods, materials, variables and controls, results, conclusion, discussion, acknowledgements, references, appendices.

NOTES:

GA1325

ACTIVITY NO.	KEY	ACTIVITY	REFER TO PAGE(S)	DATE COMPLETED
S30 (T)	IC	Discuss possible science fair topics with students. Make a written record of such topics, enter into data bank and post copy in the classroom. Encourage students to add topics. In early October, have each student choose a science fair topic to investigate.	55, 89-90	

TIPS FOR THE TEACHER

Student's Guide to Science Fair Topics and Ideas

Included on pages 89 and 90 are science fair projects that feature the use of the scientific method. These projects range from simple to complex, but all involve the solving of a real-life problem by using the scientific method. Enter the titles of the projects found on pages 89 and 90 onto a computer disc. Add or delete as the need arises. Copies of the pages can also be made and displayed in the classroom. Have students examine the list of topics and choose one to pursue by signing their names in the appropriate spaces. Have students consult the list often for updates. This practice will reduce the number of duplicate projects and keep redundancy to a minimum.

SCIENCE FAIR PROJECTS USING THE SCIENTIFIC METHOD

SEE PAGES 89 and 90 FOR EXCITING INFORMATION!

NOTES:

GA1325

SCIENCE FAIRS WITH STYLE
STUDENT'S PACKET

Name _____

School _____

(Front Cover)

SCIENCE FAIRS WITH STYLE
STUDENT'S PACKET

(Back Cover)

57

SCIENCE FAIRS WITH STYLE STUDENT'S PACKET
WITH SUGGESTED TIME LINE AND ACTIVITIES

(S)

Table of Contents

To the Students:

Having your own science fair packet will help you reach the goal of having a successful science fair experience. At the beginning of the year, your teacher will give you punched copies of selected pages that make up your Science Fairs with Style Student's Packet. Keep these pages in a three-ring binder and store in a safe place. Refer to it often while doing work on your science fair project. Your teacher may choose to give you all or some of the following pages to add to the binder.

These pages will help you become familiar with the Science Fair Mentorship Program.

These pages will help you to plan ahead, identify a problem, narrow the topic, formulate a hypothesis, locate information, collect and organize information, collect materials, do a controlled experiment using the scientific method and seek outside assistance from mentors.

GA1325

NOVEMBER:

These pages will help you to restate your topic in question form, collect data from tests, prepare an oral report, record data in diary/logbook entries, make graphs, identify and control variables in your experiment and write a rough draft of your report.

DECEMBER:

During this month, you will be finding out what happened in your experiment and recording any information and changes. You will complete a student entry form and write a rough draft of your science fair paper based on the results of your experiment.

JANUARY:

During this month, you will be stating your conclusions on what you learned from your experiment. You will have an opportunity to participate in a Program Cover Design Contest, write press releases and invitations, write a final science fair paper, build a backdrop display for your project and give a practice presentation of your talk to a judge.

FEBRUARY:

During this month you will set up your display and give an oral presentation at both the classroom and building science fairs. You will receive an award for your efforts and have an opportunity to evaluate the program.

MARCH:

During this month you will revise your project and enter it in other science fairs. You will write thank-you letters and notes. A certificate for your efforts will be awarded to you at an all-school assembly.

APRIL:

During this month you will write a short article about your science fair experiences for the school and/or other newspaper and/or publication.

SCIENCE FAIR GOALS FOR THE STUDENT

My Goals for Participation in the Science Fair Mentorship Program Are To:

1. Conduct scientific research using available resources and understanding that such research becomes a responsibility.

2. Improve my research techniques by using the scientific method.

3. Gain self-esteem and confidence in setting and reaching a realistic goal.

4. Increase my creative, critical thinking skills.

5. Develop my problem-solving skills by using technological innovations and equipment such as computers and high-speed instruments.

6. Enhance my ability to access information by using basic retrieval systems and data bases.

7. Develop a knowledge of scientists and how their contributions to science have affected science in my life.

8. Improve my communication skills and exchange, both orally and in writing, scientific ideas with teachers, parents and the general public.

9. Increase my ability to take risks.

10. Be able to accept failure as part of a science fair experiment and life in general.

11. Construct a display of my accomplishments and be recognized for such accomplishments.

12. Develop a desire to excel, go beyond my usual limits, consider science as a career and become the best person that I can be at this stage in my life.

SCIENCE FAIR PROJECTS MAY BEGIN WITH THESE
BUT SHOULD GO BEYOND . . . .

BOOK REPORTS

A book report is a project in which you identify a topic of interest and obtain a book about such a topic. The book is read and a written and/or oral report of its contents is usually done. A book report can be extended into a genuine science fair project by asking a question about a specific study or principle described in the book, designing a study and testing a hypothesis about such study or principle.

ART PROJECTS

Art projects that feature drawings or paintings of various pieces of scientific equipment or principles are often displayed at science fairs. Although not a genuine science fair project, a drawing or painting can be extended into a genuine science fair project with the actual testing of the scientific apparatus or principle drawn in an effort to actually solve a problem related to such a topic.

MODELS/MOCK-UPS

You may obtain a commerical model/mock-up or construct such a model/mock-up for a science fair project. You can demonstrate or explain a scientific principle about something or how something works. Students usually do library reading first about their topics. You then collect and assemble materials to demonstrate various scientific principles. You should design a test to discover something about the principles for a true science fair project.

HOBBIES/COLLECTIONS

Hobbies and collections are often displayed at science fairs. Rock and leaf collections are examples of this activity. You can extend these collections easily into science fair projects by posing questions, testing genuine experimental hypotheses and drawing conclusions from experiments done on such collections.

TECHNOLOGICAL INNOVATIONS

Many times you may invent things that feature unique ways to accomplish a task. Although these inventions are not genuine science fair projects, they are useful because they do require you to think about and manipulate actual materials. Science principles are demonstrated in the process as you often start with an object and make it better, or design a complicated procedure to follow or accomplish a simple task.

RESEARCH STUDIES

A research study is one in which you identify a topic of interest and conduct a library investigation to obtain as much information about the topic as possible. Computer data bases such as ERIC, MEDLINE and others can be used. Encyclopedias, books, journals, almanacs and interviews with knowledgeable people who are experienced in the topic are used. After the information is collected, you write a research paper or give an oral presentation about the research study.

The "nonscientific" projects outlined above such as book reports, art projects, models/mock-ups, hobbies/collections, technological innovations and research studies *can* be used as introductory investigations that, when pursued and extended, can lead to superior "scientific" science fair projects that use the scientific method.

GA1325

A STUDENT'S SCIENCE FAIR PROJECT IS . . . .

_____ Setting a Goal

_____ Hands-On

_____ Based on the Scientific Method

_____ Done by the Student

_____ Planned Well in Advance of the Science Fair

_____ Best If It Is an Experiment

_____ Asking the Right Questions

_____ Problem Centered

_____ Creative

_____ Inquiry Oriented

_____ Original in Approach and Presentation

_____ An Experience on How to Live with Ambiguity

_____ Not Always Knowing the Answers

_____ Involving Serendipity

_____ Self-Explanatory

_____ Exploring the Unknown

_____ Involving Other Areas Such as Art, Music and Mathematics

_____ Understanding Scientific Ideas

_____ Based on Using the Processes of Science to Solve Problems

_____ Doing Reading and Writing

_____ A Controlled Experiment

_____ Based on Easily Accessible and Often Cheap and Simple Materials

_____ Testing of Intelligent Guesses or Hypotheses

_____ Seeking Tentative Answers

_____ Collecting Data

_____ Recording Data

_____ Analyzing Data

_____ Repeating the Experiment to Verify Results

_____ Based on Conclusions Drawn from Collected Data

_____ Accurate, Correct and Valid

_____ Repeated by Others

_____ Related to One's Everyday Life

_____ Preparing a Research Paper

_____ Preparing an Exhibit That Is Attractive and Well-Organized

_____ Giving Credit to Those Who Helped You

_____ Making a Presentation to Your Classmates, Friends or Judges at a Science Fair

_____ Knowing You Have Reached a Goal

_____ Thinking About a Career in Science

_____ A Pleasant Experience

_____ A Memory That Lasts a Lifetime

GA1325

WHAT IS THE SCIENTIFIC METHOD?
The Scientific Method Features These Steps:

1.   PURPOSE

Identify a Problem

What Do You Want to Find Out?

2.   HYPOTHESIS

Make an Intelligent Guess

What Do You Think Will Happen?

3.   MATERIALS

Gather Materials Needed to Do the Experiment

What Materials Do You Need to Use?

4.   PROCEDURES

Things Done to Solve the Problem

What Will You do to Find Out the Solution to Your Problem?

5.   COLLECT DATA FROM TRIALS AND TESTS

Methods of Recording Data

What Things Can You Count and Measure?

6.   RESULTS

Observe What Happened

What Happened When You Did Your Experiment?

7.   CONCLUSIONS

Answers to the Questions

What Did You Learn from Your Experiment and How Is It Related to Your Everyday Life?

STUDENT'S GUIDE TO SCIENCE FAIR SAFETY

Because I have the right to do a science fair project, I accept the responsibility to:

- Be sure that all science fair activities are approved by my teacher, mentor and parents.
- Use patience and common sense when working with science equipment and materials.
- Report all accidents to my mentor, teacher and parents no matter how minor they are or seem to be.
- Know where the fire alarm, first aid kits and eye wash facilities are located.
- Never taste or touch chemicals unless specifically told to do so by my teacher or mentor.
- Roll up long and baggy sleeves above the elbows before doing science fair experiments.
- Wear old shirts for very messy experiments, but be careful that they are not too baggy.
- Wear safety glasses when doing experiments.
- Be alert and proceed with caution when doing science fair activities.
- Wash my hands thoroughly before and after doing any science fair experiments.
- Never drink or eat from glassware such as bottles, glasses, beakers or cylinders.
- Never "suck up" a liquid chemical with my mouth.
- Never sniff or breathe vapors from any gas or chemical.
- Never point a sharp object or a test tube at anyone or look directly into a test tube when mixing or heating chemicals.
- Review stop/drop/roll procedures for fire safety.
- Keep the floor free of spilled materials.
- Accept responsibility for the cleaning of science equipment used in the science fair projects.
- Do my share to clean up all materials after completing science fair activities in school and at home.
- Keep accurate records of my results and share these promptly with my teacher, mentor and parents.
- Complete my assignments on time and to the best of my ability.
- Observe the safety precautions listed and posted by my teacher and mentor regarding the use of fire, handling of animals and using electricity.
- Learn the meaning of each safety symbol shown below.
- Be the most responsible person that I can possibly be.
- Keep this page in my Science Fairs with Style Student's Packet and study frequently.

EXPLOSIVE SUBSTANCES

TOXIC SUBSTANCE

OXIDIZING SUBSTANCE

CORROSIVE SUBSTANCE

FLAMMABLE SUBSTANCE

RADIOACTIVE SUBSTANCE

GA1325

STUDENT'S SAFETY CONTRACT

(S)

I, _____, recognize that doing a science fair project is an important part of my life. To protect myself and others from danger, I agree to assume full responsibility for my own safety and that of others. I further agree to follow the safety guidelines outlined in Student's Guide to Science Fair Safety. In addition, I agree to conduct myself in a responsible manner at all times.

_____   _____
Student   Date

_____   _____
Parent/Guardian   Date

_____   _____
Teacher   Date

_____   _____
Mentor (if applicable)   Date

I, Betty Andon RECOGNIZE THAT DOING A SCIENCE FAIR PROJECT IS AN IMPORTANT PART OF MY LIFE.

GA1325

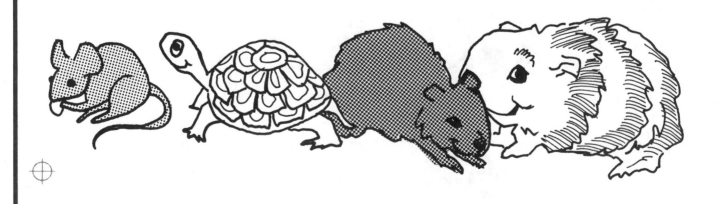 STUDENT'S GUIDELINES ON WORKING WITH ANIMALS

Animals play an important role in scientific investigations. They help scientists discover many new and important things. If you choose to use animals as part of your science fair project, you must be aware of, and obey, state laws that govern the use of animals in scientific investigations. *DO* these things if you plan to use animals in your science fair study.

1. DO get approval from your teacher, mentor and parents BEFORE you use animals in your study.

2. DO fill out a Student Vertebrate Animal Certificate BEFORE you begin your research.

3. DO have your teacher, supervisor and mentor sign the certificate BEFORE you begin your study.

4. DO attach the certificate to your science fair display at the Science Fair.

5. DO remember that animals are living things and must be treated with care and respect.

6. DO use animals only in the search for new knowledge or to prove a theory or principle.

7. DO use only tame and nonpoisonous animals in your research.

8. DO keep all animals in excellent condition.

9. DO provide animals with the proper diet. Avoid contamination of the animals' food.

10. DO provide adequate housing for the animals. Cages should be roomy. Gnawing materials and exercise devices are recommended.

11. DO provide a constant environmental temperature in the transportation of animals.

12. DO keep an animal on a restricted diet only until an observable change occurs. Then restore animal to healthy condition.

13. DO prevent others from teasing and abusing the animals.

14. DO have a plan for a permanent home for the animal after your research is completed.

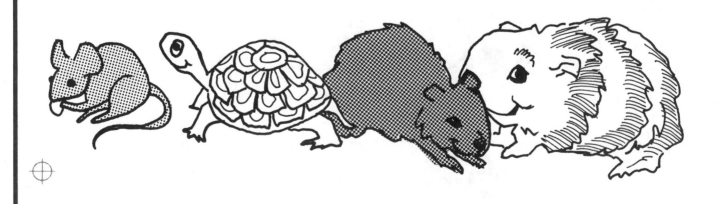

GA1325

MEALWORM MANIA

Shady Travels

Place mealworm on the X. Count the number of times the mealworm travels to squares 1, 2, 3, 4 in fifteen trials. Keep a record of your results on the chart on page 68. Note the number of travels and the types of shade chosen by your mealworm. Make a bar graph of your results. What is your mealworm's favorite shade? Then repeat the experiment using four different colored pieces of construction paper. Be sure to return your mealworm to its home for safekeeping.

Can a Mealworm Smell?

Attach four different smell stickers to each of the four corners on the inside of a shoe box lid as shown below. Make an X in the center of the shoe box lid. Place a mealworm on the X. Count the number of times the mealworm goes to each sticker. Record your results on the chart. After fifteen trials, determine the mealworm's favorite smell. Be sure to make a bar graph of your results. Return your mealworm to its home for safekeeping.

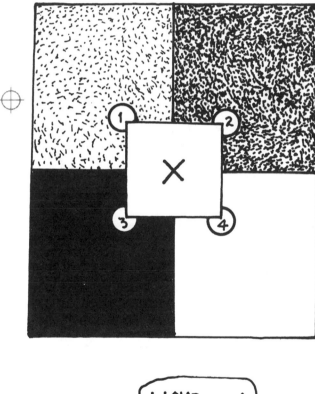

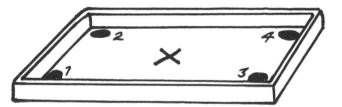

GA1325

MEALWORM MANIA DATA SHEET

Record the results of each trial in the data chart below. Then, based on the data collected, determine the mealworm's favorite color and smell.

Trial No.	Number of Shade/Color Chosen	Trial No.	Number of Smell Chosen
1.			
2.			
3.			
4.			
5.			
6.			
7.			
8.			
9.			
10.			
11.			
12.			
13.			
14.			
15.			

Conclusion: Mealworm's favorite shade/color is _____

Conclusion: Mealworm's favorite smell is _____

Guideline: The major guideline for working with mealworms that I followed when I worked with my mealworm was to _____

_____

_____

GA1325

STUDENT VERTEBRATE ANIMAL CERTIFICATE

(S)

Scientists use animals in their investigations because by studying animals, scientists discover many things. You, as a scientist, must remember that animals are living things and must be treated with care and respect. If you use live animals in your science fair project, you must complete the following certificate and give it to your teacher/mentor/supervisor *before* you begin your research. The certificate must be displayed on your display board at the Science Fair. Thank you for caring.

STUDENT ANIMAL CARE AND USE CERTIFICATION

(Note: This certificate must be displayed *with* the science fair *project*.)

Name of student _____

Name of school _____

Name of supervising teacher or mentor _____

Title of project _____

Problem and hypothesis _____

Methods or procedures _____

References (minimum of three major sources)

_____

_____

_____

Names of animals to be used _____

Number of animals to be used _____

Animals to be obtained from _____

Location of where animals will be housed _____

Cage size _____ Number of animals per cage _____

Temperature range in degrees Celsius of room where animals are to be kept _____

Frequency of cleaning cage _____

Type of bedding to be used _____

Date submitted for approval _____

Date approved _____

Signature of student _____

I certify that I have reviewed the research plan prior to the beginning of the experiment and it does comply with the Rules for Research Involving Live Vertebrate Animals.

Date _____   Signature _____

(Teacher/Supervisor/Mentor)

STUDENT'S SCIENCE FAIR GLOSSARY

Abbreviation: A short way of writing a word or group of words

Abstract: Summary giving the central parts of a larger work or the summation of an idea. Abstracts are usually 150-250 words in length.

Acknowledgements: A statement recognizing contributions by others to your present work

Analyze: To examine anything to determine its makeup

Analyzed Data: Data that comes from raw and smooth data; one draws conclusions from such data

Anonymous: Bearing no name; unknown authorship

Appendix: That which is added as a supplement

Article Report: The summation and analysis of an article written by someone else

Author: A person who writes a book, play or other work

Bar Graph: An illustration using solid bars to show relative values

Bias: Favoritism, inclination, prejudice or the tendency to foster the same

Bibliography: List of books on a certain subject

Bibliographic Data: History of books with dates, authors, editions, etc., or a list of books on a subject or by one author

Book Report: A report of a book giving the main idea or plot

Camera: A device for taking pictures by means of a lens through which rays of light pass to a sensitive plate or film

Capitalization: Proper use of capital letters

Celsius: A scale to measure temperature on which water freezes at 0°C and boils at 100°C

Check: To make sure that something is right; to stop or hold back for a short time

Citation: A quotation or the citing of a passage in a book

Clarity: Clearness; intelligibility

Classify: To arrange in classes systematically

Color, Ink: The quality of things resulting from their property or reflecting some light rays and absorbing others; to give color to; a tone or shading

GA1325

Communicate: To exchange ideas through speech, writing or a signal

Compare: To analyze one thing in terms of another; to discover resemblances and differences

Computer: An electronic calculating machine that stores information and works quickly

Conclusion: The end; an inference drawn based on the outcome of results; a final determination or answer to a question

Connect: To associate or be associated; to join or bring together; to form a line between

Contents: That which is contained, as the contents of a box; meanings, subject matter as the contents of a book. Table of Contents is a list of chapters at the beginning of a book.

Control Group: A group set up to control or monitor another group or groups upon which manipulations are performed. This group in an experiment represents the test group that has all variables standarized.

Controls: Factors that are *not* to be changed

Cover Page: The first page of a report upon which the title is placed and the name of the author. Also may contain other identifying information

Data: Facts on which reasoning is based; information

Dates: The day, month and year of an event or a happening

Dependent Variable: An event which varies according to some other happening or event. The results are linked and controlled by another factor that has also been changed.

Disc (Disk): A flat circular surface on which data is stored

Discussion: A debate; an argument pro or con

Dot Matrix: A type of printer which utilizes dots to reproduce printed matter or to encode and decode

Draft: A preliminary sketch or written document

End Note: Final thoughts appended to a report to outline future utilization of the report and possible further steps to add to its facilitation

Estimate: To guess the size, weight or cost of anything

Evaluate: To determine value; appraise; express numerically

Exhibit: To show or display

Experiment: A trial to test a theory or belief

Experimental Group: A group of subjects to which the independent variables are applied

Exposure: Act of exposing or state of being exposed; in photography, exposing a sensitized surface to light

Fahrenheit: A temperature scale having 32° as the freezing point, and 212° as the boiling point of water at sea level

GA1325

Figure: The shape or form of an object or one's body; to calculate with numbers or symbols; a numerical symbol such as 3, 5 and 7

Footnote: A note of explanation or reference at the bottom of the page

Glossary: A special list of words or phrases with a definition of use in a book

Gram: A base unit of mass in the metric system, e.g., 1000 grams in a kilogram

Graph: A diagram having lines, dots or other symbols to show relative size or the change over a period of time of variables. Graphs show raw, smooth or analyzed data.

Handwriting: Writing with the hand; that which is written by hand; a manuscript; the writing peculiarities of an individual

Heading: The title, subtitle or topic that is the beginning or top of a text

Hypothesis: Something assumed for the sake of argument; an explanation that accounts for a set of facts that can be tested by further investigation. A hypothesis tells what the experimenter thinks will happen as a result of the experiment.

Identify: To ascertain the origin, nature or definitive character of an object; to determine the taxonomic classification

Independent Variable: An event which is not affected by some other happening or event. The independent variable can be changed in an experiment without causing a change in other variables.

Infer: To derive by reasoning from facts; to conclude from evidence or premises

Information: Communicated knowledge or news; knowledge derived from study, experience or instruction

Interpretation: One's personal viewpoint based on data collected in an experiment

Introduction: The first part of a book or paper which tells you what it is about

Invertebrate: A classification of animals that do not have backbones

Issue Number: A symbol assigned to a periodical so that it can be found in a series of other periodicals or the same periodical

Justify: To demonstrate or prove to be just, right or valid

Kelvin: Pertaining to a temperature scale whose zero point is approximately -273.16°C

Keyboard: A set of control keys on a piano, typewriter or computer

Line Graph: A drawing that exhibits a relationship between two sets of numbers using lines

Liter: Liquid measure. 1000 cubic centimeters equals a liter.

Literature: A body of writings in prose or verse; the collective writings upon a given subject or particular field

Log: Daily written observations kept in a diary, notebook or journal; a record of performance or events

GA1325

Margin: The blank space around the edge of a page of printing or writing

Mass: The amount of material in something; a quantity of matter concentrated as a single body; a measurement not influenced by gravity

Materials: The substances of which anything consists; the implements and goods necessary for doing anything; any items used in an experiment

Matrix: A network of intersections between input and output leads in a computer functioning as an encoder or decoder

Mean: The middle point or situation; an approximate or adjusted average

Measure: To ascertain the dimensions or volume; to compute the extent or quantity

Median: Pertaining to the middle; constituting the middle value of a distribution with an equal amount above and below

Meter: The unit of length in the metric system; 39.37 inches equals one meter. An instrument that registers the measurement of currents through it such as water, gas and electricity.

Methods: A systematic arrangement of things or ideas; a way of doing something

Mode: Manner, way or method of doing or acting; the value or item appearing most frequently in a series of observations or statistical data

Notes: Brief explanatory comment; written reminders for yourself or someone else; single musical sound

Null: Zero; nothing; having no force or value; pertaining to a math set having no members or to zero magnitude

Numbers: Words, symbols or figures to show how many

Observe: To keep in view; take notice of; watch carefully

Observation: What one sees while doing any experiment; observations lead to raw data

Pagination: The act of making into pages; the serial numbers used; the paging

Paper: An essay, treatise or scholarly dissertation on any subject

Personal Communication: Personal contact and interview with an individual expert as opposed to relying upon written reports

Photographs: Images, especially a positive print, recorded by a camera and reproduced on photosensitive paper

Plurals: The forms of a word denoting more than one—cats, kittens, children

Predict: To say what is likely to happen in the future; forecast

Printer: One that prints; a person whose occupation is printing; the part of a computer which produces printed matter

Probability: That which is likely to happen; a number expressing the likelihood of occurrence of a specific event

GA1325

Problem: A question for solution; a difficulty for which an answer is needed

Procedure: A manner of taking action; a way of conducting an experiment; the steps taken when an experiment is done

Proposal: A planned procedure

Qualitative Analysis: Analysis made without measurement; subjective

Quantitative Analysis: Analysis made with measurement instruments

Question: To ask repeatedly for answers so as to discover facts or solutions; an inquiry, interrogation

Raw Data: Figures, observations, results of experiments and other data which have not been refined by analysis or organization and applied to the problem or suggested hypothesis

Read: To examine and grasp the meaning of written or printed characters, words and sentences

Record: The facts in the history of anything; cylinder or disk from which sounds are reproduced by a phonograph; to set down for future reference

Reference: A source of information or authority

Reference Citation: A citation which gives information about where a particular quote may be found so the reader can verify accuracy or gain additional information on the subject

Relationship: The condition of being related; a logical or natural association between two or more things

Research: The process of gathering information on a subject by reviewing sources of information

Research Notes: Written records of observations, computations and the study of the problems, which are accumulated to become the material for the solution of the problem or hypothesis

Research Report: The final formal report which is the result of your studies and manipulations

Results: Consequences, effects of action; something that happens because of some action or happening; often are graphs and tables that represent raw, smooth and analyzed data

Rewrite: To look over again; to study again; to write a notice of a book or article

Scientific Method: The totality of principles and processes necessary for scientific investigation; rules for concept formation, conduct of observations and experiments and validation of observations and experiments, and validation of hypotheses by observation and experiment. In essence, one uses valid subjects, variables and controls and records results when using this method.

Serendipity: Making fortunate and expected discoveries by accident

Smooth Data: Tables and graphs that combine information from raw tables and graphs

Spacing: The act of arranging by spaces; a system or allowance for intervals; a space or spaces, as in printed matter

Statistics: Figures or numbers as they are used in classifying and explaining facts

Style Guide: A guide which is available which will give instructions as to how to prepare a report in a particular style or mode

GA1325

Subheadings: One of the small divisions of a writing or printing or the titles of such a division

Summary: A briefer form of a document or composition; presenting its principle features in a small space

Symbol: An emblem or sign; anything that represents something else. Figures are symbols for numbers, e.g., + means "addition" in mathematics.

Tables: Written way of presenting raw, smooth or analyzed data

Telephoto Lens: Lens which brings distant objects within distinct vision

Text: A topic or theme; a version of a book or story; the main part of a printed book

Think: To form a concept; imagine; to form a judgment; to use judgment, reason, imagination as opposed to mere sense perception

Time: Measure of duration, as by hours, days, years, ages; to measure the duration of action

Title: The name of an article, book, poem, picture or the like

Topic Report: A report which confines itself to one general topic or theme

Typewriting: The act, process or skill of using a typewriter; copy produced by typewriting; typescript

Unknown: Not known; unfamiliar; not identified or ascertained; a quantity of unknown numerical value in mathematics

Variable: Changing, unreliable; changeable, fickle, unsteady, inconsistent; anything subject to change; something that is changed to test the hypothesis or something that changes as a result of testing the hypothesis

Vertebrate: Classification of animals with backbones

Volume: The amount of space occupied by an object, as measured in cubical units; mass or bulk; a single book; how loud the sound is

Volume Number: A number assigned to a book so that it can be located in a series of similar books in the Library of Congress, on the shelves of local libraries and school libraries. The most common classification is the Dewey Decimal System.

Weight: The measure of the heaviness or mass of an object; the gravitational force exerted by the earth or other celestial body on an object; influence; importance; authority

Wide Angle Lens: A lens that has a relatively short focal length and permits an angle of view wider than approximately seventy (70) degrees

Word Processing: A system of producing typewritten documents, such as business letters, by use of automated typewriters and electronic text-editing equipment

Wordiness: Using more words than are necessary to convey meaning; redundancy

Write: To make intelligible symbols with a pointed tool on a surface; to form words, phrases, sentences

X Axis: The horizontal axis in Cartesian coordinates

Y Axis: The vertical axis in Cartesian coordinates

Zoom Lens: A camera lens whose focal length can be changed rapidly, allowing rapid change in the size of an image

GA1325

STUDENT'S GUIDE TO SCIENCE FAIR SYMBOLS
AND ABBREVIATIONS

Term	Symbol	Note
absolute	A	
alternating current	a.c.	
ampere	A	
ampere-hour	A-h	
angstrom	A°	
atomic weight	at.wt.	
boiling point	b.p.	
British thermal unit	Btu	
calorie	cal	
centimeter	cm	
cubic centimeter	cm^3	
decibel	db	
degree Celsius	°C	
degree Fahrenheit	°F	
degree Kelvin	°K	
direct current	d.c.	
Farad	F	
freezing point	f.p.	
gallon	gal.	
gram	g	
hectare	ha	
hertz	Hz	do not use cycles per second
horsepower	hp	
hour	h	
infrared	i.r.	
joule	J	
kilocalorie	kcal	
kilogram	kg	
kilometer	km	
liter	l	use entire word if confusing
lumen	lm	
melting point	m.p.	
meter	m	
microgram	ug	
micrometer	um	
miles per hour	mph	
milliampere	mA	
millivolt	mV	
molar (contentration)	M	underlined or italicized
nanometer	nm	
newton	N	

GA1325

Term	Symbol	Note
normal (concentration)	$\underline{N}$	underlined or italicized
ohm	$\underline{\Omega}$	
ounce	oz.	
parts per million	ppm	mg/l is preferred
pascal	Pa	
per	/	
percent	%	
pounds per square inch	pounds/in	
probability	$\underline{P}$	underlined or italicized
probably error	pe	
relative humidity	r.h.	
revolutions per minute	rpm	
second (time)	s	
species, singular	spp.	only after genus name
standard atmosphere	atm	
standard deviation	SD	
standard error	SE	
standard temperature and pressure	s.t.p.	
ultraviolet	u.v.	
volt	V	
volume	vol	
watt	W	
week	wk	
weight	wt.	
year	yr	

REQUIREMENTS: STUDENT'S SCIENCE FAIR CONTRACT

I, (the undersigned), do hereby contract for a science fair project and agree to the following conditions:

A. I will follow the basic principles of scientific investigation:
    1. Conduct research and collect data on my chosen topic
    2. Set up and conduct experiments in this area
    3. Construct a stable means of exhibiting my information and experiment

B. I will also construct a display board to exhibit my project at the Science Fair on _____ . By this I understand that I will meet the following deadlines unless previously arranged:
    1. I will have my project set up in the _____ by _____ p.m., _____, 19 _____ .
    2. I will remove my project no earlier than _____ on the evening of _____, 19 _____ .

C. I will have an Official Entry Card, which will be provided to me, attached to the right-hand side of my display along with an approved Student Vertebrate Animal Certificate if I use live animals in my study.

D. I will include in my exhibit a brief summary of my project, its purpose and a written paper of my study.

E. I will present a brief explanation of my project to the judges on _____ , 19 _____ . I will honestly attempt to answer with utmost sincerity and courtesy any questions the judges might ask me.

F. I understand that I will be judged on the following items:
    1. scientific thought: use of the scientific method
    2. research report
    3. physical display
    4. oral presentation
    5. attendance at science fair

G. I further acknowledge that if because of some extreme unforeseen circumstances my experiment cannot be concluded I may, under mutual agreement with my teacher, be reassigned to do a research paper on a related topic. I must give notification of this before _____, 19 _____ .

H. I also understand that this contract is in effect whether I am present in school or not. Termination of this contract is only possible by an extenuating circumstance such as withdrawal from school, death in the family or a serious illness certified by a doctor that I am unable to perform the work.

I hereby agree to the conditions and terms of this contract and have been given sufficient time to question any part of this contract. My signature implies complete understanding of this contract.

Signed_____   Contract date_____

Title of project (subject to approval)_____
Note: It is understood by the student that the topic is subject to change in wording but not in theme.

_____   _____
Signature of student   Signature of parent/guardian

_____   _____
Signature of teacher   Signature of mentor (if applicable)

GA1325

STUDENT'S MONTHLY SCIENCE FAIR PROJECT COMPLETION SCHEDULE

Name _____ School _____

Keep this schedule in a place where it is seen often.

Assignment	Date Due	Date Completed	Comments
1. Understand Judging Criteria			
2. Understand Scientific Method			
3. Preview Sample Program			
4. Review Project Idea and Question			
5. Identify a Problem			
6. Review of Literature			
7. State Hypothesis			
8. Project Proposal Written			
9. Locate Information			
10. Collect and Organize Data			
11. Keep a Journal			
12. Analyze and Interpret Results			
13. Research Report Written			
14. Construct Graphs, Tables and Diagrams			
15. Write Abstract			
16. Write Title Page, Table of Contents and References			
17. Build Project Display			
18. Develop Oral Presentation			
19. Present Project			
20. Evaluation of Project			
21. Revise Project			
22. Enter Project in Science Fairs at Local, State and/or National Levels			
23. Write Article to Share with Others			

GA1325

CRITERIA FOR JUDGING SCIENCE FAIR PROJECTS

There are many methods of judging science fair projects. This one, based on 100 points, will be used by the judges at the Science Fair.

Criteria	Points	My Points
A. Scientific Thought: Use of the Scientific Method 1. Student performed experiment in which data were collected and analyzed by using the scientific method.	1 2 3 4 5	
2. Student set up experiment carefully and kept an accurate record of the data in a journal, diary or logbook.	1 2 3 4 5	
3. Student's conclusion is logical and justifiable.	1 2 3 4 5	
4. Experiment is an original idea, unique and creatively done.	1 2 3 4 5	
5. Summary shows title, question, hypothesis, materials, procedures, results and conclusions.	1 2 3 4 5	
B. Research Report 1. Includes title page, table of contents, abstract, write-up of procedures, background information and bibliography.	1 2 3 4 5	
2. Background information shows student has conducted research on the topic.	1 2 3 4 5	
3. Report is displayed and written with correct use of spelling and grammar.	1 2 3 4 5	
4. Abstract is interesting and helpful.	1 2 3 4 5	
5. Bibliography is related to topic and written in correct form.	1 2 3 4 5	
C. Physical Display 1. Student has a well-constructed backdrop to display the project.	1 2 3 4 5	
2. Display tells story of the project accurately.	1 2 3 4 5	
3. Display is appealing and is neatly done with correct spelling.	1 2 3 4 5	
4. Display shows components of science fair project.	1 2 3 4 5	
D. Attendance at Science Fair Student is present at display and greets judge on time.	1 2 3 4 5	
E. Oral Presentation 1. Student gives a clear explanation about the research conducted.	1 2 3 4 5	
2. Oral presentation is coherent and well organized.	1 2 3 4 5	
3. Oral presentation had effective use of visual aids.	1 2 3 4 5	
4. Student answers questions accurately and honestly.	1 2 3 4 5	
5. Oral presentation made in time allotted with all phases discussed.	1 2 3 4 5	
	Possible Total	**Student Total**

Levels of Performance:
5 = Superior   4 = Excellent   3 = Good   2 = Satisfactory   1 = Fair   Points = [100]   Points = [ ]
Comments: Use reverse side for written comments and notes.

GA1325

STUDENT'S GUIDE
ON HOW TO DO A HIGH-QUALITY SCIENCE FAIR PROJECT

S

Date _____

Dear Student:

The excitement of participating in the Science Fair Mentorship Program is one of the many benefits of doing a science fair project. Some of you may study with very knowledgeable people in the community called "mentors," who will help you with your project. To prepare you for this experience, a review of the steps necessary to plan and carry out a high-quality science fair project is necessary. These steps are outlined below.

PLAN AHEAD

Preparing a project schedule will help you budget your time to meet certain deadlines. If you know the deadline for submitting a report for a particular task, then start with those dates and work backwards. Use a calendar and check with your teacher and/or mentor to help you set up your schedule.

IDEAS: IDENTIFY THE NEW PROBLEM

Coming up with an idea for your research project is often a difficult step. Do some brainstorming with your friends and classmates. Check current newspapers and popular magazines for lead articles that focus on current ideas such as lasers and energy. Read the tables of contents of recent science magazines to see what leading researchers are currently doing in science. While on vacation you may visit museums, parks, historical sites and other recreational areas where something will suggest an idea for your project. Talk to family members and neighbors about their work. Visit community events such as fairs. Consider your hobbies and crafts. Use as many events as possible to come up with ideas for your project.

NARROW THE TOPIC

Once you have some idea of your area of interest, you should begin to narrow the topic. A serious error of first-time investigators is trying to do too much. You'll be able to do a better job if you narrow the topic. For example, in order to ask a question about a topic such as energy, you will need to understand if the topic can be broken down into smaller units. Soon you will reach a part of the topic that is limited enough to allow you to proceed until you begin to exhaust all available sources of information. A broad topic such as energy could be divided into sources, uses and the physics of energy. Sources could include natural gas, oil, nuclear, coal, solar and wind. If you are particularly interested in wind, you'll soon discover that you can be even more specific. Projects on wind may be concerned with availability, economics, environmental aspects, regulations and engineering. Engineering may be limited to one question such as "How does blade design affect the performance of a wind turbine?"

GA1325

FORMULATE HYPOTHESIS: MAKE AN INTELLIGENT GUESS

A hypothesis is a statement of what you expect will happen in your experiment. You may state, for example, that the more blades or vanes on a wind turbine, the faster it will turn. A hypothesis should state precisely what will be tested. Formulating a hypothesis will help you design your experiment so you'll know what to measure and what data will be needed in your study.

LOCATE INFORMATION VIA LIBRARY RESEARCH

Once you have set up a schedule, chosen an idea for your project, limited your topic, identified a problem and stated a hypothesis, you need to make a thorough search for additional information to help you learn as much as possible about your topic. This information is needed to refine your experimental approach. Expand your search for information beyond your school. Consider the many resources available in your community—public libraries, businesses and industries, governmental agencies, trade and professional organizations, colleges and universities, museums and nature centers. Use your local library to find more information. Although advanced research requires access to various data bases in research laboratories, you'll find that your local library will give you access to a world of information if you take the time to ask. Your first stop in the library will probably be the card catalog which is often on computer terminals. The computer will show various sources of books and materials arranged by author, title and subject. On-line catalogs and data bases using a CD-ROM may be searched rapidly on your topic. These on-line sources are useful to find publications which may be borrowed through a library loan from other libraries. The card catalog will list circulating books which are usually stored on long rows of shelves or stacks. You can also use the card catalog to find noncirculating reference books. Reference books include science encyclopedias, which can be used as a starting point in your research to get an overview of the subject. Top-quality researchers, however, must use many other sources of information since encyclopedias are general and seldom useful beyond the early stages of the work. Handbooks of standards, formulas and data will help you determine whether your results are similar to those obtained over the years by researchers. Newspaper and magazine indexes give you an access to a broad range of publications. Once the reference is located, you will need to find a microfilm or microfiche and view it with a special reader. You can even make a hard copy of it for your later reference. Nearly every library will have the *Readers' Guide to Periodical Literature* which allows you to find popular publications with articles on your subject. Abstract publications provide extensive listings of research reports in technical papers presented at meetings or published in scientific and engineering journals. Although not always available in local libraries, most college libraries have abstract publications on chemistry, biology, mathematics, physics, social sciences, energy and the environment. Technical journals and weekly magazines give you the latest findings of researchers in many fields of science. Another library source is the pamphlet or vertical file. Often very useful items can be found here which don't seem to fit in with other parts of the library system.

LOG: COLLECT AND ORGANIZE DATA

An important step in your science fair project is the collection and organization of data and other information. Be sure to budget adequate time. Consider also how you'll record information. Purchase a notebook that will serve as a log or diary for all of your observations. Make accurate entries. Feel free to include more information than you think is needed. Later, you may find out that at one time something seemed unimportant, but later it is just what you need to explain some unexpected results. Record the date and time of all entries in your log. You may also find that a tape recorder, various cameras and other media such as word processing are useful to record observations.

PROCEDURES: DESIGN INVESTIGATION

There are many methods of collecting data. Choose one method or a combination of methods that is the best for testing your hypothesis. Some of these methods include:

1. **A Simple Controlled Experiment.** This is an experiment in which there is only one group or subject that gets the experimental treatment. The control group does not get the experimental treatment but is otherwise treated the same.

2. **Counterbalancing or Cross-Over Design Experiment.** This is a controlled experiment which is done twice with the same subjects. The second time the groups are crossed over, thus the control becomes the experimental and the experimental becomes the control.

3. **Blind and Double-Blind Experiments.** In a blind experiment, the subject, although being knowledgeable about the experiment does not know if he/she is a part of the control group or the experimental group. In a double-blind experiment, both the experimenter and the subject are uninformed as to which group received the treatment.

4. **Case Study.** A case study is a detailed observation for a study of an individual or an event.

5. **Anecdotal Record.** An anecdotal record is one's personal experience written as a story.

6. **Naturalistic Observation.** A naturalistic observation is a viewing and recording of a natural situation such as people, animals, societies and communities which are viewed with the least amount of disturbance to the subjects.

7. **Survey.** A survey is the systematic sampling of opinions or collection of data from a designated group of people, plants or animals.

Whatever method you use to collect data, be sure it is the best one for testing your hypothesis.

GA1325

LOCATE EQUIPMENT AND MATERIALS

Before you begin your experiment you should list and locate all equipment and materials you need. If your school doesn't have the equipment and you can't borrow it locally and can't afford to purchase it, consider writing a proposal to a local community service organization for possible funding. First, write for a proposal guide. Second, follow the guidelines carefully. Third, write the proposal and then submit your proposal to the organization. Many local groups will help you if you try.

ANALYZE AND INTERPRET RESULTS

The results of your experiment should be summarized as accurately as possible in appropriate ways. Use tables, graphs and the power of the computer to analyze your findings. Describe what relationship exists between the variables. Consider your sampling methods. Were they adequate to generate sufficient data? Do you need to go back and report certain trials or tests to make sure your samples weren't contaminated? Was the experiment a reliable test of the hypothesis? Will the same results occur if the experiment was done again? Ask your math teacher to help with statistical analysis to prove whether your sampling techniques and the amount of data you collected are valid.

WRITE REPORT

No project would be complete without the preparation of a written report. Physically, your report should have several parts including an accurate title page, table of contents page, abstract page, introduction including background information, statement of the problem and hypothesis, experimental design, analysis of results including tables and graphs, conclusion, references and finally an appendix. Ask your English teacher for help in the preparation of your report. You may also use various guides for writing reports. Use a word processor to write your report; it saves valuable time.

DISPLAY

If you plan to use your project at the Science Fair, you need to prepare a display in addition to preparing a written report. Accuracy of displayed information is important. The display should represent the sequence of your report and be a graphic and concise representation of your research. Although the exact contents of your display will vary, depending on the nature of your project, be sure to include the following elements: title, abstract, background information including problem and hypothesis, experimental design results (including tables and graphs), conclusions and implications for further research, project log, research report, experimental apparatus and samples.

MAKE ORAL PRESENTATION

Effective oral presentations are essential to top-quality science fair projects. In an oral presentation, you'll be asked to summarize your research. Don't memorize your speech. An effective way to present your material is to use your display as a backdrop for your oral presentation. Use note cards to make sure you've covered all the parts of your work. See page 204 for tips on how to make an oral presentation to judges.

The excitement of participating in a Science Fair Mentorship Program is a sharp contrast to the stillness of the libraries, but they are both experiences you will enjoy when you look back on your accomplishments. As you plan your project, remember these important steps: plan ahead, search for ideas, narrow your topic, identify your problem, state your hypothesis, locate information, collect and organize data, analyze and interpret results, write a report, build a display, make your presentation and be confident and proud of your work. If you follow these suggestions, you'll be well on your way to planning a successful science fair project. Your project will open up a whole world of opportunities for you. Your future will be bright and personally rewarding.

Sincerely,

_____

_____

Parent/Guardian Signature

Modified from the videotape *Planning Your Science Project*. Copyright © 1984 by The Ohio Academy of Science, 445 King Avenue, Columbus, OH 43201. Used with permission.

STUDENT'S GUIDE
ON HOW TO WRITE A SCIENCE FAIR REPORT

A

Includes your name, school and title of research topic.

B

Features a list of the major sections in the paper. Should be done last when you have all the pages numbered and organized.

C

A shortened version, usually 150-200 words, of your own research paper

D

A statement about what others have found out about the problem you are investigating

E

A list of books, periodicals and other reference materials used in your background research to find out what others have done related to your topic

F

Precisely state the problem or question you are attempting to answer. "The problem of this research study is . . . ."

G

State what you expected to happen or what is to be proved by your work.

H

State how the project was done. Include the steps you followed when you did your experimentation.

GA1325

STUDENT'S GUIDE
ON HOW TO WRITE A SCIENCE FAIR REPORT

I
List all materials that you used in your research. These may include things that you built, used or borrowed. Include all audiovisual materials such as photography, too. Be sure to include a computer if you used one.

J
Describe the things that you changed and those that you tried to control. Identify both the control and experimental groups.

K
Include all data that you collected using charts, models, diagrams, computer programs, videotapes, photographs and tables that you created when you did the experiment.

L
State what you found out as a result of doing the project. Tell how the research data either supported or denied your hypothesis or guess.

M
State the practical value of your research. Also state how your research findings could be used in future research. Tell about new questions that came about as a result of your research.

N
List full names and titles of all people who helped you in your research and what they contributed to your research study.

O
A final list of books, periodicals and other materials used in your study

P
Include any extra related information and materials directly related to the topic and research study. Include copies of any required forms here.

STUDENT'S GUIDE
ON HOW TO WRITE A SCIENCE FAIR REPORT

In the blank next to each statement in Column A, write the letter found on the science fair card that best matches that statement. The first one is done for you. Then in Column B, write the steps in the correct order. The first one is done for you.

Column A

_____A_____ Title Page

_____ Abstract

_____ Background Bibliography

_____ Statement of Hypothesis

_____ Procedures and Methods

_____ Statement of Problem

_____ Background Research

_____ Table of Contents

_____ Appendices

_____ Materials

_____ Acknowledgements

_____ Results

_____ Conclusion

_____ Discussion

_____ Variables and Controls

_____ References

Column B

1. _____Title Page_____

2. _____

3. _____

4. _____

5. _____

6. _____

7. _____

8. _____

9. _____

10. _____

11. _____

12. _____

13. _____

14. _____

15. _____

16. _____

STUDENT'S GUIDE
TO SCIENCE FAIR TOPICS AND IDEAS

IDEA	
1. What Are the Effects of Various Temperatures on Seed Germination?	
2. How Does Sugar Affect the Growth of Yeasts?	
3. What Is the Effect of Moon Phases on Seed Germination?	
4. Under Which Color of Light Do Plants Grow the Best?	
5. What Is the Effect of Auto Exhaust on Plant Growth?	
6. What Effects Does Temperature Have on the Activity of Earthworms?	
7. In Which Type of Material Will Plants Grow the Best?	
8. How Do Mealworms React to a Light Stimulus?	
9. Can Earthworms Tell Left from Right?	
10. What Is the Effect of Salt on the Growth of Plants?	
11. Does Adding Bleach to Water Affect Fungus Growth?	
12. Do Snails or Earthworms Travel Faster?	
13. How Is the Behavior of Ants Affected by Coffee Grounds?	
14. Do Apples of Various Types Have the Same Number of Seeds?	
15. How Much Water Is in an Orange?	
16. How Do Sound Waves Affect Plant Growth?	
17. What Is the Effect of Magnetism on Seed Germination?	
18. What Affects the Biodegradability of Various Detergents?	
19. What Effects Does Barometric Pressure Have on Grades?	
20. Does Sugar Prolong the Life of Cut Flowers?	
21. What Effect Does the Amount of Salt Have on the Floatability of an Egg?	

STUDENT'S GUIDE
TO SCIENCE FAIR TOPICS AND IDEAS

IDEA	
22. What Effects Does Salt Have on Ice at Different Temperatures?	
23. Which Type of Cheese Grows Mold the Fastest?	
24. How Is the Taste of a Cookie Affected by the Absence of One Ingredient?	
25. How Does Salt Affect the Rate of Temperature Change in Water?	
26. Which Antacid Is Really the Best?	
27. What Is the pH of Rain and/or Snow?	
28. Which Materials Absorb the Most Water?	
29. Which Brand of Diaper Absorbs the Most Moisture?	
30. Which Brand of Popcorn Pops the Most Kernels?	
31. Which Brand of Popcorn Pops the Fastest?	
32. Which Brand of Raisin Cereal Has the Most Raisins?	
33. How Much Vitamin C Is in Various Types of Orange Juice?	
34. Which Type of Juice Cleans Pennies the Best?	
35. Which Type of Cleaner Removes Ink Stains the Best?	
36. Which Brand of Paper Toweling Is the Strongest?	
37. Which Brand of Paper Toweling Is the Best Overall?	
38. What Materials Provide the Best Insulation?	
39. What Are the Effects of Weather on Painted Surfaces?	
40. What Is the Best Concrete Mixture?	
41. Will a Metal or Wooden Baseball Bat Hit a Ball Farther?	
42. Which Type of Battery Will Run a Toy the Longest?	

GA1325

O P P F = October
                Planning
                Parent
                Focus

THE SCIENCE FAIR TEACHER COMMUNICATES WITH PARENTS

91

GA1325

ACTIVITY NO.	KEY	ACTIVITY	REFER TO PAGE(S)	DATE COMPLETED
O1 (T)	OC	Design a Science Fairs with Style Parents' Packet. Draft a cover letter to parents that explains the contents of the parents' packet.	92, 99-113, 102	

TIPS FOR THE TEACHER

Science Fairs with Style Parents' Packet

The second of five packets, Science Fairs with Style Parents' Packet, is found on pages 99 to 113. Make copies of the packet and distribute to parents. In addition to front and back covers, the packet contains a cover letter (p. 102); a parents' volunteer letter (p. 103); a scrounge and save letter (p. 104); a letter and list of requirements, criteria and time lines (pp. 105-111); Guidelines for a Science Fair Display (p. 112) and an evaluation form to be completed after the science fair program is over (p. 113).

In the cover letter encourage parents to read both the parents' *and* student's packets carefully. Urge parents to return the three signed documents as soon as possible so their youngsters can begin their science fair projects. The signed documents include

1. Student's Safety Contract (p. 65)
2. Student's Science Fair Contract (p. 78)
3. Student's Guide on How to Do a High-Quality Science Fair Project (pp. 81-85)

NOTES:

ACTIVITY NO.	KEY	ACTIVITY	REFER TO PAGE(S)	DATE COMPLETED
O2 (T)	OC	Include in the Science Fairs with Style Parents' Packet a follow-up copy of the Parents' Volunteer Letter sent to the parents in August.	22, 93, 103	

TIPS FOR THE TEACHER

Parents' Volunteer Letter

The Parents' Volunteer Letter to be included in the parents' packet is identical to the one on page 22 that was sent to the parents in August. This letter is included as a follow-up to remind the parents of your need for their help in the Science Fair Mentorship Program. Your request for help can be extended further by including the scounge and save letter (see page 104) in the parents' packet. Key materials for use in the Science Fair Student's Packet may be acquired with the use of this letter.

NOTES:

ACTIVITY NO.	KEY	ACTIVITY	REFER TO PAGE(S)	DATE COMPLETED
O3 (T)	OC	Include in the Science Fairs with Style Parents' Packet a personal letter that outlines the requirements, criteria and time line for the program.	94, 105-108	

TIPS FOR THE TEACHER

Parents' Guide to Requirements, Criteria and Time Line

The letter on page 105 is intended to inform the parents of the basic student requirements, criteria in judging science fair projects and overall time line for the Science Fair. Encourage parents to become involved and support the youngsters in their science fair activities. With everyone working together, the Science Fair Mentorship Program can be a huge success.

NOTES:

GA1325

ACTIVITY NO.	KEY	ACTIVITY	REFER TO PAGE(S)	DATE COMPLETED
O4 Ⓣ	OC	Include in the Science Fairs with Style Parents' Packet a copy of the article "How Can I Help My Child with a Science Fair Project?"	95, 109-111	

TIPS FOR THE TEACHER
"How Can I Help My Child with a Science Fair Project?"

Insert a copy of the article "How Can I Help My Child with a Science Fair Project?" in the parents' packet. This article presents tips on how parents can help their youngsters in the Science Fair Mentorship Program. Encourage parents to read the article and support their youngsters in developing science fair projects—being ever so careful not to do the projects for the children.

NOTES:

GA1325

ACTIVITY NO.	KEY	ACTIVITY	REFER TO PAGE(S)	DATE COMPLETED
O5 (T)	OC	Include in the Science Fairs with Style Parents' Packet a copy of Guidelines for a Science Fair Display.	96, 112	

TIPS FOR THE TEACHER

Guidelines for a Science Fair Display

Basic guidelines for a science fair display are found on page 112. Insert this page into the parents' packet. Encourage parents to help their children find sturdy materials for project displays. Emphasize that the display should be of an appropriate size, neither too large nor too small. Dimensions are included in the parents' packet and should be followed closely.

SOURCES OF SCIENCE FAIR DISPLAY BOARDS

There are many kinds of sturdy materials that can be used in making science fair display boards. Some of these include plywood, Masonite, pegboard, foam board, corkboard, particle board and triple wall. For information on foam boards, write to

Showboard Project Display Boards
Showboard, Inc.
2602 Delcon Street
Tampa, FL 33609

Triple wall (three-layered cardboard) is a strong, sturdy material. It can also be used for display boards. For information on triple wall, write to

Tri-Wall Containers, Inc.
Butler, IN 46721

*Cardboard carpentry is a hands-on, activity-based approach to basic carpentry principles and techniques utilizing triple-thick corrugated cardboard and simple tools. Many types of science fair apparatus and materials can be built using triple wall. For information on cardboard carpentry, write to

Learning Things, Inc.
68A Broadway, P.O. Box 436
Arlington, MA 02174

Note: For information on how to purchase the book *Cardboard Carpentry*, write to JED and Associates, P.O. Box 7143 RC, Toledo, OH 43615.

NOTES:

GA1325

ACTIVITY NO.	KEY	ACTIVITY	REFER TO PAGE(S)	DATE COMPLETED
O6 (T)	OC	Include in the Science Fairs with Style Parents' Packet a parent evaluation form to be returned at the end of the Science Fair Mentorship Program.	97, 113	

TIPS FOR THE TEACHER

Science Fair Mentorship Program Evaluation Form

Include a copy of the evaluation form found on page 113 in the parents' packet. This form is to be completed by the parents at the conclusion of the Science Fair Mentorship Program. The numbers below the appropriately checked blanks may be added to determine a total score. This score will represent the parents' view on the effectiveness of the Science Fair Mentorship Program. The lower the numerical score, the more favorable the rating. Group the open-ended responses into various categories such as items liked the best about the program, least, and specific suggestions for improvement of the program. Subcategories may range from doing the experiment, writing the paper, building the display, giving an oral presentation and evaluating the program. Share comments with parents, judges and members of the media. Use all constructive comments to improve next year's Science Fair Mentorship Program.

NOTES:

GA1325

ACTIVITY NO.	KEY	ACTIVITY	REFER TO PAGE(S)	DATE COMPLETED
O7 (T)	OC	Make copies of the complete Science Fairs with Style Parents' Packet. Distribute packets to the parents.	98-113	

TIPS FOR THE TEACHER
Science Fairs with Style Parents' Packet

The Science Fairs with Style Parents' Packet, the second in a series of five packets featured in this book, contains fifteen pages including information on how parents can become actively involved in support of their children in the Science Fair Mentorship Program. Make copies of the parents' packet for each parent. These parents' packets may be distributed to the parents by the children, or you can give them directly to the parents at an open house or parent-teacher conference. Encourage the parents to read *both* the parents' and student's packets and subsequently return signed copies of (1) Student's Safety Contract, (2) Student's Science Fair Contract and (3) Student's Guide on How to Do a High-Quality Science Fair Project.

NOTES:

SCIENCE FAIRS WITH STYLE
PARENTS' PACKET

Name _____

Address _____

(Front Cover)

SCIENCE FAIRS WITH STYLE
PARENTS' PACKET

(Back Cover)

Table of Contents

GA1325

ABOUT THE PARENTS' PACKET

Date _____

Dear Parents:

This science fair packet is designed to help you and your child have a successful science fair experience. Your role is a crucial one in the success of your child. This packet contains information in additon to what is found in the Science Fairs with Style Student's Packet. You are encouraged to read this packet and the student's packet carefully. Please sign the appropriate documents found in the student's packet and return them as soon as possible.

Included in the parents' packet are the following items:

1. Parents' Volunteer Letter

2. Parents' Scrounge and Save Letter

3. Parents' Guide to Requirements, Criteria and Time Line

4. Article entitled "How Can I Help My Child with a Science Fair Project?"

5. Guidelines for a Science Fair Display

6. Science Fair Mentorship Program Evaluation Form

Included in the student's packet are the following documents that we ask you and your youngster to sign and return to us as soon as possible:

1. Student's Safety Contract (p. 65)

2. Student's Science Fair Contract (p. 78)

3. Student's Guide on How to Do a High-Quality Science Fair Project (pp. 81-85)

Thank you for your assistance.

Sincerely,

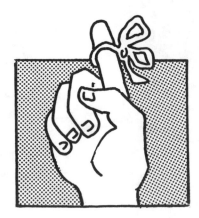

PARENTS' VOLUNTEER LETTER

(P)

Date _____

Dear Parents:

   In your child's study of science this year, we will be involved in a unique Science Fair Mentorship Program. As avid teachers of science, our major goal is to offer your child an opportunity to conduct a scientific research study under the careful guidance of a mentor, a person experienced in a subject area. Last year some students worked with physicians, veterinarians and engineers. The results of their efforts were displayed at our annual Science Fair in February.

   In order to reach our goal of having a successful Science Fair Mentorship Program, we need your help. Below is a Science Fair Volunteer Form. Please check the tasks that you could do to help us reach our goal. Clip the form and return it to us by the date shown on the form. We will organize volunteers in groups by tasks. You will receive further information throughout the year on our progress.

   Thank you for your support.

                                        Sincerely,

SCIENCE FAIR VOLUNTEER FORM

I would like to volunteer for the following activity(ies) involved in the Science Fair Mentorship Program:

_____ Be a member of the Science Fair Committee   _____ Organize field trips to research sites
_____ Contact librarians   _____ Be a science fair mentor
_____ Contact judges   _____ Donate science periodicals and books
_____ Contact community mentors   _____ Contact members of the media
_____ Help set up gym for Science Fair   _____ Supervise students setting up projects
_____ Help supply and dispense refreshments   _____ Donate science equipment
_____ Be a classroom helper   _____ Supervise students during judging
_____ Develop science fair program   _____ Contact guest speakers
_____ Help construct display boards   _____ Help in fund-raising
_____ Contact retired people for assistance   _____ Distribute copy of this form to anyone
_____ Other   who would be of help

Name _____   Address _____

Telephone (work) _____ (home) _____   Please return by _____.

PARENTS' SCROUNGE AND SAVE LETTER

Date _____

Dear Parents:

   In your child's study of science this year, we will be involved in a unique Science Fair Mentorship Program. As avid teachers of science, our goal is to offer your youngster an opportunity to conduct scientific research that will culminate in a science fair project.

   In order to reach our goal, we need your help. Below is a list of items that you may have in your home. If you are willing to donate any of these items, please send them to school with your youngsters by _____.

   Thank you for your support.

                              Sincerely,

paint	6-volt batteries
poster board	dry cells
35mm film	wire
videotapes	scales and balances
audio cassette tapes	measuring cups
slide trays	plastic containers
electrical cords	models and collections

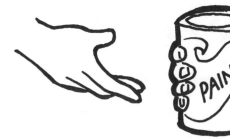

GA1325

PARENTS' GUIDE TO REQUIREMENTS, CRITERIA AND TIME LINE

Date _____

Dear Parents:

In your child's study of science this year, we will be involved in a unique Science Fair Mentorship Program. As avid teachers of science, our goal is to offer your child an opportunity to conduct scientific research that will culminate in a science fair project.

In order to reach our goal, we need your help. Enclosed in this packet are copies of the Student's Science Fair Contract that lists the requirements of the program; Criteria for Judging Science Fair Projects, which will be followed when judging your child's science fair project; and a Week-to-Week Schedule of Science Fair Activity for October Through February. This schedule will enable you to know what is required of your child each week.

Please read and sign the three appropriate documents that your child brings home. Have your child return the signed documents to school as soon as possible.

Thank you for your support.

Sincerely,

(P)

REQUIREMENTS: STUDENT'S SCIENCE FAIR CONTRACT

I, (the undersigned), do hereby contract for a science fair project and agree to the following conditions:

A. I will follow the basic principles of scientific investigation:
   1. Conduct research and collect data on my chosen topic
   2. Set up and conduct experiments in this area
   3. Construct a stable means of exhibiting my information and experiment

B. I will also construct a display board to exhibit my project at the Science Fair on _____ .
   By this I understand that I will meet the following deadlines unless previously arranged:
   1. I will have my project set up in the _____ by _____ p.m.,
      _____ , 19 _____ .
   2. I will remove my project no earlier than _____ on the evening of _____ ,
      19 _____ .

C. I will have an Official Entry Card, which will be provided to me, attached to the right-hand side of my display along with an approved Student Vertebrate Animal Certificate if I use live animals in my study.

D. I will include in my exhibit a brief summary of my project, its purpose and a written paper of my study.

E. I will present a brief explanation of my project to the judges on _____ , 19 _____ .
   I will honestly attempt to answer any questions the judges might ask me with utmost sincerity and courtesy.

F. I understand that I will be judged on the following items:
   1. scientific thought: use of the scientific method
   2. research report
   3. physical display
   4. oral presentation
   5. attendance at science fair

G. I further acknowledge that if because of some extreme unforeseen circumstances my experiment cannot be concluded I may, under mutual agreement with my teacher, be reassigned to do a research paper on a related topic. I must give notification of this before _____ ,
   19 _____ .

H. I also understand that this contract is in effect whether I am present in school or not. Termination of this contract is only possible by an extenuating circumstance such as withdrawal from school, death in the family or a serious illness certified by a doctor that I am unable to perform the work.

I hereby agree to the conditions and terms of this contract and have been given sufficient time to question any part of this contract. My signature implies complete understanding of this contract.

Signed _____ Contract date _____

Title of project (subject to approval) _____

Note: It is understood by the student that the topic is subject to change in wording but not in theme.

_____   _____
Signature of student   Signature of parent/guardian

_____   _____
Signature of teacher   Signature of mentor (if applicable)

GA1325

CRITERIA FOR JUDGING SCIENCE FAIR PROJECTS

There are many methods of judging science fair projects. This one, based on 100 points, will be used by the judges at the Science Fair.

Criteria	Points	My Points
A. Scientific Thought: Use of the Scientific Method 1. Student performed experiment in which data were collected and analyzed by using the scientific method.	1 2 3 4 5	
2. Student set up experiment carefully and kept an accurate record of the data in a journal, diary or logbook.	1 2 3 4 5	
3. Student's conclusion is logical and justifiable.	1 2 3 4 5	
4. Experiment is an original idea, unique and creatively done.	1 2 3 4 5	
5. Summary shows title, question, hypothesis, materials, procedures, results and conclusions.	1 2 3 4 5	
B. Research Report 1. Includes title page, table of contents, abstract, write-up of procedures, background information and bibliography.	1 2 3 4 5	
2. Background information shows student has conducted research on the topic.	1 2 3 4 5	
3. Report is displayed and written with correct use of spelling and grammar.	1 2 3 4 5	
4. Abstract is interesting and helpful.	1 2 3 4 5	
5. Bibliography is related to topic and written in correct form.	1 2 3 4 5	
C. Physical Display 1. Student has a well-constructed backdrop to display the project.	1 2 3 4 5	
2. Display tells story of the project accurately.	1 2 3 4 5	
3. Display is appealing and is neatly done with correct spelling.	1 2 3 4 5	
4. Display shows components of science fair project.	1 2 3 4 5	
D. Attendance at Science Fair Student is present at display and greets judge on time.	1 2 3 4 5	
E. Oral Presentation 1. Student gives a clear explanation about the research conducted.	1 2 3 4 5	
2. Oral presentation is coherent and well organized.	1 2 3 4 5	
3. Oral presentation had effective use of visual aids.	1 2 3 4 5	
4. Student answers questions accurately and honestly.	1 2 3 4 5	
5. Oral presentation made in time allotted with all phases discussed.	1 2 3 4 5	
	Possible Total	**Student Total**

Levels of Performance:
5 = Superior   4 = Excellent   3 = Good   2 = Satisfactory   1 = Fair   Points = 100   Points = [ ]
Comments: Use reverse side for written comments and notes.

GA1325

WEEKLY OCTOBER THROUGH FEBRUARY TIME LINE
Week-to-Week Schedule of Science Fair Activity
for October Through February

Week No. Due	OCTOBER ACTIVITY
1	Review sample projects of past science fair activities for ideas.
2	Topic selection is due. Register name of topic with your teacher.
3	Identify a problem that you would like to solve. Narrow the topic. Formulate a hypothesis by making an intelligent guess.
4	Find out what others have done to solve the problem. Go to the library. Read books and articles on the topic. Turn in a list of these materials to your teacher.

	NOVEMBER ACTIVITY
1	Meet with mentor to begin science fair activity. Make an oral presentation to your mentor that features your ideas.
2	Collect data from trials and tests that you do to solve the problem.
3	Keep a journal of all science fair activity both in and out of school.
4	Rough draft of an outline of your paper is due to your teacher. Include all topic headings. Have your mentor, parents and your teacher sign your outline.

	DECEMBER ACTIVITY
1	Written progress report on the results of your experiment is due to your teacher and mentor.
2	Begin to analyze the results of your experiment by making graphs, charts and using other statistical analyses of data.
3	Prepare an oral report on your project for presentation to a judge or members of the class.
4	Rough draft of your written science fair paper is due to your teacher and mentor.

	JANUARY ACTIVITY
1	With feedback from your teacher and mentor, draw final conclusions from your study.
2	Write and type final science fair paper to be given to your teacher and mentor.
3	Construct a backdrop display to exhibit your science fair project at the Science Fair in February.
4	Make a practice audio and/or videotape of your science fair presentation for the judges.

	FEBRUARY ACTIVITY
1	Complete entry form that includes name, project title, project number and signatures from student, parents and mentor is due to your teacher. Write an abstract of your study to be sent to judges prior to the day of the Science Fair.
2	Present science fair project for classroom Science Fair. Revise as needed for school Science Fair.
3	Present science fair project at school Science Fair. RELAX.
4	Complete Science Fair Mentorship Program Evaluation Form. Revise science fair project and enter into other science fairs at local, district, state and national levels.

GA1325

How Can I Help My Child With a Science Fair Project?

(P)

JEROME E. De BRUIN
University of Toledo

(A few tips teachers can give parents who ask this important question.)

How can I help my child with a science fair project? Teachers have often heard this question. They have responded with tips that range from going to the library to check out books or actually helping the child with the project—valuable advice, but there is much more parents can do to help their children.

Following are ideas that you can suggest to parents to help their children and, in the process, become partners in the learning process with you and the children. Though employing these tips takes little educational training, it does take time. It's well worth it. Some of the suggestions may seem quite obvious to you, but you can't assume that parents will know them and follow them all. If tips are given to answer parents' specific questions rather than used as condescending remarks, they can help build good relationships between the home and school. Consider sending parents a list of recommendations similar to this one, being sure to include a letter that tells the purpose of the list of tips.

1. Be Positive. When a person displays a positive feeling towards something, it encourages in others a similarly positive feeling towards that something. If you have a positive attitude toward the science fair project, your children will develop that same positive attitude. Try to be positive about your children's work. Praise them when they succeed. Be there to help them when they are having problems. They need your support and encouragement. Feeling, touching, and responding to your children in a positive manner really does help.

2. Be Aware of the Boy-Girl Syndrome. Science is for boys and English is for girls. Right? No! Wrong. Stocking an aquarium and hatching chick eggs are important activities for both boys and girls. Try to eliminate sex-role stereotypes. Perhaps Mom could take the youngsters to a quarry to dig fossils while Dad whips up a salad for a nutritious meal. This practice helps promote the idea early in your children's lives that science projects can be cooperatively done and thoroughly enjoyed by *all* members of the family.

3. Be Aware of the Perfect Parent Syndrome. Human beings are not perfect; we all make mistakes. Allow your children to make mistakes, and then help them capitalize on these mistakes and learn from them. Jean Piaget once said that children learn more from their mistakes and wrong answers than they do from correct ones. The same holds true for adults. Permit your children to make mistakes, but be sure they profit from them.

4. Be Honest with Your Children. Your children will ask many questions to which you may not know the answers. Be open and genuine in your responses. *Say* that you don't know the answer if you really don't know, but offer to help locate a source of information for possible answers and then follow through. Recently, after an exciting science lesson, a pint-sized second-grade girl tugged on my pants leg and asked, "Do bears go to the bathroom when they hibernate?" I assured her that I really didn't know for sure but offered to pursue the question further with her. Together, we called the zookeeper, who provided us with limited information but encouraged us to continue our investigation. We dug deeper and found an animal

GA1325

physiology book that supplied more detailed information. The search for information continued with interesting ideas being discovered. The net result: we learned together from our experience—and a great deal at that. (By the way, *do* bears really go to the bathroom when they hibernate? Yes, but only in small amounts because of low metabolic rate during hibernation, according to our expert.)

5. Look Around You. Coming up with ideas for a project can be difficult, but it won't be if you look around you. Do you grow plants in your home or garden? Do you have small animals? Do you travel to recreational areas, the zoo, or the beach? If so, these areas are excellent starting points for launching a science fair project. Observe and discuss with your children what is happening around them in their immediate surroundings. Take your children to parks, science centers, farms, zoos, art museums, airports, factories, quarries, and pet shops to obtain further ideas for a project.

6. Seek Out People to Help You. Contact people who have expertise in science and upon whom you can call to help with ideas on how to get started or help while the project is in progress. Does your child have a favorite teacher in school or a relative who may help? High school science teachers and university science professors have ideas and may be willing to lend a hand. Local businesses and industries often have educational services divisions that are excellent sources for ideas. Keep a record of science fair ideas and materials that you obtain from each source along with the names of key personnel and their telephone numbers for handy reference. Then, contact these people for help.

7. Get Books for Your Children. Join and use the free public library. Take your children to the library and help them obtain library cards. Select and check out books on how to do science fair projects. These books are excellent resources for starter ideas and do provide pertinent information that can be used in the development of a project. Books are fine, because they often tell you how to do the project but will carry you and your child only so far. Actual materials that your children can feel, touch, and work with are much better when actually doing the project.

8. Collect and Save Materials. Collect materials from all sources. Think before you throw anything away. Could it be used for the science fair project? Guide your children in gathering materials, and develop ways to use and care for these materials. Such items as egg cartons, scrap pieces of lumber, and boxes are handy materials to collect for a project.

9. Work with Materials. The single most important idea to remember, when working on a project, is that your children must be free to work with actual materials. Inexpensive everyday household materials often work the best. Your children will enjoy mixing powders, growing plants, breeding fish, or building out of scrap cardboard a maze for a pet gerbil. Encourage your children to "mess about" with these ideas and materials instead of merely reading about scientific discoveries in a book. Put the following ancient Chinese proverb into action:

> I hear and I forget;
> I see and I remember;
> I do and I understand.

10. Allow Time for Thinking and Exploring Alone. You will want to provide ample time for your children to be alone. During this time your children will explore, ask questions, and think about what is being done. It is important to be patient with your children during this period of incubation. Keep the atmosphere relaxed. Be a good listener and learn right along with your children. Praise your children and help out, but be ever so careful not to do for them many things that they can do for themselves. Remember, it's your child's project; not yours.

11. Stress "How-To" Skills. You will want your children to develop some very special skills, called "process" skills, while working on a science fair project. These skills should be stressed before the specific science facts. Some of these skills include observing, classifying, comparing, sorting, describing, inferring, and using space-time relationships. Your children will learn a great deal from observing an aquarium or an ant hill, classifying animals by color and size, describing an experiment, making guesses about what might happen when solutions are added to various powders, and sketching the moon for a month. Encourage your children to use and extend all possible senses when learning the processes of science. Facts, too, are important, but the processes that your children use when arriving at science facts are more helpful because your children can use them to solve problems that come up in everyday life. A sense of accomplishment is gained and a positive self-concept is developed in your children.

12. Examine Moral-Related Issues. It is healthy to help your children examine moral and values related issues that may arise during the course of a science fair project. Your children may ask why scientists sometimes sacrifice animals for experimentation purposes or why waters become polluted. Gather information about these topics. Then help your children explore the reasons experiments are conducted by scientists in various situations in an effort to improve the life of man on earth.

13. Daily Log of Research Activity. You and your children will want to keep accurate records of research activity while doing a science fair project. Information should be collected and recorded at regular intervals. You may want to help your children keep a record of personal feelings about the project which then can be used in writing a paper for a local science fair.

14. Paper. You will want to encourage your children to use the daily log when writing a paper for a science fair project. The written paper should include a description of the problem studied, some guesses on how to solve the problem, the methods used for collecting information, testing procedures, and some tentative findings or conclusions. After

the paper is written, help your children plan and develop an attractive display. Then, go over some possible questions that people may ask your children while the project is exhibited at the fair.

15. The Fair. It is vitally important that you and your children go to the science fair together. Help your children set up the project. Take photographs of their work and other entrants' projects. Save these ideas for future science projects. Have your children develop a scrapbook of ideas. Encourage them to chat with others about their projects. Ideas breed ideas. We learn from each other.

16. Follow-Up. After the science fair is over, you will want to urge your children to continue further research on the current project, dig a bit deeper, or explore another project. Talk about the possibilities. Share. Evaluate past projects and plan future ones. Stress the importance of scientific research done for the betterment of mankind. Give a science fair project a try and let me know how you and your children are doing.

Science Activities, Volume 17, Number 3, pages 109-111, September-October 1980. Reprinted with permission of the Helen Dwight Reid Educational Foundation. Published by Heldref Publications, 4000 Albemarle St., N.W., Washington, D.C. 20016. Copyright © 1980.

GUIDELINES FOR A SCIENCE FAIR DISPLAY

The following includes ideas on how a science fair project should be displayed. A typical science fair display looks like this:

The display board should be durable and made out of triple wall, cardboard, tagboard, Masonite, pressed wood or other self-supporting material. If three pieces need to be joined, connect them with inexpensive hinges or tape. The sides should measure 22" (55 cm) wide and 60" (150 cm) high, the back 30" (75 cm) wide and 60" (150 cm) high. Space is limited so adhere to these dimensions. Please notify me if your youngster's project requires special things like a computer, running water or electrical outlets. The display should have the following elements:

- Title
- Abstract
- Experimental design
- Background information including problem and hypothesis
- Results including tables and graphs of data
- Conclusion(s)
- Technical report
- Logbook
- Equipment, samples or other items from project activity

Help your child transport the project to and from school on time. The displays will be set up for _____ school day(s). Students will need to set up their displays in the _____ of the school between _____ and _____ . The displays are to be taken down between _____ and _____ .

Thank you for your help in this unique Science Fair Mentorship Program. Please join us and enjoy the rewards of your child's dedicated efforts.

GA1325

SCIENCE FAIR MENTORSHIP PROGRAM EVALUATION FORM

(P)

For each of the paired items listed below, place an X on the line that best represents your feelings about the Science Fair Mentorship Program.

Example: The Science Fair Mentorship Program was

Hot __X__ _____ _____ _____ _____ _____ _____ Cold
    (1)   (2)   (3)   (4)   (5)   (6)   (7)

1. **Interesting** _____ _____ _____ _____ _____ _____ _____ **Boring**
    (1) (2) (3) (4) (5) (6) (7)

2. **Important** _____ _____ _____ _____ _____ _____ _____ **Useless**
    (1) (2) (3) (4) (5) (6) (7)

3. **Informative** _____ _____ _____ _____ _____ _____ _____ **Worthless**
    (1) (2) (3) (4) (5) (6) (7)

4. **Complete** _____ _____ _____ _____ _____ _____ _____ **Incomplete**
    (1) (2) (3) (4) (5) (6) (7)

5. **Mixed Up** _____ _____ _____ _____ _____ _____ _____ **Smooth**
    (7) (6) (5) (4) (3) (2) (1)

6. **A Downer** _____ _____ _____ _____ _____ _____ _____ **An Upper**
    (7) (6) (5) (4) (3) (2) (1)

7. **Selfish** _____ _____ _____ _____ _____ _____ _____ **Unselfish**
    (7) (6) (5) (4) (3) (2) (1)

8. **Enough Time** _____ _____ _____ _____ _____ _____ _____ **Not Enough Time**
    (1) (2) (3) (4) (5) (6) (7)

9. **Light** _____ _____ _____ _____ _____ _____ _____ **Dark**
    (1) (2) (3) (4) (5) (6) (7)

10. **Negative** _____ _____ _____ _____ _____ _____ _____ **Positive**
    (7) (6) (5) (4) (3) (2) (1)

11. **High** _____ _____ _____ _____ _____ _____ _____ **Low**
    (1) (2) (3) (4) (5) (6) (7)

12. **Bad** _____ _____ _____ _____ _____ _____ _____ **Good**
    (7) (6) (5) (4) (3) (2) (1)

13. **Liked** _____ _____ _____ _____ _____ _____ _____ **Disliked**
    (1) (2) (3) (4) (5) (6) (7)

14. **Black** _____ _____ _____ _____ _____ _____ _____ **White**
    (7) (6) (5) (4) (3) (2) (1)

15. **Fast** _____ _____ _____ _____ _____ _____ _____ **Slow**
    (1) (2) (3) (4) (5) (6) (7)

On the other side of this page, list responses to the following: (1) Things I like(d) best about the Science Fair Mentorship Program; (2) Things I like(d) least about the Science Fair Mentorship Program and (3) Suggestions for improvement of the Science Fair Mentorship Program. **Note:** Please return this form as soon as possible to the Director of the Science Fair Mentorship Program or place in the Return Box on the day of the Science Fair. Thank you.

GA1325

ACTIVITY NO.	KEY	ACTIVITY	REFER TO PAGE(S)	DATE COMPLETED
O8 (T)	OC	Review copy of the Weekly October Through February Time Line at parent-teacher conferences. Inquire about progress made on project.	108, 114, 121	

TIPS FOR THE TEACHER

Conferences and Science Fair Time Line

An open house in early fall or parent-teacher conferences in October are ideal times to inquire with parents about their child's progress on the development of a high-quality science fair project. Review monthly (page 79) and weekly schedules (page 108) of science fair activity. Inquire with parents on progress made and effectiveness of Science Fairs with Style Parents' Packet. Answer any question in a straightforward manner. Be sure to thank the parents for their involvement in the Science Fair Mentorship Program and encourage them to contribute their efforts on behalf of their children.

NOTES:

GA1325

STUDENT'S MONTHLY SCIENCE FAIR PROJECT COMPLETION SCHEDULE

Name_____ School _____

Keep this schedule in a place where it is seen often.

Assignment	Date Due	Date Completed	Comments
1. Understand Judging Criteria			
2. Understand Scientific Method			
3. Preview Sample Program			
4. Review Project Idea and Question			
5. Identify a Problem			
6. Review of Literature			
7. State Hypothesis			
8. Project Proposal Written			
9. Locate Information			
10. Collect and Organize Data			
11. Keep a Journal			
12. Analyze and Interpret Results			
13. Research Report Written			
14. Construct Graphs, Tables and Diagrams			
15. Write Abstract			
16. Write Title Page, Table of Contents and References			
17. Build Project Display			
18. Develop Oral Presentation			
19. Present Project			
20. Evaluation of Project			
21. Revise Project			
22. Enter Project in Science Fairs at Local, State and/or National Levels			
23. Write Article to Share with Others			

ACTIVITY NO.	KEY	ACTIVITY	REFER TO PAGE(S)	DATE COMPLETED
O9 (T)	OC	Ask other teachers to save their students' work for possible extension into science fair projects.	36, 116	

TIPS FOR THE TEACHER

Students' Work and Science Fairs

Because of the *interdisciplinary* nature of science, post an announcement that encourages teachers from all disciplines to save high-quality work done by students. With permission from the students, these works can often be extended into worthwhile science fair projects. For example, a high-quality study on nutrition in home economics could be developed further into an interesting science fair project.

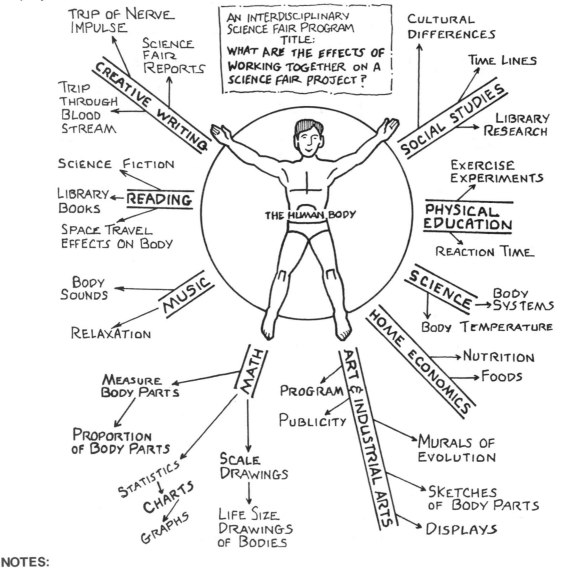

NOTES:

GA1325

ACTIVITY NO.	KEY	ACTIVITY	REFER TO PAGE(S)	DATE COMPLETED
O10 (T)	OC	Alert librarians at public library of assignment of science fair topics. Seek assistance on the acquisition and availability of science fair projects, books and materials.	28, 30, 117	

TIPS FOR THE TEACHER
Public Library

The public library can offer you and your students a wealth of information and serve as a source of inspiration. Discuss your science fair program early in the year with the public librarian. Ask the librarian to show you the collection of science titles including resource books, reference books, abstracts, vertical files, filmstrips, videotapes and laser discs. Ask whether CD-ROM and computer searches of data bases are available. Obtain a copy of the library hours and circulation rules for checkout of materials. Distribute these to students in the classroom. Inquire whether the highest-quality science fair projects may be displayed in the public library for public viewing after the Science Fair is over. Thank the librarian and pledge that you will keep the librarian current in what you and your students are doing in the classroom.

Extension: Large data bases such as The Source and CompuServe can be accessed for a list of resources on various topics. Check the rates, however, for use of the data bases. Plan your searches carefully because you will be charged for the length of time that you use the data bases. Have the printout of citations mailed to you to lower the cost of the search.

Note: Name of public librarian: _____

Address: _____

Phone _____

PUBLIC LIBRARIAN
Contact me early!

NOTES:

GA1325

ACTIVITY NO.	KEY	ACTIVITY	REFER TO PAGE(S)	DATE COMPLETED
O11 ⓣ	OC	Meet with school librarian. Arrange a library time for students to be shown science fair reference materials. Arrange to have reference materials checked out for classroom use.	118-119	

TIPS FOR THE TEACHER

School Library

The school library can also offer you and your students a wealth of information and serve as a source of inspiration. Contact and meet with the librarian early in the year to discuss your science fair program. Ask the librarian to show you the collection of science titles including resource books, reference materials, abstracts, vertical files, filmstrips, computer hardware and software, videotapes and laser discs. Ask whether CD-ROM and computer searches of data bases are available. Obtain information on library hours and circulation rules for check-out of materials. Ask whether an in-service session for teachers and students could be held and if special study schedules and hours for science fair students could be initiated. Ask whether the librarian could set up a science fair center in the library and keep a record of science fair projects in progress. Inquire if the librarian could review library and study skills that focus on interdisciplinary science fair projects. Inquire whether the highest-quality science fair projects may be displayed in the library after the Science Fair is over. Review Student's Library Checklist (page 119) with the librarian. Ask for suggestions. Then assign the page to the students. Be sure to thank the librarian and pledge that you will keep the librarian current on what you and your students are doing in the classroom.

Note: Name of school librarian: _____

Address: _____

Phone: _____

NOTES:

GA1325

STUDENT'S LIBRARY CHECKLIST

(S)

Name: _____

Science Fair Topic: _____

Title: _____

Key Descriptor Words: _____

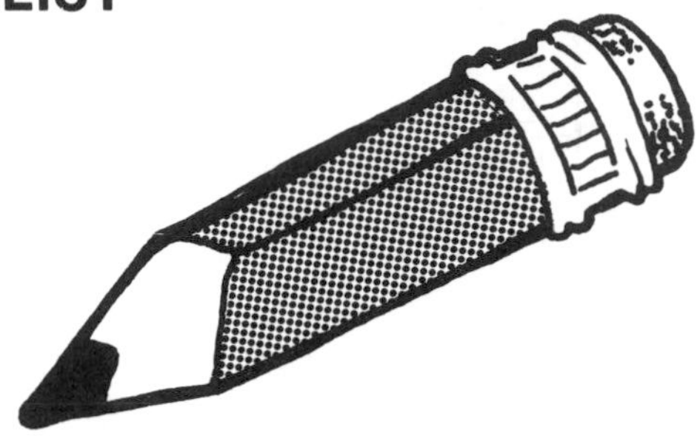

Items to Locate in the Library	Check ✓ When Found
A. CARD CATALOG Author, title and subject of circulating nonfiction and noncirculating reference books	
B. INDEXES Author's name and subject heading. *Readers' Guide to Periodical Literature*	
C. NEWSPAPER AND MAGAZINE INDICES	
D. SCIENCE ENCYCLOPEDIAS	
E. HANDBOOKS Chemistry, biology, physics and others	
F. ABSTRACTS Biological, chemical, mathematical, social sciences, environmental, energy	
G. JOURNALS	
H. COMPUTERIZED DATA BASES Including on-line card catalogs, The Source, CompuServe and CD-ROM such as ERIC.	
I. VERTICAL FILE Collection of brochures, magazine articles and other resource materials on specific subject areas	
J. OTHER Films, filmstrips, laser discs, posters, charts	

GA1325

ACTIVITY NO.	KEY	ACTIVITY	REFER TO PAGE(S)	DATE COMPLETED
O12 (T)	OC	Locate and reserve a vacant school room where students can store their science fair projects.	31, 120, 241	

TIPS FOR THE TEACHER
Vacant Storage Room

If students are permitted to work on science fair projects under adult supervision at school, ask the principal to reserve a vacant room in the school where science fair projects can be stored. If space is unavailable, science fair projects need to be done under adult supervision at home or at the site designated by a mentor.

NOTES:

GA1325

ACTIVITY NO.	KEY	ACTIVITY	REFER TO PAGE(S)	DATE COMPLETED
O13 (T)	IC	Develop with, and give to, students a week-to-week schedule that outlines the nature of science fair activities with expected deadlines to be met.	108, 114, 121	

TIPS FOR THE TEACHER
Week-to-Week Schedule

In early October, review Week-to-Week Schedule of Science Fair Activity for October Through February. A copy of the weekly time line (see page 108) is found in the parents' packet. Remind students that the title of their topic needs to be registered with you. The development of a hypothesis is encouraged after students visit the library to learn what others have done on the topic.

Extension: Make a chart of the following sources of information. Review chart with students. Post in the classroom for all to use.

Sources of Information

Airports
Books
Data Bases
Encyclopedias
Government Publications
Industry
Institutes
Local Newspaper
Magazines
Military
Museums
National Newspapers
Professional Journals
Public Library
Research Centers
Retired Individuals
Scholarly Journals
School Library
Seaquariums
University Library
Zoos

NOTES:

GA1325

ACTIVITY NO.	KEY	ACTIVITY	REFER TO PAGE(S)	DATE COMPLETED
O14 (T)	IC	Review process of conducting a science fair project using the scientific method.	63, 122	

TIPS FOR THE TEACHER
Review of the Scientific Method

Doing experiments with various pendulums is an excellent way to involve students in the process of conducting a science fair investigation. Review steps followed in the scientific method on page 63: Purpose, Hypothesis, Materials, Procedures Including Variables, Collection of Data, Results and Conclusions. Discuss each step. Inform students that they will be doing a controlled experiment using various pendulums.

NOTES:

ACTIVITY NO.	KEY	ACTIVITY	REFER TO PAGE(S)	DATE COMPLETED
O15 (T)	IC	Teach students the scientific method by performing a controlled experiment. Stress problem solving, hands-on lab experience with data collection.	123-125	

TIPS FOR THE TEACHER
Controlled Experiment Using the Scientific Method

This problem solving, hands-on lab experiment entitled A Swinging Time involves a controlled experiment on pendulums.

Do A Swinging Time in small groups. Make and distribute copies of page 124, A Swinging Time Using the Scientific Method. Review the word *pendulums* in the blank marked Topic Area. Inform students that they will study the problem of whether the length of the string has any effect on how many times the pendulum swings back and forth. Review the purpose of the experiment on the recording sheet. Have students develop a hypothesis in which they make a guess in order to answer the question "How does the length of the pendulum affect the number of times it swings back and forth?" Have students write their hypotheses in the blank. Gather these materials: lead sinkers for bob, stopwatch, string, meterstick and tape. Review procedure. Define *variable* as a factor that is manipulated or changed in an experiment (length of string), a *control* as things that are kept the same (time and starting height). Have the students test their hypotheses. Hold bob and string parallel to the floor. Release the bob. Count the number of swings it takes in fifteen seconds. Repeat using different lengths of strings. Have students record all data on page 125, A Swinging Time Data Sheet. Analyze data to determine whether the results support or refute the students' hypotheses. Then have the students write one conclusion based on the results of this activity. Include in the conclusion a statement on how this experiment is related to activities in everyday life such as various pendulums in clocks.

NOTES:

GA1325

A SWINGING TIME USING THE SCIENTIFIC METHOD

Use the spaces provided to record information about your science fair project. If you need more room, use the back of this sheet.

TOPIC AREA— _____ **Pendulums** _____

PURPOSE—Identify a Problem: What do you want to find out about pendulums? I want to find out if the length of the string affects the number of swings of a pendulum.

HYPOTHESIS—Make an Intelligent Guess: What do you think will happen?
___ I think . . . _____

MATERIALS—Gather Materials: What materials do you need to use?
_____

PROCEDURES—Things Done to Solve the Problem: What will you do to find the solution to your problem?
_____

  Variable: Things that change _____

  Control: Things that are kept the same _____

COLLECT DATA FROM TRIALS AND TESTS—Methods of Recording Data: What things can you count and measure?
_____

RESULTS—Observe What Happened: What happened when you did your experiment?
_____

CONCLUSIONS—Answers to the Question: What did you learn from your experiment?
_____

How can the results of this experiment be applied to your activities in everyday life?
_____

GA1325

A SWINGING TIME DATA SHEET

String Length	4″ (10 cm)	8″ 20 cm)	12″ (30 cm)	16″ (40 cm)	20″ (50 cm)	24″ (60 cm)	28″ (70 cm)	32″ (80 cm)	36″ (90 cm)	40″ (100 cm)

Swings Per 15 Seconds

Shade in the number of swings recorded for each length of string in the chart below. Remember to count the number of swings in fifteen seconds for each length of string.

NUMBER OF SWINGS											
10											
9											
8											
7											
6											
5											
4											
3											
2											
1											
0											
in cm	0″ 0	4″ 10	8″ 20	12″ 30	16″ 40	20″ 50	24″ 60	28″ 70	32″ 80	36″ 90	40″ 100

What seems to be the effect of varying the length of the string on the number of swings of the pendulum? How is this related to activities in your everyday life?

GA1325

ACTIVITY NO.	KEY	ACTIVITY	REFER TO PAGE(S)	DATE COMPLETED
O16 (T)	IC	Require students to write a summary of the results of their controlled experiment. Include a question, hypothesis, materials, procedures, results in a chart or graph form and a conclusion based on the data collected.	124-126, 128	

TIPS FOR THE TEACHER

Writing a Summary

Have students look up the term *summary* in their Student's Science Fair Glossary. Define the term as "a briefer form of a document or composition that presents the principal features in a small space." Using the previously completed pages, A Swinging Time Using the Scientific Method (p. 124) and A Swinging Time Data Sheet (p. 125), have the students write one-page summaries of the results of their controlled experiments on pendulums. Emphasize that the writing of the summaries of the controlled experiments will prepare the students to write summaries of the results for their own science fair projects. Be certain that the summaries contain all parts of the study ranging from the statement of the question through drawing a conclusion based on the data collected.

Extension: Writing summaries is an excellent way to introduce students to the computer, word processing skills and various types of data base software. This activity will be extended further when students begin to make information cards when they choose their final topics on page 128.

NOTES:

ACTIVITY NO.	KEY	ACTIVITY	REFER TO PAGE(S)	DATE COMPLETED
O17 ⓣ	IC	Help students narrow down and finally choose a manageable science fair topic to investigate.	126-127	

TIPS FOR THE TEACHER
Narrow the Topic

Once students have identified an area of interest, help them to narrow down their topic to a specific part of the total area of study. Students will often try to do too much, so encourage them to narrow their topics with the use of flowcharts. For example, if a student shows an interest in the sea, the topic can be narrowed as such: sea—uses—food—animals—humans. Encourage students to be *specific* in the selection of a topic. From the flowchart, the following topic may evolve: "What Are the Effects of Fish Oil on Cardiovascular Performance?" Emphasize that students should study a small part of a much larger whole in the development of their science fair projects.

NOTES:

GA1325

ACTIVITY NO.	KEY	ACTIVITY	REFER TO PAGE(S)	DATE COMPLETED
O18 (T)	IC	Have students choose, then begin to work on their science fair topics in earnest.	128, 153	

TIPS FOR THE TEACHER
Choosing a Final Science Fair Topic

   An effective technique used to help students choose their topics is to have them identify two favorite topics they would like to investigate. Students must write both topics in question or statement form on cards. Have students then choose the best topic knowing that the question or statement may change in the future. Inform the students that after a subsequent meeting with their teacher and/or mentor in early November, they will once again restate their science fair topics in question or statement form.

Extension: Using a computer, have students write their questions or statements on cards which are generally available for any tractor feed printer. Encourage students to record information using a word processor or data base. Facts can later be rearranged for writing various science fair reports. Encourage students to use their software to rearrange facts. Have a spelling checker available for their use.

NOTES:

ACTIVITY NO.	KEY	ACTIVITY	REFER TO PAGE(S)	DATE COMPLETED
O19 (T)	IC	Have students write a letter to a knowledgeable person in the community asking for assistance in the science fair study.	129-130	

TIPS FOR THE TEACHER
Letter to a Mentor

As students begin to work on their science fair projects, they will need assistance. Encourage them to write a knowledgeable person asking for such assistance. An acceptable letter includes these components:

1. Return address, telephone number and date

2. Shows evidence that student has used local library resources

3. Request is very specific and shows how student has narrowed the topic.

4. Student sends a description of the project and a summary of the background information collected. The person responding will less likely duplicate the information already collected.

5. Clearly shows that student has done advanced planning and is committed to the study

Mentors may be recruited from various community organizations, businesses and research facilities such as those found at airports, animal clinics, botanical gardens, colleges and universities, city government agencies, hospitals, industries, nature centers, retirees, zoos and others found in your local telephone book. See page 130 for a sample letter to a mentor.

Extension: Encourage students to use the word processor to write letters to mentors.

NOTES:

GA1325

(S)

Name _____

Street _____

City, State, Zip _____

Telephone (____) _____

Date _____

Dr. T. J. Sneva
Professor
Department of Mechanical Engineering
Our University
Theirtown, OH 43606
U.S.A.

Dear Dr. Sneva:

I am doing a research project on the control of emissions in automobiles. I have exhausted the resources at my school library, the local public library and the nearby college library.

An automobile mechanic at a local auto dealership suggested that you might be able to help me locate recent test data on the use of legal mechanisms to control emissions. I am specifically interested in how well these mechanisms control emissions at different levels of humidity and temperature over different periods of time. Do you have any recent reports or data which you could share with me? Would you be willing to talk with me about this request?

To help you respond to my questions, I have enclosed my research plan and a summary of the background information I have collected.

Thank you for your consideration of my request.

Sincerely,

Jerry DeBruin

Jerry DeBruin

Enc.

N P C F = November
Planning
Community
Focus

THE SCIENCE FAIR TEACHER COMMUNICATES WITH COMMUNITY MEMBERS

131

GA1325

ACTIVITY NO.	KEY	ACTIVITY	REFER TO PAGE(S)	DATE COMPLETED
N1 (T)	OC	Make copies of the Science Fairs with Style Community Member's Packet. Distribute to various community organizations, businesses and agencies.	132-133, 148	

TIPS FOR THE TEACHER

Science Fairs with Style Community Member's Packet

The third of five packets, Science Fairs with Style Community Member's Packet, is found on pages 133 to 148 in this book. Make copies of the packet and distribute to various community organizations, businesses and agencies, especially to those who feature retired people who may be willing to help in the program. In addition to front and back covers, the packet contains a cover letter (p. 136), a community member's volunteer letter (p. 137), a request to become a mentor for a science student (p. 138), an appeal for funding and materials (pp. 140 and 141), a guide for science fair activity (pp. 142-146) and an evaluation form (p. 148) to be completed and returned to the teacher after the Science Fair is completed.

In the cover letter, encourage members of the community to become actively involved in the Science Fair by acting as volunteers and/or mentors for science fair students. Mentors may be recruited from various community organizations, businesses and research facilities such as those found at airports, animal clinics, botanical gardens, colleges and universities, city government agencies, hospitals, industries, nature centers, retirees, zoos and others found in your local telephone book.

NOTES:

GA1325

SCIENCE FAIRS WITH STYLE
COMMUNITY MEMBER'S PACKET

Name _____

Affiliation _____

(Front Cover)

SCIENCE FAIRS WITH STYLE
COMMUNITY MEMBER'S PACKET

(Back Cover)

SCIENCE FAIRS WITH STYLE
COMMUNITY MEMBER'S PACKET

Table of Contents

GA1325

ABOUT THE COMMUNITY MEMBER'S PACKET

Date _____

Dear Community Member:

   This science fair packet is written to inform you of our unique Science Fair Mentorship Program. As avid teachers of science, our major goal is to involve our students with various members of the community in an effort to conduct high-quality science fair projects. Your role as a mentor is a crucial one for the success of these students and for our community as a whole.

Included in the community member's packet are the following items:

   1. Community Member's Volunteer Letter

   2. Mentor Volunteer Form: Adopt a Young Scientist

   3. Letter of Appeal for Funding

   4. Community Member's Scrounge and Save Letter

   5. Community Member's Guide to Science Fair Requirements, Criteria and Time Line

   6. Student's Science Fair Project Completion Schedule

   7. Guidelines for a Science Fair Display

   8. Science Fair Mentorship Program Evaluation Form

   We hope that you will read the packet carefully and consider helping us in this unique program. If interested, please call us at _____ by _____ , _____ .

Sincerely,

COMMUNITY MEMBER'S VOLUNTEER LETTER

C

Date _____

Dear Community Member:

In our students' study of science this year, we will be involved in a unique Science Fair Mentorship Program. As avid teachers of science, our major goal is to afford students an opportunity to conduct a scientific research study under the careful guidance of a mentor, a person experienced in a subject area. Last year some youngsters worked with physicians, veterinarians and engineers. The results of their efforts were displayed at our annual Science Fair in February.

In order to reach our goal of having a successful Science Fair Mentorship Program, we need your help. Below is a Science Fair Volunteer Form. Please check the tasks that you could do to help us reach our goal. Clip the form and return it to us by the date shown on the form. We will organize volunteers in groups by tasks. You will receive further information throughout the year on our progress.

Thank you for your support.

Sincerely,

_____

SCIENCE FAIR VOLUNTEER FORM

I would like to volunteer for the following activity(ies) involved in the Science Fair Mentorship Program:

_____ Be a member of the Science Fair Committee
_____ Contact librarians
_____ Contact judges
_____ Contact community mentors
_____ Help set up gym for Science Fair
_____ Help supply and dispense refreshments
_____ Be a classroom helper
_____ Develop science fair program
_____ Help construct display boards
_____ Contact retired people for assistance
_____ Other

_____ Organize field trips to research sites
_____ Be a science fair mentor
_____ Donate science periodicals and books
_____ Contact members of the media
_____ Supervise students setting up projects
_____ Donate science equipment
_____ Supervise students during judging
_____ Contact guest speakers
_____ Help in fund-raising
_____ Distribute copy of this form to anyone who would be of help

Name _____ Address _____

Telephone (work) _____ (home) _____ Please return by _____

GA1325

MENTOR VOLUNTEER FORM: ADOPT A YOUNG SCIENTIST

Date _____

Dear Prospective Mentor:

This school year we are involved in a unique Science Mentorship Program for students. As avid teachers of science, our major goal in the program is to afford students an opportunity to conduct a science research study under the careful guidance of a mentor, an experienced person knowledgeable in a subject area. The results of the students' research efforts will be displayed at our annual Science Fair in February.

In order to reach our goal of having a successful Science Fair Mentorship Program, we need your help in the identification of knowledgeable people in the fields listed below who may be interested in acting as mentors for our students.

General Areas of Research Interests	**Name, Address, Phone No. of Possible Mentor**
_____ Anatomy: Human and Nonhuman	_____
_____ Astronomy	_____
_____ Behavioral and Social Sciences	_____
_____ Biochemistry	_____
_____ Biomedical Engineering	_____
_____ Botany	_____
_____ Chemistry	_____
_____ Computers	_____
_____ Earth Science	_____
_____ Embryology/Developmental Biology	_____
_____ Engineering	_____
_____ Environmental Sciences	_____
_____ Genetics	_____
_____ Health	_____
_____ Lasers	_____
_____ Mathematics	_____
_____ Medicine	_____
_____ Microbiology	_____
_____ Microscopy	_____
_____ Molecular Biology	_____
_____ Nutrition	_____
_____ Pathology	_____
_____ Pharmacology	_____
_____ Physiology	_____
_____ Physics	_____
_____ Space Science	_____
_____ Veterinary Science	_____
_____ Zoology	_____
_____ Other	_____

Please read page 139 for further information on the role of the mentor. Please consider being a mentor yourself. Check the appropriate space and return this letter to me as soon as possible. Thank you.

Sincerely,

GA1325

THE ROLE OF THE SCIENCE FAIR MENTOR

A science fair mentor is a member of the community knowledgeable in a subject matter area who is willing to share his/her experience with a junior scientist. In our Science Fair Mentorship Program, the student is paired with the science fair mentor who helps the student conduct a scientific investigation that leads to a science fair project and display. Meeting at mutually agreed upon times, the mentor, acting in the role of an advisor, assists the student with the following tasks:

1. selecting a manageable topic

2. determining resources needed

3. selecting an appropriate title and posing it as a question

4. planning on-site, long-range experiments and/or demonstrations

5. completing research

6. filling out progress reports

7. writing a 100 to 150-word abstract

8. being interviewed by others

9. collecting data

10. building a display or exhibit

11. written report

12. oral presentation

13. meeting with classroom teacher and student

14. meeting periodically to review project with the student

15. Other _____

Being a mentor for a young scientist is a rewarding way for scholars to become involved in and return to society the benefits that society once gave to them. Students need role models to emulate. Won't you adopt a young scientist and be a part of our Science Fair Mentorship Program? The rewards are many. Thank you.

GA1325

LETTER OF APPEAL FOR FUNDING TO SUPPORT
A UNIQUE SCIENCE FAIR MENTORSHIP PROGRAM FOR STUDENTS

Date _____

Dear _____ :

    This school year we are involved in a unique Science Fair Mentorship Program for students. As avid teachers of science, our major goal in the program is to offer students an opportunity to conduct a science research study under the careful guidance of a mentor, an experienced person knowledgeable in a subject matter area. A mentor may be a physician, veterinarian or engineer. The results of the students' research efforts will be displayed at our annual Science Fair in February.

    In order to reach our goal of having a successful Science Fair Mentorship Program, we need your help. Below is a list of items that we will need. We hope that you will support our program with a contribution and/or materials, and thus give our students an opportunity to participate in this unique program.

    Our first annual Science Fair will be held on _____ , _____ at _____ . Please join us to view the accomplishments of these students, all of whom are a result of being placed in an environment in which they could be the very best that they could be. Thank you.

Sincerely,

Item	Quantity	Item	Quantity
Stencils	8 sets	Duplicating paper	5 reams
Paint	10 pints	Stationery	Asstd.
Rubber cement	10 bottles	Electrical cords	10
Markers	10 sets	Exhibit paper	5 packets
Construction paper	20 packs	35mm film	20 rolls
Poster board	30 sheets	Videotapes	10
Note cards (4" x 6")	10 packs	Audio cassette tapes	10
Masking tape	30 rolls	Slide trays	2
Glue	10 bottles	Computer discs	30
Thick cardboard or Masonite (60" x 74")	30 sheets	Computer paper	2 cartons

*Your gifts to educational institutions are often tax deductible to the amount limited by law.

Thank you.

COMMUNITY MEMBER'S SCROUNGE AND SAVE LETTER

Date _____

Dear Community Member:

In our students' study of science this year, we will be involved in a unique Science Fair Mentorship Program. As avid teachers of science, our major goal in the program is to offer students an opportunity to conduct scientific research that will result in a science fair project which will be displayed at our annual Science Fair in February.

In order to reach our goal, we need your help. Below is a list of items that you may have in your possession. If you have any of these items in limited or large quantities, that you are willing to donate, please deliver them to school by _____ , or call us at _____ , and we will pick them up.

Thank you for your support.

Sincerely,

Item	Quantity	Item	Quantity
Stencils	8 sets	Duplicating paper	5 reams
Paint	10 pints	Stationery	Asstd.
Rubber cement	10 bottles	Electrical cords	10
Markers	10 sets	Exhibit paper	5 packets
Construction paper	20 packs	35mm film	20 rolls
Poster board	30 sheets	Videotapes	10
Note cards (4" x 6")	10 packs	Audio cassette tapes	10
Masking tape	30 rolls	Slide trays	2
Glue	10 bottles	Computer discs	30
Thick cardboard or		Computer paper	2 cartons
Masonite (60" x 74")	30 sheets		

*Your gifts to educational institutions are often tax deductible to the amount limited by law.

Thank you.

BE A SUPER SCROUNGER LIKE ME!

COMMUNITY MEMBER'S GUIDE
TO SCIENCE FAIR REQUIREMENTS, CRITERIA AND TIME LINE

Date _____

Dear Community Member:

   In our students' study of science this year, we will be involved in a unique Science Fair Mentorship Program. As avid teachers of science, our major goal is to offer students an opportunity to conduct a scientific research that will result in a science fair project which will be displayed at our Science Fair in February.

   In order to reach our goal, we need your help. Enclosed in this packet are copies of the Student's Science Fair Contract that lists the requirements of the program; Criteria for Judging Science Fair Projects, which will be followed when judging the student's science fair project; and a Week-to-Week Schedule of Science Fair Activity for October Through February so you know what is required of the students each week.

   I hope that you will read the enclosed documents and consider helping us in our program. If you have any questions, feel free to call us at _____ . Thank you for your support.

Sincerely,

NOTES:

GA1325

I, (the undersigned), do hereby contract for a science fair project and agree to the following conditions:

A. I will follow the basic principles of scientific investigation:
    1. Conduct research and collect data on my chosen topic
    2. Set up and conduct experiments in this area
    3. Construct a stable means of exhibiting my information and experiment

B. I will also construct a display board to exhibit my project at the Science Fair on _____. By this I understand that I will meet the following deadlines unless previously arranged:
    1. I will have my project set up in the _____ by _____ p.m., _____ , 19 _____ .
    2. I will remove my project no earlier than _____ on the evening of _____ , 19 _____ .

C. I will have an Official Entry Card, which will be provided to me, attached to the right-hand side of my display along with an approved Student Vertebrate Animal Certificate, if I use live animals in my study.

D. I will include in my exhibit a brief summary of my project, its purpose and a written paper of my study.

E. I will present a brief explanation of my project to the judges on _____, 19 _____ . I will honestly attempt to answer with utmost sincerity and courtesy any questions the judges might ask me.

F. I understand that I will be judged on the following items:
    1. Scientific thought: use of the scientific method
    2. Research report
    3. Physical display
    4. Oral presentation
    5. Attendance at science fair

G. I further acknowledge that if because of some extreme unforeseen circumstances my experiment cannot be concluded I may, under mutual agreement with my teacher, be reassigned to do a research paper on a related topic. I must give notification of this before _____ , 19 _____ .

H. I also understand that this contract is in effect whether I am present in school or not. Termination of this contract is only possible by an extenuating circumstance such as withdrawal from school, death in the family or a serious illness certified by a doctor that I am unable to perform the work.

I hereby agree to the conditions and terms of this contract and have been given sufficient time to question any part of this contract. My signature implies complete understanding of this contract.

Signed_____   Contract date_____

Title of project (subject to approval)_____
Note: It is understood by the student that the topic is subject to change in wording but not in theme.

_____   _____
Signature of student   Signature of parent/guardian

_____   _____
Signature of teacher   Signature of mentor (if applicable)

CRITERIA FOR JUDGING SCIENCE FAIR PROJECTS

There are many methods of judging science fair projects. This one, based on 100 points, will be used by the judges at the Science Fair.

Criteria	Points	My Points
A. Scientific Thought: Use of the Scientific Method 1. Student performed experiment in which data were collected and analyzed by using the scientific method.	1 2 3 4 5	
2. Student set up experiment carefully and kept an accurate record of the data in a journal, diary or logbook.	1 2 3 4 5	
3. Student's conclusion is logical and justifiable.	1 2 3 4 5	
4. Experiment is an original idea, unique and creatively done.	1 2 3 4 5	
5. Summary shows title, question, hypothesis, materials, procedures, results and conclusions.	1 2 3 4 5	
B. Research Report 1. Includes title page, table of contents, abstract, write-up of procedures, background information and bibliography.	1 2 3 4 5	
2. Background information shows student has conducted research on the topic.	1 2 3 4 5	
3. Report is displayed and written with correct use of spelling and grammar.	1 2 3 4 5	
4. Abstract is interesting and helpful.	1 2 3 4 5	
5. Bibliography is related to topic and written in correct form.	1 2 3 4 5	
C. Physical Display 1. Student has a well-constructed backdrop to display the project.	1 2 3 4 5	
2. Display tells story of the project accurately.	1 2 3 4 5	
3. Display is appealing and is neatly done with correct spelling.	1 2 3 4 5	
4. Display shows components of science fair project.	1 2 3 4 5	
D. Attendance at Science Fair Student is present at display and greets judge on time.	1 2 3 4 5	
E. Oral Presentation 1. Student gives a clear explanation about the research conducted.	1 2 3 4 5	
2. Oral presentation is coherent and well organized.	1 2 3 4 5	
3. Oral presentation had effective use of visual aids.	1 2 3 4 5	
4. Student answers questions accurately and honestly.	1 2 3 4 5	
5. Oral presentation made in time allotted with all phases discussed.	1 2 3 4 5	
	Possible Total	**Student Total**

Levels of Performance:
5 = Superior   4 = Excellent   3 = Good   2 = Satisfactory   1 = Fair   Points = [100]   Points = [ ]
Comments: Use reverse side for written comments and notes.

GA1325

WEEKLY OCTOBER THROUGH FEBRUARY TIME LINE
Week-to-Week Schedule of Science Fair Activity
for October Through February

Week No. Due	OCTOBER ACTIVITY
1	Review sample projects of past science fair activities for ideas.
2	Topic selection is due. Register name of topic with your teacher.
3	Identify a problem that you would like to solve. Narrow the topic. Formulate a hypothesis by making an intelligent guess.
4	Find out what others have done to solve the problem. Go to the library. Read books and articles on the topic. Turn in a list of these materials to your teacher.

	NOVEMBER ACTIVITY
1	Meet with mentor to begin science fair activity. Make an oral presentation to your mentor that features your ideas.
2	Collect data from trials and tests that you do to solve the problem.
3	Keep a journal of all science fair activity both in and out of school.
4	Rough draft of an outline of your paper is due to your teacher. Include all topic headings. Have your mentor, parents and your teacher sign your outline.

	DECEMBER ACTIVITY
1	Written progress report on the results of your experiment is due to your teacher and mentor.
2	Begin to analyze the results of your experiment by making graphs, charts and using other statistical analyses of data.
3	Prepare an oral report on your project for presentation to a judge or members of the class.
4	Rough draft of your written science fair paper is due to your teacher and mentor.

	JANUARY ACTIVITY
1	With feedback from your teacher and mentor, draw final conclusions from your study.
2	Write and type final science fair paper to be given to your teacher and mentor.
3	Construct a backdrop display to exhibit your science fair project at the Science Fair in February.
4	Make a practice audio and/or videotape of your science fair presentation for the judges.

	FEBRUARY ACTIVITY
1	Complete entry form that includes name, project title, project number and signatures from student, parents and mentor is due to your teacher. Write an abstract of your study to be sent to judges prior to the day of the Science Fair.
2	Present science fair project at classroom Science Fair. Revise as needed for school Science Fair.
3	Present a science fair project at school Science Fair. RELAX.
4	Complete Science Fair Mentorship Program Evaluation Form. Revise science fair project and enter into other science fairs at local, district, state and national levels.

GA1325

STUDENT'S MONTHLY SCIENCE FAIR PROJECT COMPLETION SCHEDULE

Name _____   School _____

Keep this schedule in a place where it is seen often.

Assignment	Date Due	Date Completed	Comments
1. Understand Judging Criteria			
2. Understand Scientific Method			
3. Preview Sample Program			
4. Review Project Idea and Question			
5. Identify a Problem			
6. Review of Literature			
7. State Hypothesis			
8. Project Proposal Written			
9. Locate Information			
10. Collect and Organize Data			
11. Keep a Journal			
12. Analyze and Interpret Results			
13. Research Report Written			
14. Construct Graphs, Tables and Diagrams			
15. Write Abstract			
16. Write Title Page, Table of Contents and References			
17. Build Project Display			
18. Develop Oral Presentation			
19. Present Project			
20. Evaluation of Project			
21. Revise Project			
22. Enter Project in Science Fairs at Local, State and/or National Levels			
23. Write Article to Share with Others			

GA1325

GUIDELEINES FOR A SCIENCE FAIR DISPLAY

The following includes ideas on how a science fair project should be displayed. A typical science fair display looks like this:

The display board should be durable and made out of triple wall, cardboard, tagboard, Masonite, pressed wood or other self-supporting material. If three pieces need to be joined, connect them with inexpensive hinges or tape. The sides should measure 22″ (55 cm) wide and 60″ (150 cm) high, the back 30″ (75 cm) wide and 60″ (150 cm) high. Space is limited so adhere to these dimensions. Please notify me if your youngster's project requires special things like a computer, running water or electrical outlets. The display should have the following elements:

- Title
- Abstract
- Experimental design
- Background information including problem and hypothesis
- Results including tables and graphs of data
- Conclusions(s)
- Technical report
- Logbook
- Equipment, samples or other items from project activity

Help your child transport the project to and from school on time. The displays will be set up for _____ school day(s). Students will need to set up their displays in the _____ of the school between _____ and _____. The displays are to be taken down between _____ and _____.

Thank you for your help in this unique Science Fair Mentorship Program. Please join us and enjoy the rewards of your child's dedicated efforts.

GA1325

SCIENCE FAIR MENTORSHIP PROGRAM EVALUATION FORM

For each of the paired items listed below, place an X on the line that best represents your feelings about the Science Fair Mentorship Program.

Example: The Science Fair Mentorship Program was

Hot	X							Cold
	(1)	(2)	(3)	(4)	(5)	(6)	(7)	

1.	**Interesting**	___	___	___	___	___	___	___	**Boring**
		(1)	(2)	(3)	(4)	(5)	(6)	(7)	
2.	**Important**	___	___	___	___	___	___	___	**Useless**
		(1)	(2)	(3)	(4)	(5)	(6)	(7)	
3.	**Informative**	___	___	___	___	___	___	___	**Worthless**
		(1)	(2)	(3)	(4)	(5)	(6)	(7)	
4.	**Complete**	___	___	___	___	___	___	___	**Incomplete**
		(1)	(2)	(3)	(4)	(5)	(6)	(7)	
5.	**Mixed Up**	___	___	___	___	___	___	___	**Smooth**
		(7)	(6)	(5)	(4)	(3)	(2)	(1)	
6.	**A Downer**	___	___	___	___	___	___	___	**An Upper**
		(7)	(6)	(5)	(4)	(3)	(2)	(1)	
7.	**Selfish**	___	___	___	___	___	___	___	**Unselfish**
		(7)	(6)	(5)	(4)	(3)	(2)	(1)	
8.	**Enough Time**	___	___	___	___	___	___	___	**Not Enough Time**
		(1)	(2)	(3)	(4)	(5)	(6)	(7)	
9.	**Light**	___	___	___	___	___	___	___	**Dark**
		(1)	(2)	(3)	(4)	(5)	(6)	(7)	
10.	**Negative**	___	___	___	___	___	___	___	**Positive**
		(7)	(6)	(5)	(4)	(3)	(2)	(1)	
11.	**High**	___	___	___	___	___	___	___	**Low**
		(1)	(2)	(3)	(4)	(5)	(6)	(7)	
12.	**Bad**	___	___	___	___	___	___	___	**Good**
		(7)	(6)	(5)	(4)	(3)	(2)	(1)	
13.	**Liked**	___	___	___	___	___	___	___	**Disliked**
		(1)	(2)	(3)	(4)	(5)	(6)	(7)	
14.	**Black**	___	___	___	___	___	___	___	**White**
		(7)	(6)	(5)	(4)	(3)	(2)	(1)	
15.	**Fast**	___	___	___	___	___	___	___	**Slow**
		(1)	(2)	(3)	(4)	(5)	(6)	(7)	

On the other side of this page, list responses to the following: (1) Things I like(d) best about the Science Fair Mentorship Program; (2) Things I like(d) least about the Science Fair Mentorship Program and (3) Suggestions for improvement of the Science Fair Mentorship Program. **Note:** Please return this form as soon as possible to the Director of the Science Fair Mentorship Program or place in the Return Box on the day of the Science Fair. Thank you.

GA1325

ACTIVITY NO.	KEY	ACTIVITY	REFER TO PAGE(S)	DATE COMPLETED
N2 (T)	OC	Follow up on distribution of packets. Identify community members who will act as mentors. Match mentors with students, based on student interests. Review duties of mentor.	139, 149	

TIPS FOR THE TEACHER

Follow-Up Letter to a Mentor

Write this letter to all who have agreed to act as mentors. The letter should state student's name, address and topic area to be studied.

Date _____

Dear _____ :

A special thanks to all those who have agreed to act as a mentor for a _____ grade student in our Science Fair Mentorship Program. You may recall that our major goal in the program is to offer students an opportunity to conduct a scientific study under the guidance of a mentor, an experienced person knowledgeable in a subject matter area.

Listed on the card below is the student's name, address, telephone number and name of the topic to be studied. The student will contact you soon to begin work on the science fair project study.

Thank you for your willingness to help a student in this worthwhile program. If you have any questions, feel free to call me anytime at _____ .

Sincerely,

Name of Student:

_____

Address:

_____

_____

Telephone:

_____

Topic:

_____

GA1325

ACTIVITY NO.	KEY	ACTIVITY	REFER TO PAGE(S)	DATE COMPLETED
N3 (T)	OC	Using a computer, prepare a spread sheet that has the names, addresses and telephone numbers of mentors, teachers and assigned students. Record titles of science fair projects.	89-90, 150, 221	

TIPS FOR THE TEACHER
Data Base for Student-Mentor Activity

A computer will help you to develop a data bank of names of mentors, teachers and students with titles of science fair projects. These can be displayed throughout the duration of the Science Fair Mentorship Program. Your spread sheet may look like this:

Mentor Last, First	Address & Phone No.	Student Last, First	Address & Phone No.	Title of Project	Teacher Last, First	Address & Phone No.

NOTES:

GA1325

ACTIVITY NO.	KEY	ACTIVITY	REFER TO PAGE(S)	DATE COMPLETED
N4 (T)	OC	Using a computer, prepare a ten-week class record of weekly meetings with mentors. Have students check the week in which they met with their mentors.	150-151, 155	

TIPS FOR THE TEACHER

Record of Meetings with Mentors

Use this record of weekly attendance after students have been assigned to various mentors. Your attendance sheet may look like this:

Student Last, First	Mentor Last, First	Wk. 1	Wk. 2	Wk. 3	Wk. 4	Wk. 5	Wk. 6	Wk. 7	Wk. 8	Wk. 9	Wk. 10

NOTES:

GA1325

ACTIVITY NO.	KEY	ACTIVITY	REFER TO PAGE(S)	DATE COMPLETED
N5 (T)	IC	Review week-to-week schedule for October. Follow week-to-week science fair schedule for November.	79, 108, 152	

TIPS FOR THE TEACHER
Week-to-Week Schedule

Review page 79, Student's Monthly Science Fair Project Completion Schedule and page 108, a Weekly October Through February Time Line. Make copies of page 108. Review activities for October and note student progress. Introduce November activities. Encourage students to keep diaries or journals of their research activities as a basis for rough drafts of their written papers which should be signed by their mentors and parents and turned into you by late December. After you review the pages, rough drafts may be returned to students in early January for final revisions.

NOTES:

GA1325

ACTIVITY NO.	KEY	ACTIVITY	REFER TO PAGE(S)	DATE COMPLETED
N6 (T)	IC	Have students restate their science fair topics in question or statement form.	127-128, 153	

TIPS FOR THE TEACHER
Science Fair Topic Questions and Statements

Introduce page 154, My Science Fair Question/Statement. Review how to narrow down an area of study until one question or statement is investigated. Encourage students to restate their science fair topics based on their experiences with mentors, materials and resources at hand. Polish the questions/statements. Have students write their questions or statements in the boxes on page 154. Students may also want to write their questions in a large question mark to be displayed in the classroom or on statement cards to be kept by the teacher in a card file box for all to consult.

NOTES:

GA1325

MY SCIENCE FAIR QUESTION/STATEMENT

Name _____

Write the question that you have chosen for your science fair topic on the lines or in the question mark.

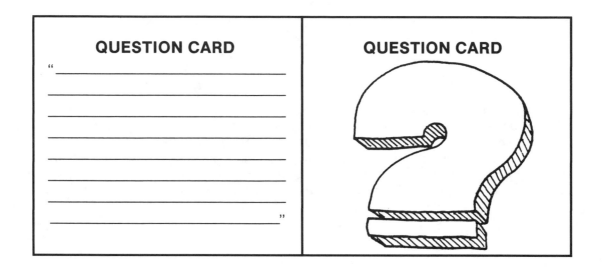

QUESTION CARD

" _____
_____
_____
_____
_____
_____
_____ "

QUESTION CARD

A STATEMENT OF MY SCIENCE FAIR TOPIC

Write a clear statement(s) of your science fair topic here.

STATEMENT CARD

_____
_____
_____
_____
_____
_____
_____

ACTIVITY NO.	KEY	ACTIVITY	REFER TO PAGE(S)	DATE COMPLETED
N7 (T)	IC	Have students give three-minute oral reports on the initial exploration of science fair topics with mentors.	155, 184, 228-229	

TIPS FOR THE TEACHER

Oral Reports

This activity encourages students to do long-range planning in preparation for oral presentations in December, January and February. Limit the oral report to three minutes so students are concise and narrow their topics further. Have students use this format as a guide for their three-minute presentations. Students should use note cards and cite sources of information in their presentations.

FORMAT FOR THREE-MINUTE ORAL PRESENTATION

"Hello. My name is _____. I am a _____ grade student at _____ School. The question I am trying to answer is _____

_____

My hypothesis is _____. I investigated the works of _____ and

_____

_____ to find out what they did on the topic. The procedure that I'm using to test my hypothesis is _____. I have learned _____

_____ thus

far as a result of my investigation."

Extension: Encourage students to use visual aids in their oral presentations, such as showing the audience the cutout question mark with the question written inside the question mark shown on page 154. Students may also begin to use the overhead projector with various transparencies to illustrate the steps followed in their research study.

NOTES:

GA1325

ACTIVITY NO.	KEY	ACTIVITY	REFER TO PAGE(S)	DATE COMPLETED
N8 (T)	IC	Have students list identified resources for project and review notes on note cards or computer. Organize outline of paper. Include all topic headings. Have mentor sign outline of paper. Alert students that rough draft of paper is due in late November.	86-88, 156	

TIPS FOR THE TEACHER
Writing the Rough Draft

As a result of their three-minute oral presentations, have students turn in a minimum of two sources of information with note cards that contain information germane to the topic. Review pages 86, 87 and 88, Student's Guide on How to Write a Science Fair Report. Focus on cards D, E, F, G, H, I, J and O as students begin to write rough drafts of their written papers. If applicable, have mentor sign the rough draft. Inform students that a second rough draft of the written paper is due in late November.

Extension: Encourage students to write all rough drafts and the final science fair research paper by using a word processor or data base software. Have students print out their latest version of their reports for the rough drafts. Emphasize that students should make a backup diskette of all files, notes and citations that were included in the rough draft. Show students how many word processing and data base programs will allow them to combine a number of files into one. This is especially useful when creating smooth or combined data from raw data. See pages 157, 159, 160 and 161 for such exercises.

NOTES:

GA1325

ACTIVITY NO.	KEY	ACTIVITY	REFER TO PAGE(S)	DATE COMPLETED
N9 (T)	IC	Have students continue their investigations. Emphasize the recording of observations in a diary/logbook.	157-161	

TIPS FOR THE TEACHER

Sample Diary/Logbook Page

Copy and give students copies of page 158, Sample Diary/Logbook Page. Inform students that there are many ways to record data using many different formats. A computer is often used for such purpose. Introduce the Sample Diary/Logbook Page. Note that the right half of the page is for written comments, the left half is for charts of data, drawings and sketches. Emphasize that pages should be numbered in the upper right corner for easy reference.

Extension: Collect information from students on the months in which they were born. Make a chart on the board similar to the one below. This data will be used for an exercise on graphing found on pages 160 and 161.

Month of Birth

	Jan.	Feb.	Mar.	Apr.	May	June	July	Aug.	Sept.	Oct.	Nov.	Dec.
Number of Students	5	5	5	5	5	5	5	5	5	5	5	5
	4	4	4	4	4	4	4	4	4	4	4	4
	3	3	3	3	3	3	3	3	3	3	3	3
	2	2	2	2	2	2	2	2	2	2	2	2
	1	1	1	1	1	1	1	1	1	1	1	1
	0	0	0	0	0	0	0	0	0	0	0	0

NOTES:

GA1325

SAMPLE

DIARY/LOGBOOK PAGE

Use the space below to keep an accurate record of your observations. Collect and record data. Make additional notes about your observations and feelings. Try your hand at drawing your favorite scene, cartoon, doodle, mind bender, bumper sticker, T-shirt saying or postage stamp. You may also want to write a poem, letter, limerick or compose a story about your fantasies, dreams, insights or other creative ideas. All these techniques will lead to a high-quality science fair project.

SCIENCE DIARY & LOG

NAME _____

DATE _____

ACTIVITY NO.	KEY	ACTIVITY	REFER TO PAGE(S)	DATE COMPLETED
N10 (T)	IC	Teach students new skills as the need arises, for example, graphing and recording of results. Review variables and controls.	87, 159-161	

TIPS FOR THE TEACHER
Graphing and Recording of Data

Review cards J and K on page 87 in the Student's Guide on How to Write a Science Fair Report. Make copies of and give students page 160. Review meaning of results. On the data chart have students circle the number of students who were born each month. On the graph at the bottom of the page, have students plot the data for each month. Connect the dots to complete the line graph. Ask the students to interpret the results shown on the line graph. For example, how many students were born in the month of July? In which month were the fewest students born? Be sure students label both the horizontal and vertical parts of the graph, plot their data points and connect the points to make a complete line graph.

Extension: Repeat the exercise. Use same data and have students make a bar graph on page 161. Shade in squares to represent data on the bar graph. Discuss variables that may be operating when more or less births occur in each month. Review Variables and Controls card on page 87. Discuss. Make copies and give students page 162, P.S.: A Final Word About Variables and Controls. Have the students read the page carefully. Discuss samples of independent and dependent variables. Have students write both the independent and dependent variables in the boxes on page 162 for further reference.

J. Variables and Controls
Describe the things you changed and those that you tried to control. Identify both the control and experimental groups.

K. Results
Include all data that you collected using charts, models, diagrams, computer programs, videotapes, photographs and tables that you created when you did the experiment.

NOTES:

GA1325

Card K, page 87

Results: Include all data that you collected using charts, models, diagrams, computer programs, videotapes, photographs and tables that you created when you did the experiment.

Data Chart

Month of Birth

	Jan.	Feb.	Mar.	Apr.	May	June	July	Aug.	Sept.	Oct.	Nov.	Dec.
5	5	5	5	5	5	5	5	5	5	5	5	5
4	4	4	4	4	4	4	4	4	4	4	4	4
3	3	3	3	3	3	3	3	3	3	3	3	3
2	2	2	2	2	2	2	2	2	2	2	2	2
1	1	1	1	1	1	1	1	1	1	1	1	1
0	0	0	0	0	0	0	0	0	0	0	0	0

Number of Students (vertical axis label)

Line Graph

5											
4											
3											
2											
1											
0											

Number of Students (vertical axis label)

Jan. Feb. Mar. Apr. May June July Aug. Sept. Oct. Nov. Dec.

Month of Birth

Name _____ **Date** _____

GA1325

Card K, page 87

Results: Include all data that you collected using charts, models, diagrams, computer programs, videotapes, photographs and tables that you created when you did the experiment.

Data Chart

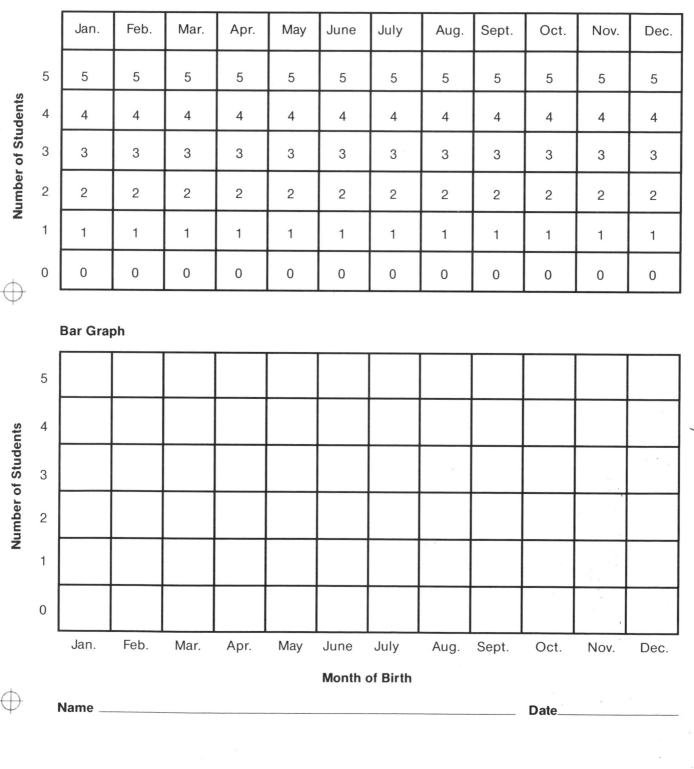

Month of Birth

	Jan.	Feb.	Mar.	Apr.	May	June	July	Aug.	Sept.	Oct.	Nov.	Dec.
5	5	5	5	5	5	5	5	5	5	5	5	5
4	4	4	4	4	4	4	4	4	4	4	4	4
3	3	3	3	3	3	3	3	3	3	3	3	3
2	2	2	2	2	2	2	2	2	2	2	2	2
1	1	1	1	1	1	1	1	1	1	1	1	1
0	0	0	0	0	0	0	0	0	0	0	0	0

Number of Students

Bar Graph

5												
4												
3												
2												
1												
0												

| Jan. | Feb. | Mar. | Apr. | May | June | July | Aug. | Sept. | Oct. | Nov. | Dec. |

Number of Students

Month of Birth

Name _____ **Date** _____

GA1325

(S) P.S.: A FINAL WORD ABOUT VARIABLES AND CONTROLS

Your project should include a *controlled experiment*. If your experiment is done under carefully controlled conditions, what will happen? You, as the experimenter, can change certain conditions and observe how the condition of your subject is affected or changed. This experimentation provides a method for testing your hypothesis.

It is wise to get some help from your teacher and/or mentor who has experience in scientific experimentation.

Your experimental design depends upon the experiment that you are doing. Plants and animals will require different equipment and procedures than motors, soil and the weather.

Whatever experiment you do, there will probably be many *variables*. Two types of variables in simple controlled experiments are

1. **Independent Variable:** The experimenter changes something to observe what will happen. The "thing" that is changed is the independent variable.

2. **Dependent Variable:** The experimenter changes something to observe what will happen. The "things" that are changed may cause something else to happen. The "something else" is the dependent variable.

A variable, then, is something that is changed or shows change in an experiment. There are a number of ways to control variables. In a simple experiment, you might have an *experimental group* and a *control group*. You can check all variables which might change the outcome of the experiment, but you are not testing for that change. Be sure both your control group and your experimental group are treated the same (except for the one variable which you are purposely changing in the experimental group). You must be very careful not to be *biased*. This means you accidentally, or unintentionally, favor the experimental group.

Remember that different types of experiments require different types of controls. Get help from your teacher and/or mentor if you are not sure how to control your variables. Then list the independent and dependent variables in your study in the boxes below.

INDEPENDENT VARIABLE

DEPENDENT VARIABLE

GA1325

D P J F = December
Planning
Judges
Focus

THE SCIENCE FAIR TEACHER COMMUNICATES WITH JUDGES

GA1325

ACTIVITY NO.	KEY	ACTIVITY	REFER TO PAGE(S)	DATE COMPLETED
D1 (T)	OC	Identify and contact judges.	132, 164	

TIPS FOR THE TEACHER
Sources to Tap for Judges

Judges play an important role in the success of a Science Fair Mentorship Program. Contact these people for judging at the Science Fair.

	Date Contacted	Yes	No	Name	Area
I. School administrative office					
A. Superintendent					
B. Assistant superintendent					
C. Curriculum supervisors					
D. School board members					
E. Principals					
F. School nurses					
II. Personnel from surrounding districts					
A. Teachers					
B. Principals					
C. Curriculum staff					
III. Community					
A. Medical fields					
1. Optometrists					
2. Veterinarians					
3. Dental hygienists					
4. Dentists					
5. Doctors					
6. Nurses					
7. Pharmacists					
8. Lab technicians					
B. Business fields and technical fields					
1. Manufacturers					
2. Public utilities					
3. Research and development laboratories					
4. Engineering consulting firms					
5. Architects					
6. Lawyers					
C. Colleges, universities, and technical and vocational schools					
1. Professors					
2. Graduate students					
3. Undergraduate students					
D. Government					
1. City and county engineers					
2. Water and sewage treatment personnel					
3. Agricultural agents and health departments					
4. Airport and port authority					
5. Zoos					
6. Botanical gardens					
E. Senior citizens organizations					
1. Retired people					
F. Scientific trade and professional organizations					
1. Technical societies					

NOTES:

GA1325

ACTIVITY NO.	KEY	ACTIVITY	REFER TO PAGE(S)	DATE COMPLETED
D2 ⓣ	OC	Make copies of Science Fairs with Style Judge's Packet. Distribute copies to those who have volunteered to be science fair judges.	165, 167-176	

TIPS FOR THE TEACHER

Science Fairs with Style Judge's Packet

The fourth of five packets, Science Fairs with Style Judge's Packet, is found on pages 166 to 176. Make copies of the packet and distribute to judges after initial contact has been made. In addition to front and back covers, the packet contains A Preliminary Letter to Science Fair Judges (p. 169), the Weekly October Through February Time Line (p. 170), a Sample Record of Projects to Judge (p. 171), criteria and background information on the judging process (pp. 172-173), a Final Science Fairs with Style Day Letter to Judges (p. 174), Next Year's Judge Volunteer Form and a Science Fair Mentorship Program Evaluation Form. In all meetings with the judges, encourage them to become actively involved in the Science Fair Mentorship Program by becoming a judge and recruiting others to do the same.

NOTES:

GA1325

SCIENCE FAIRS WITH STYLE
JUDGE'S PACKET

Name _____

Affiliation _____

(Front Cover)

SCIENCE FAIRS WITH STYLE
JUDGE'S PACKET

(Back Cover)

SCIENCE FAIRS WITH STYLE JUDGE'S PACKET

Table of Contents

A PRELIMINARY LETTER TO SCIENCE FAIR JUDGES

Date _____

Dear Science Fair Judge:

   This science fair packet is written to inform you of our unique Science Fair Mentorship Program. As avid teachers of science, we are conducting a science fair that features the display of student exhibits. Students responsible for the exhibits have worked on a science project with mentors in the community. The students, with assistance from mentors and parents, have worked very hard to produce high-quality projects. The time has come for these projects to be judged. We ask you for your help.

   We will be having our Science Fair on _____ from _____ to _____ . In order to evaluate each student's project properly, we need judges who have some knowledge of science and an interest in helping with our Science Fair Mentorship Program. You are invited to serve as a judge for this year's Science Fair. The schedule for judging the Science Fair is listed below.

		Time
1.	Judges meet to discuss judging procedures and criteria.	_____
2.	Judges evaluate exhibits.	_____
3.	Scores are tabulated.	_____
4.	Awards are presented.	_____

   We hope that you will take the time to complete this form and be a judge. We hope to meet you on _____ at _____ .

Sincerely,

- -

Please detach and return to _____ **by** _____ .

Name _____ Phone _____

Address _____

Occupation _____

_____ Yes, I will serve as a judge.
_____ I am unable to serve as a judge at this time.

_____ I would like more information about the Science Fair before I make a decision about judging.

Science Categories: (Please circle one or more of the following science areas that you feel comfortable judging.)

Animals (Zoology)	Energy	Astronomy	Mathematics
Plants (Botany)	Weather	Health Science	Computers
Chemistry	Geology	Human Biology	Others:
Physics	Oceanography	Environmental Science	_____

GA1325

J

WEEKLY OCTOBER THROUGH FEBRUARY TIME LINE
Week-to-Week Schedule of Science Fair Activity
for October Through February

Week No. Due	OCTOBER ACTIVITY
1	Review sample projects of past science fair activities for ideas.
2	Topic selection is due. Register name of topic with your teacher.
3	Identify a problem that you would like to solve. Narrow the topic. Formulate a hypothesis by making an intelligent guess.
4	Find out what others have done to solve the problem. Go to the library. Read books and articles on the topic. Turn in a list of these materials to your teacher.

	NOVEMBER ACTIVITY
1	Meet with mentor to begin science fair activity. Make an oral presentation to your mentor that features your ideas.
2	Collect data from trials and tests that you do to solve the problem.
3	Keep a journal of all science fair activity both in and out of school.
4	Rough draft of an outline of your paper is due to your teacher. Include all topic headings. Have your mentor, parents and your teacher sign your outline.

	DECEMBER ACTIVITY
1	Written progress report on the results of your experiment is due to your teacher and mentor.
2	Begin to analyze the results of your experiment by making graphs, charts and using other statistical analyses of data.
3	Prepare an oral report on your project for presentation to a judge or members of the class.
4	Rough draft of your written science fair paper is due to your teacher and mentor.

	JANUARY ACTIVITY
1	With feedback from your teacher and mentor, draw final conclusions from your study.
2	Write and type final science fair paper to be given to your teacher and mentor.
3	Construct a backdrop display to exhibit your science fair project at the Science Fair in February.
4	Make a practice audio and/or videotape of your science fair presentation for the judges.

	FEBRUARY ACTIVITY
1	Complete entry form that includes name, project title, project number and signatures from student, parents and mentor is due to your teacher. Write an abstract of your study to be sent to judges prior to the day of the Science Fair.
2	Present science fair project at classroom Science Fair. Revise as needed for school Science Fair.
3	Present science fair project at school Science Fair. RELAX.
4	Complete Science Fair Mentorship Program Evaluation Form. Revise science fair project and enter into other science fairs at local, district, state and national levels.

GA1325

SAMPLE

RECORD OF PROJECTS TO JUDGE

Number of Projects _____

Titles of Projects

_____   _____

_____   _____

_____   _____

Scoring Per Project

SAMPLE ABSTRACT FORM

Approximately one week *before* the actual science fair, you will receive a student-written *abstract* of each project you are to judge. The form, with a sample abstract, looks like this:

Name: ___Brown, Jason___   ID-Exhibit No.: ___29___

School: ___St. Mary's___   Room No.: ___210___

Grade: ___6___   Teacher: ___Mrs. Benedict___

Project Title: ___The Effects of a Missing Ingredient in Chocolate Chip Cookies___

The *purpose* of this experiment was to determine the effects, if any, of a missing ingredient on the appearance and taste of chocolate chip cookies. The *procedure* included making five batches of chocolate chip cookies: the control group with no missing ingredient and four experimental groups with a single missing ingredient in each—vanilla, brown sugar, white sugar and flour. Tests of both sight and taste were developed for the study. The *results* showed that the experimental cookies, especially those with no flour, when compared to the control group, changed *appearance* the most according to the testers. Four of the five batches had a different *taste* when compared to the control group. Cookies with no flour had the worst taste followed by those with no vanilla, no brown sugar and no white sugar. The major *conclusion* found in the study was that a missing ingredient does have a significant effect on the *appearance* and taste of chocolate chip cookies. Future research needs to focus on the effects of a missing ingredient on nonchocolate chip cookies.

J

CRITERIA FOR JUDGING SCIENCE FAIR PROJECTS

There are many methods of judging science fair projects. This one, based on 100 points, will be used by the judges at the Science Fair.

Criteria	Points	My Points
A. Scientific Thought: Use of the Scientific Method 1. Student performed experiment in which data were collected and analyzed by using the scientific method.	1 2 3 4 5	
2. Student set up experiment carefully and kept an accurate record of the data in a journal, diary or logbook.	1 2 3 4 5	
3. Student's conclusion is logical and justifiable.	1 2 3 4 5	
4. Experiment is an original idea, unique and creatively done.	1 2 3 4 5	
5. Summary shows title, question, hypothesis, materials, procedures, results and conclusions.	1 2 3 4 5	
B. Research Report 1. Includes title page, table of contents, abstract, write-up of procedures, background information and bibliography.	1 2 3 4 5	
2. Background information shows student has conducted research on the topic.	1 2 3 4 5	
3. Report is displayed and written with correct use of spelling and grammar.	1 2 3 4 5	
4. Abstract is interesting and helpful.	1 2 3 4 5	
5. Bibliography is related to topic and written in correct form.	1 2 3 4 5	
C. Physical Display 1. Student has a well-constructed backdrop to display the project.	1 2 3 4 5	
2. Display tells story of the project accurately.	1 2 3 4 5	
3. Display is appealing and is neatly done with correct spelling.	1 2 3 4 5	
4. Display shows components of science fair project.	1 2 3 4 5	
D. Attendance at Science Fair Student is present at display and greets judge on time.	1 2 3 4 5	
E. Oral Presentation 1. Student gives a clear explanation about the research conducted.	1 2 3 4 5	
2. Oral presentation is coherent and well organized.	1 2 3 4 5	
3. Oral presentation had effective use of visual aids.	1 2 3 4 5	
4. Student answers questions accurately and honestly.	1 2 3 4 5	
5. Oral presentation made in time allotted with all phases discussed.	1 2 3 4 5	
	Possible Total	**Student Total**

Levels of Performance:
5 = **Superior**   4 = **Excellent**   3 = **Good**   2 = **Satisfactory**   1 = **Fair**

Comments: Use reverse side for written comments and notes.

Points = [100]   Points = [   ]

ABOUT THE JUDGING EXPERIENCE

Your attitude and conduct determine the success of a student at the Science Fair. It is vital that you understand your role as a judge. We hope that you will have a genuine interest in students and offer much encouragement and guidance to them as they pursue learning in various fields of science. The following tips are offered to help you with this task. (You may want to select a project *not* assigned to you and do a trial run first.)

1. You will be paired with another judge. You may determine the final score as a team, or you may judge each project independently and average the scores.

2. Introduce yourself as you approach the student. Establish a friendly rapport to reduce the student's anxiety.

3. Put the student at ease by asking an introductory question such as "How did you get interested in your project?"

4. Ask questions of the student that pertain only to the project itself and at the level of the student.

5. Assume an active listening role as the student presents the results of the project.

6. Ask questions about sources of information, materials, tools, construction and types of assistance enlisted in preparation of the project.

7. Read the abstract *before* meeting the student. During the presentation, check the *quality* of the written paper. Also, check the construction of materials used in the project and the physical display itself. Be sure to ask the students what the results of the study were and how the project is related to activities in their everyday lives.

8. Note the size of the population and determine if the results can be applied to a larger population. Check the bibliography to determine the depth and scope of background information.

9. Consider the grade level of the student before judging and assigning a final score.

10. Thank the student for the opportunity to judge his/her science fair project.

11. Assign a tentative rating for each criterion item. Discuss with your partner a score for each criterion item. Conduct this discussion far from the student. Agree on each point. Do *not* disclose the score to the student at the time of judging.

12. Give your final ratings to the members in the tally room for final check and assignment of ribbon if applicable.

13. Complete biographical information form giving pertinent information on willingness to judge at next year's Science Fair.

14. Tell your friends about your experience. Encourage them to contact the director of the Science Fair and volunteer to judge science fair projects next year.

Thank you.

(J)

FINAL SCIENCE FAIRS WITH STYLE DAY LETTER TO JUDGES

Date _____

Dear Science Fair Judge:

   The long awaited Science Fair is here. Thank you for your willingness to participate in this event as a judge. Final briefing of judges and assignment of teams will take place on _____ at _____ . The judges' meeting will begin promptly at _____ . Judges' packets are to be picked up between _____ and _____ . Judging is to begin at _____ . Parking is available at _____ . If an emergency occurs prior to the day, please try to get a substitute or contact me at _____ .

   Enclosed are abstracts of projects that you are to judge. Criteria sheets for judging are found in your packet. Each judging team has no more than six projects. Also, enclosed in the packet is a copy of About the Judging Experience and the criteria by which the students are to be evaluated. Familiarize yourself with the interpretations of the judging criteria and the contents of the abstracts. We hope these will assist you in your preparation for judging.

   For the deliberations and discussions done by the judging teams, Room _____ has been reserved for your use. Refreshments will be available in or near this room. A schedule for the day is enclosed. If this is your first time judging, contact one of the hosts who will direct you to where the projects are set up, the tally room and the judges' meeting room.

   Thank you for your important contribution to the success of the Science Fair. If you have any questions, please call me at home _____ or at school _____ . Have a great day on _____ , 19 _____ .

See you then.

                                 Sincerely,

GA1325

NEXT YEAR'S JUDGE VOLUNTEER FORM

Thank you for being a judge at this year's Science Fair. We hope that you have had a rewarding experience and that you return next year. Please complete this form and leave it with a representative in the tally room. Thank you for your support.

We will be having our Science Fair next year on _____ from _____ to _____ . In order to evaluate each student's project properly, we need judges who have some knowledge of science and an interest in helping with our Science Fair Mentorship Program.

You are invited to serve as a judge for next year's Science Fair. The schedule for judging the Science Fair is listed below.

	Date	Time
1. Judges meet to discuss judging procedures and criteria.	_____	_____
2. Judges evaluate exhibits.	_____	_____
3. Scores are tabulated.	_____	_____
4. Awards are presented.	_____	_____

We hope that you will take the time to complete this form and be a judge. We hope to meet you on _____ at _____ .

Sincerely,

- -

Please detach and return to _____ **by** _____ .

Name _____ Phone _____

Address _____

Occupation _____

_____ Yes, I will serve as a judge.   _____ I would like more information about the
_____ I am unable to serve as a judge   Science Fair before I make a decision
       at this time.   about judging.

Science Categories: (Please circle one or more of the following science areas that you feel comfortable judging.)

Animals (Zoology)	Energy	Astronomy	Mathematics
Plants (Botany)	Weather	Health Science	Computers
Chemistry	Geology	Human Biology	Others:
Physics	Oceanography	Environmental Science	_____

GA1325

SCIENCE FAIR MENTORSHIP PROGRAM EVALUATION FORM

For each of the paired items listed below, place an X on the line that best represents your feelings about the Science Fair Mentorship Program.

Example: The Science Fair Mentorship Program was

Hot	X							Cold
	(1)	(2)	(3)	(4)	(5)	(6)	(7)	

#		(1)	(2)	(3)	(4)	(5)	(6)	(7)	
1.	Interesting								Boring
2.	Important	(1)	(2)	(3)	(4)	(5)	(6)	(7)	Useless
3.	Informative	(1)	(2)	(3)	(4)	(5)	(6)	(7)	Worthless
4.	Complete	(1)	(2)	(3)	(4)	(5)	(6)	(7)	Incomplete
5.	Mixed Up	(1)	(2)	(3)	(4)	(5)	(6)	(7)	Smooth
6.	A Downer	(7)	(6)	(5)	(4)	(3)	(2)	(1)	An Upper
7.	Selfish	(7)	(6)	(5)	(4)	(3)	(2)	(1)	Unselfish
8.	Enough Time	(7)	(6)	(5)	(4)	(3)	(2)	(1)	Not Enough Time
9.	Light	(1)	(2)	(3)	(4)	(5)	(6)	(7)	Dark
10.	Negative	(1)	(2)	(3)	(4)	(5)	(6)	(7)	Positive
11.	High	(7)	(6)	(5)	(4)	(3)	(2)	(1)	Low
12.	Bad	(1)	(2)	(3)	(4)	(5)	(6)	(7)	Good
13.	Liked	(7)	(6)	(5)	(4)	(3)	(2)	(1)	Disliked
14.	Black	(1)	(2)	(3)	(4)	(5)	(6)	(7)	White
15.	Fast	(7)	(6)	(5)	(4)	(3)	(2)	(1)	Slow
		(1)	(2)	(3)	(4)	(5)	(6)	(7)	

On the other side of this page, list responses to the following: (1) Things I like(d) best about the Science Fair Mentorship Program; (2) Things I like(d) least about the Science Fair Mentorship Program and (3) Suggestions for improvement of the Science Fair Mentorship Program. **Note:** Please return this form as soon as possible to the Director of the Science Fair Mentorship Program or place in the Return Box on the day of the Science Fair. Thank you.

ACTIVITY NO.	KEY	ACTIVITY	REFER TO PAGE(S)	DATE COMPLETED
D3 (T)	OC	Using a computer, prepare a spread sheet that has the names, addresses, telephone numbers and areas of expertise of judges who have volunteered to judge science fair projects.	169, 177	

TIPS FOR THE TEACHER

Data Base of Candidates for Judging

NAME	ADDRESS	PHONE NO.	SCIENCE AREA OF EXPERTISE	COMMENTS

NOTES:

GA1325

ACTIVITY NO.	KEY	ACTIVITY	REFER TO PAGE(S)	DATE COMPLETED
D4 (T)	OC	Invite a science fair judge to class to discuss what a judge looks for in a high-quality science fair project.	80-178	

TIPS FOR THE TEACHER

Invite a Judge to Class

After initial distribution of the Science Fairs with Style Judge's Packets, invite an experienced science fair judge to class to discuss what a science fair judge looks for in a high-quality science fair project. In class, have the judge review the Criteria for Judging Science Fair Projects (p. 80) and the project itself (p. 147). If possible, videotape the judge's presentation and show the tape to other students as they begin preparation for the Science Fair.

NOTES:

GA1325

ACTIVITY NO.	KEY	ACTIVITY	REFER TO PAGE(S)	DATE COMPLETED
D5 Ⓣ	OC	Design a student entry form that includes name, date, teacher, grade level, project title, project description, project hypothesis and blanks for student, parents, teacher and mentor (if applicable) signatures.	179, 232	

TIPS FOR THE TEACHER

Student Entry Form

Name: _____ Date: _____

Teacher: _____ Grade: _____

Project Title: _____

Project Description (be brief): _____

_____

_____

Project Hypothesis: _____

_____

Project Area (Circle one.):

Animal (Zoology)	Plants (Botany)	Energy	Weather	Geology
Human Biology	Chemistry	Physics	Mathematics	Behavioral Science
General Science	Oceanography	Astronomy	Health Science	Environmental Science
Computers	Other_____			

Project Type (Check one.):

_____ **Experimental:** Forming a hypothesis (question) about something the student doesn't know the answer to, doing an actual scientific experiment, making observations, collecting data and reaching conclusions.

(OPTIONAL)

_____ **Scientific Investigations:** Science in a show and tell format. The student knows what is going to happen when he or she begins investigation. Includes models, mock-ups, kits, collections, hobbies, art projects, book reports, posters and library research studies.

Will your project require electricity? _____ Yes _____ No

Will your project require running water? _____ Yes _____ No

Will your project require a computer? _____ Yes _____ No

Your project should include the following items: (1) Exhibit that can stand by itself, (2) Research paper with bibliography, (3) Abstract (one-page summary, with bibliography), (4) Materials necessary for the exhibit, (5) Oral presentation (3 to 5 minutes) and (6) Diary/Logbook of daily work.

Return this form to your teacher by _____ .

Student's signature _____ Date _____

Teacher's signature _____ Date _____

Mentor's signature _____ Date _____

Parents only: My child, _____, has permission to participate in the Science Fair.

Signed_____ Date_____

GA1325

ACTIVITY NO.	KEY	ACTIVITY	REFER TO PAGE(S)	DATE COMPLETED
D6 (T)	OC	Design a final report form that includes number (name optional), project title, grade, hypothesis, methods, summary of observations and conclusion(s).	86-87, 180, 225	

TIPS FOR THE TEACHER

Final Report Form

Have students complete this form in preparation for the Science Fair.

STUDENT FINAL REPORT FORM
Room Number
ID-Exhibit No.
Project Title
Grade
Hypothesis
Methods
Summary
Conclusion(s)

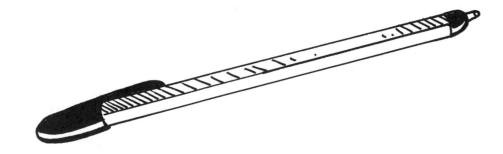

NOTES:

ACTIVITY NO.	KEY	ACTIVITY	REFER TO PAGE(S)	DATE COMPLETED
D7 Ⓣ	IC	Follow week-to-week science fair schedule for December.	108, 181	

TIPS FOR THE TEACHER
Week-to-Week Science Fair Schedule for December

WEEK	ACTIVITY
1	Continue to collect data from on-going tests to solve the problem.
2	Continue data collection in an effort to solve the problem. Work on rough draft of final paper.
3	End data collection. Begin to analyze data. Construct graphs, tables and diagrams of data collected. Include these in rough draft of final paper.
4	Rough draft of all parts of the paper due to the teacher. Attach the signed copy of the outline of the paper done in November to the rough draft of your final paper.

NOTES:

GA1325

ACTIVITY NO.	KEY	ACTIVITY	REFER TO PAGE(S)	DATE COMPLETED
D8 (T)	IC	Teach students new skills as need arises, for example, statistical analysis of data and methods used in presenting the data.	70-75, 182	

TIPS FOR THE TEACHER
Statistical Analyses

Introduce basic statistics to students. Review hypothesis and how such hypothesis is tested. Have students refer to the student's Science Fair Glossary on pages 70-75. Discuss the words *mean*, *median* and *mode* found on page 73. For a handy reference see *Statistics for Students*, by Harold Baal published by Communications Planning Consultants, Box 327, Lakefield, ON CANADA KOLAHO.

Extension: Introduce students to various spread sheet programs that are available. These spread sheet programs allow one to perform many functions such as sum, count, average, minimum, maximum, means, medians, modes and standard deviations if needed.

NOTES:

GA1325

ACTIVITY NO.	KEY	ACTIVITY	REFER TO PAGE(S)	DATE COMPLETED
D9 (T)	IC	Using diaries/logbooks for background information, have students describe their meetings with mentors and/or other resource personnel.	155, 183	

TIPS FOR THE TEACHER
Meetings with Mentors

Assist students in making oral presentations based on significant events recorded in their science diaries/logbooks. Explain that a scientific log is much like a diary which eventually leads to a comprehensive scientific journal. Note that in a journal, one writes down everything one does, observes and thinks about. Review three-minute oral presentations given by students in November (see page 155). Using effective oral presentation skills, have students first rewrite a significant passage from their diaries/logbooks and then orally present their experiences to the class. Videotape or tape-record these experiences. Review the tapes to improve student communication skills in preparation for the Science Fair.

NOTES:

GA1325

ACTIVITY NO.	KEY	ACTIVITY	REFER TO PAGE(S)	DATE COMPLETED
D10 (T)	IC	Have students develop a five-minute oral and one-page written progress report on their science fair projects.	184, 204	

TIPS FOR THE TEACHER
Progress Report

Review sections of Student's Guide on How to Write a Science Fair Report as outlined on pages 87 and 88. Note that a rough draft of the report is due at the end of December. Review principles of an effective oral presentation as outlined on page 155. Have students fill in the blanks and note any changes that have occurred in their research design since November.

FORMAT FOR FIVE-MINUTE ORAL PRESENTATION

"My name is _____ . I am a _____ grade student at _____ School. The question I am trying to answer is _____ _____ .

My hypothesis is _____ .
I investigated the works of _____
and _____ to learn what they did on the topic. The first procedure
that I used to test my hypothesis was _____ . I changed
my procedure to _____ . I learned _____
_____
as a result of my initial investigations and _____
as a result of my further investigations. I changed _____ in
my study. I might conclude _____
_____ from my study."

Extension: Encourage students to continue to develop and use visual aids in their oral presentations. Such aids may include transparencies, slides, computer-generated graphics and videotapes of their research activity. Videotape and/or audiotape the students' presentations for later analysis.

NOTES:

ACTIVITY NO.	KEY	ACTIVITY	REFER TO PAGE(S)	DATE COMPLETED
D11 Ⓣ	IC	Have students report changes in plans, ideas, books read, computer searches of data bases and note cards written.	117-119, 185	

TIPS FOR THE TEACHER

Reporting Changes

Design a copy of this form for your students. Have students add references and note any changes in plans, ideas, works read, computer searches done and note cards written. Use reverse side for additional changes and information.

BOOK

From a Book
Author(s)   1. _____
                      Last   First   Middle
              2. _____
              3. _____
              4. _____

Title _____

City Where Published _____

Publisher _____

Year Published_____ Page(s) Used_____

ARTICLE

From an Article in a Periodical
Author(s)   1. _____
                      Last   First   Middle
              2. _____
              3. _____
              4. _____

Title of Article _____

Name of Periodical_____ Volume No._____

Year Published_____ Page(s) Used_____

PERSONAL COMMUNICATION

From Personal Communication
Name _____
                 Last   First   Middle

☐ Interview   ☐ Letter   ☐ Discussion with Mentor

Title of Affiliation _____

Date of Communication _____

GA1325

ACTIVITY NO.	KEY	ACTIVITY	REFER TO PAGE(S)	DATE COMPLETED
D12 (T)	IC	Have each student write and turn in a rough draft of his/her paper based on observations, experimentation and revision of data in diary/logbook.	86-87, 186	

TIPS FOR THE TEACHER
Rough Draft of Paper

Review Student's Guide on How to Write a Science Fair Report on pages 86 and 87. Require each student to turn in a rough draft of his/her paper including information on cards A-P by the end of December. Read rough drafts and return them to the students in early January for revisions before the Science Fair.

Extension: As part of the rough draft, have students include graphs and charts of data. Introduce students to a computer software package such as those in a dot-matrix printer and/or a 12-pen plotter. Have students use software packages to improve the presentation of graphs and charts in their papers.

NOTES:

THE SCIENCE FAIR TEACHER COMMUNICATES WITH MEMBERS OF THE MEDIA

GA1325

ACTIVITY NO.	KEY	ACTIVITY	REFER TO PAGE(S)	DATE COMPLETED
J1 (T)	OC	Contact members of the media (newspapers, television, radio, managers of malls, grocery stores and banks) to place science fair announcements on electronic message boards and bulletin boards. Invite them to "cover" the Science Fair with announcements, press releases, and television and radio "spots."	188, 205, 209	

TIPS FOR THE TEACHER
Contact Members of the Media

Members of the media play an important role in the success of the Science Fair Mentorship Program. Contact the following members of the media. Ask them to publicize your program.

	Date Contacted	Yes	No	Maybe	Contact Person	Phone
I. **Members of the Media**						
A. Television						
B. Radio						
C. Newspapers						
II. **Members of the Community**						
A. Managers of Malls						
B. Grocery Stores						
C. Banks						
D. Dry Cleaners						
E. Restaurants						
III. **Scientific Trade and Professional Organizations**						
IV. **Other**						

NOTES:

GA1325

ACTIVITY NO.	KEY	ACTIVITY	REFER TO PAGE(S)	DATE COMPLETED
J2 (T)	OC	Make copies of the Science Fairs with Style Members of the Media Packet. Distribute to members of the media who have responded to your request to "cover" the event.	189-206	

TIPS FOR THE TEACHER

Science Fairs with Style Members of the Media Packet

The fifth and final packet, Science Fairs with Style Members of the Media Packet, is found on pages 190 to 206. Make copies of the packet. Distribute to members of various media outlets after initial contact has been made. In addition to front and back covers, the packet contains A Personal Letter to Members of the Media (p. 193), Media Member's Volunteer Letter (p. 194), Letter of Appeal for Funding (p. 195), Media Member's Scrounge and Save Letter (p. 197), Media Member's Guide to Science Fair Requirements (p. 199), Criteria (p. 200), Time Line (p. 201), Guidelines for a Science Fair Display (p. 203), Guidelines for an Oral Presentation (p. 204), a Sample Press Release (p. 205) and a Science Fair Mentorship Program Evaluation Form (p. 206). In all contacts with the media, urge them to publicize the Science Fair. Ask members of the media to assist students in techniques for effective oral presentations and displays. In addition, seek assistance from the media in helping students write effective press releases that publicize the Science Fair.

NOTES:

GA1325

SCIENCE FAIRS WITH STYLE
MEMBERS OF THE MEDIA PACKET

Name _____

Affiliation _____

(Front Cover)

SCIENCE FAIRS WITH STYLE
MEMBERS OF THE MEDIA PACKET

(Back Cover)

Table of Contents

VIDEO
science fairs with style

A PERSONAL LETTER TO MEMBERS OF THE MEDIA

(M)

Date _____

Dear Member of the Media:

This science fair packet is written to inform you of our unique Science Fair Mentorship Program. As avid teachers of science, our major goal is to have our students work with various community members in an effort to develop high-quality science fair projects. Your role as a member of the media is a crucial one for the success of these students and for our community as a whole. Included in this media packet are the following items:

1. Media Member's Volunteer Form
2. Letter of Appeal for Funding
3. Media Member's Scrounge and Save Letter
4. Media Member's Guide to Science Fair Requirements, Criteria and Time Line
5. Requirements: Student's Science Fair Contract
6. Criteria for Judging a Science Fair Project
7. Student's Weekly October Through February Time Line
8. Student's Monthly Science Fair Project Completion Schedule
9. Guidelines for a Science Fair Display
10. Guidelines for an Oral Presentation to Judges
11. Sample Science Fairs with Style Press Release
12. Science Fair Mentorship Program Evaluation Form

We hope that you will read the packet carefully and consider helping our students with suggested tips on how to write press releases, deliver effective oral presentations and construct eye-catching visual displays of the results of their science fair projects. If you can help in any way, please check the activity(ies) below and return the form to us as soon as possible. If you have any questions, please feel free to call us anytime at _____ (school) _____ (home).

Thank you for your support.

Sincerely,

MEDIA MEMBER'S VOLUNTEER FORM

Name _____ Phone _____

Address _____

Occupation _____

Yes, I would like to volunteer to help students with the following activities:

_____ Writing effective press releases
_____ Delivering exciting oral presentations
_____ Other
_____

_____ Constructing eye-catching visual science fair displays
_____ Visiting the classroom as a resource speaker

(M) MEDIA MEMBER'S VOLUNTEER LETTER

Date _____

Dear Member of the Media:

   In science this year, we will be involved in a unique Science Fair Mentorship Program. As avid teachers of science, our major goal is to afford students an opportunity to conduct a scientific research study under the careful guidance of a mentor, a person experienced in a subject area. Last year, some students worked with physicians, veterinarians and engineers. The results of their efforts were displayed at our annual Science Fair in February.

   In order to reach our goal of having a successful Science Fair Mentorship Program, we need your help. Below is a Science Fair Volunteer Form. Please check the tasks that you could do to help us reach our goal. Clip the form and return it to us by the date shown on the form. We will organize volunteers in groups by tasks. You will receive further information throughout the year on our progress.

   Thank you for your support.

                                        Sincerely,

_____

SCIENCE FAIR VOLUNTEER FORM

I would like to volunteer for the following activity(ies) involved in the Science Fair Mentorship Program:

_____ Be a member of the Science Fair Committee   _____ Organize field trips to research sites
_____ Contact librarians   _____ Be a science fair mentor
_____ Contact judges   _____ Donate science periodicals and books
_____ Contact community mentors   _____ Contact members of the media
_____ Help set up gym for Science Fair   _____ Supervise students setting up projects
_____ Help supply and dispense refreshments   _____ Donate science equipment
_____ Be a classroom helper   _____ Supervise students during judging
_____ Develop science fair program   _____ Contact guest speakers
_____ Help construct display boards   _____ Help in fund-raising
_____ Contact retired people for assistance   _____ Distribute copy of this form to anyone
_____ Other _____   who would be of help

Name _____ Address _____

Telephone (work) _____ (home) _____ Please return by _____

GA1325

LETTER OF APPEAL FOR FUNDING

Date _____

Dear _____ :

    This school year we are involved in a unique Science Fair Mentorship Program for students. As avid teachers of science, our major goal is to afford students an opportunity to conduct a scientific research study under the careful guidance of a mentor, an experienced person knowledgeable in a subject matter area. The results of the students' research efforts will be displayed at our annual Science Fair in February.

    In order to reach our goal of having a successful Science Fair Mentorship Program, we need your help. Enclosed is a prioritized listing of materials that we will need. We hope that you will support our program with a contribution and/or materials and thus help our students by providing them with this unique opportunity.

    Our first annual Science Fair will be held on _____ , _____ , at _____ . Please join us to view the accomplishments of these students, all of which are a result of being placed in an environment in which they could be the very best that they could be. If you have any questions, please call us at _____ (school) or _____ (home).

    Thank you for your support.

Sincerely,

GA1325

SAMPLE

PRIORITIZED LISTING OF MATERIALS NEEDED FOR THE SCIENCE FAIR MENTORSHIP PROGRAM PER CLASS (30)

Item	Number Needed	Cost Per	Total	Priority No.
Triple-wall backboards	30	$ 4.00	$120.00	1
Stencils	8 sets	5.00	40.00	1
Paint	10 pints	4.00	40.00	1
Rubber cement	10 bottles	3.00	30.00	1
Markers	10 sets of 12	11.00	110.00	1
Construction paper	20 packs	2.50	50.00	1
Poster board	30	1.50	45.00	1
Note cards	10 packs	3.00	30.00	1
Judges' packets	6	6.00	36.00	1
Masking tape	30 rolls	2.00	60.00	1
Film (35mm)	10 rolls	6.00	60.00	1
Film developing	10 rolls	6.00	60.00	1
Videotapes	10	6.00	60.00	1
Audio cassette tapes	10	4.00	40.00	1
Slide trays	2	15.00	30.00	1
Computer discs	30	3.00	90.00	1
Computer paper	2 cartons	40.00	80.00	1
Exhibit paper	5 packets	9.00	45.00	2
Duplicating paper	5 reams	7.00	35.00	1
Stationery & thank-you notes	Asstd.	30.00	30.00	1
Ribbons & awards	30	5.00	150.00	1
Certificates of appreciation	30 (5 per pack)	3.00	15.00	1
Electrical cords	10	8.00	80.00	1
Photo albums	2	12.00	24.00	1
Reference books	20	10.00	200.00	1
Postage	—	—	150.00	1
Transportation to labs	3 trips	variable	100.00	2
Miscellaneous science supplies	Asstd.	variable	280.00	1
Refreshments	Variety for 100 people	1.50 per person	250.00	1
			$2340.00	

*Prices are approximate and subject to change based on time, location and number of items requested.

NOTES:

GA1325

MEDIA MEMBER'S SCROUNGE AND SAVE LETTER

Date _____

Dear Member of the Media:

In our students' study of science this year, we will be involved in a unique Science Fair Mentorship Program. As avid teachers of science, our goal is to offer an opportunity to conduct scientific research that will culminate in a science fair project which will be displayed at our annual Science Fair in February.

In order to reach our goal, we need your help. Below is a list of items that you may have in your possession. If you have any of these items in limited or large quantities that you are willing to donate, please send them to school by _____ or call us at _____ and we will pick them up.

Thank you for your support.

Sincerely,

Item	Quantity	Item	Quantity
Stencils	8 sets	Duplicating paper	5 reams
Paint	10 pints	Stationery	Asstd.
Rubber cement	10 bottles	Electrical cords	10
Markers	10 sets	Exhibit paper	5 packets
Construction paper	20 packs	35mm film	20 rolls
Poster board	30 sheets	Videotapes	10
Note cards(4" x 6")	10 packets	Audio cassette tapes	10
Masking tape	30 rolls	Slide trays	2
Glue	10 bottles	Computer discs	30
Thick cardboard or		Computer paper	2 cartons
Masonite (60" x 74")	30 sheets		

*Your gifts to educational institutions are often tax deductible to the amount limited by law.

Thank you.

GA1325

MEDIA MEMBER'S GUIDE
TO SCIENCE FAIR REQUIREMENTS, CRITERIA AND TIME LINE

Date _____

Dear Member of the Media:

In our study of science this year, we will be involved in a unique Science Fair Mentorship Program. As avid teachers of science, our goal is to offer students an opportunity to conduct scientific research that will culminate in a science fair project which will be displayed at our annual Science Fair in February.

In order to reach our goal, we need your help. Enclosed in your packet are copies of the Student's Science Fair Contract that lists the requirements of the program; Criteria for Judging Science Fair Projects, which will be followed when judging science fair projects; and a Week-to-Week Schedule of Science Fair Activity for October Through February. It is hoped that these documents will inform you of what is required each week of our students in the program.

Please read the appropriate documents that describe our program. We hope that you will publicize our program through various media channels and outlets.

Thank you for your support.

Sincerely,

NOTES:

REQUIREMENTS: STUDENT'S SCIENCE FAIR CONTRACT (M)

I, (the undersigned), do hereby contract for a science fair project and agree to the following conditions:

A. I will follow the basic principles of scientific investigation:
    1. Conduct research and collect data on my chosen topic
    2. Set up and conduct experiments in this area
    3. Construct a stable means of exhibiting my information and experiment

B. I will also construct a display board to exhibit my project at the Science Fair on _____ .
    By this I understand that I will meet the following deadlines unless previously arranged:
    1. I will have my project set up in the _____ by _____ p.m.,
       _____ , 19 _____ .
    2. I will remove my project no earlier than _____ on the evening of
       _____ , 19 _____ .

C. I will have an Official Entry Card, which will be provided to me, attached to the right-hand side of my display along with an approved Student Vertebrate Animal Certificate if I use live animals in my study.

D. I will include in my exhibit a brief summary of my project, its purpose and a written paper of my study.

E. I will present a brief explanation of my project to the judges on _____ , 19 _____ .
    I will honestly attempt to answer with utmost sincerity and courtesy any questions the judges might ask me.

F. I understand that I will be judged on the following items:
    1. Scientific thought: use of the scientific method
    2. Research report
    3. Physical display
    4. Oral presentation
    5. Attendance at science fair

G. I further acknowledge that if because of some extreme unforeseen circumstances my experiment cannot be concluded I may, under mutual agreement with my teacher, be reassigned to do a research paper on a related topic. I must give notification of this before _____ , 19 _____ .

H. I also understand that this contract is in effect whether I am present in school or not. Termination of this contract is only possible by an extenuating circumstance such as withdrawal from school, death in the family or a serious illness certified by a doctor that I am unable to perform the work.

I hereby agree to the conditions and terms of this contract and have been given sufficient time to question any part of this contract. My signature implies complete understanding of this contract.

Signed_____   Contract date_____

Title of project (subject to approval)_____
Note: It is understood by the student that the topic is subject to change in wording but not in theme.

_____   _____
Signature of student   Signature of parent or guardian

_____   _____
Signature of teacher   Signature of mentor (if applicable)

GA1325

CRITERIA FOR JUDGING SCIENCE FAIR PROJECTS

There are many methods of judging science fair projects. This one, based on 100 points, will be used by the judges at the Science Fair.

Criteria	Points	My Points
A. Scientific Thought: Use of the Scientific Method 1. Student performed experiment in which data were collected and analyzed by using the scientific method.	1 2 3 4 5	
2. Student set up experiment carefully and kept an accurate record of the data in a journal, diary or logbook.	1 2 3 4 5	
3. Student's conclusion is logical and justifiable.	1 2 3 4 5	
4. Experiment is an original idea, unique and creatively done.	1 2 3 4 5	
5. Summary shows title, question, hypothesis, materials, procedures, results and conclusions.	1 2 3 4 5	
B. Research Report 1. Includes title page, table of contents, abstract, write-up of procedures, background information and bibliography.	1 2 3 4 5	
2. Background information shows student has conducted research on the topic.	1 2 3 4 5	
3. Report is displayed and written with correct use of spelling and grammar.	1 2 3 4 5	
4. Abstract is interesting and helpful.	1 2 3 4 5	
5. Bibliography is related to topic and written in correct form.	1 2 3 4 5	
C. Physical Display 1. Student has a well-constructed backdrop to display the project.	1 2 3 4 5	
2. Display tells story of the project accurately.	1 2 3 4 5	
3. Display is appealing and is neatly done with correct spelling.	1 2 3 4 5	
4. Display shows components of science fair project.	1 2 3 4 5	
D. Attendance at Science Fair Student is present at display and greets judge on time.	1 2 3 4 5	
E. Oral Presentation 1. Student gives a clear explanation about the research conducted.	1 2 3 4 5	
2. Oral presentation is coherent and well organized.	1 2 3 4 5	
3. Oral presentation had effective use of visual aids.	1 2 3 4 5	
4. Student answers questions accurately and honestly.	1 2 3 4 5	
5. Oral presentation made in time allotted with all phases discussed.	1 2 3 4 5	
	Possible Total	**Student Total**

Levels of Performance:
5 = Superior   4 = Excellent   3 = Good   2 = Satisfactory   1 = Fair   Points = [100]   Points = [ ]
Comments: Use reverse side for written comments and notes.

GA1325

WEEKLY OCTOBER THROUGH FEBRUARY TIME LINE
Week-to-Week Schedule of Science Fair Activity
for October Through February

Week No. Due	OCTOBER ACTIVITY
1	Review sample projects of past science fair activities for ideas.
2	Topic selection is due. Register name of topic with your teacher.
3	Identify a problem that you would like to solve. Narrow the topic. Formulate a hypothesis by making an intelligent guess.
4	Find out what others have done to solve the problem. Go to the library. Read books and articles on the topic. Turn in a list of these materials to your teacher.

	NOVEMBER ACTIVITY
1	Meet with mentor to begin science fair activity. Make an oral presentation to your mentor that features your ideas.
2	Collect data from trials and tests that you do to solve the problem.
3	Keep a journal of all science fair activity both in and out of school.
4	Rough draft of an outline of your paper is due to your teacher. Include all topic headings. Have your mentor, parents and your teacher sign your outline.

	DECEMBER ACTIVITY
1	Written progress report on the results of your experiment is due to your teacher and mentor.
2	Begin to analyze the results of your experiment by making graphs, charts and using other statistical analyses of data.
3	Prepare an oral report on your project for presentation to a judge or members of the class.
4	Rough draft of your written science fair paper is due to your teacher and mentor.

	JANUARY ACTIVITY
1	With feedback from your teacher and mentor, draw final conclusions from your study.
2	Write and type final science fair paper to be given to your teacher and mentor.
3	Construct a backdrop display to exhibit your science fair project at the Science Fair in February.
4	Make a practice audio and/or videotape of your science fair presentation for the judges.

	FEBRUARY ACTIVITY
1	Complete entry form that includes name, project title, project number and signatures from student, parents and mentor is due to your teacher. Write an abstract of your study to be sent to judges prior to the day of the Science Fair.
2	Present science fair project at classroom Science Fair. Revise as needed for school Science Fair.
3	Present science fair project at school Science Fair. RELAX.
4	Complete Science Fair Mentorship Program Evaluation Form. Revise science fair project and enter into other science fairs at local, district, state and national levels.

GA1325

STUDENT'S MONTHLY SCIENCE FAIR PROJECT COMPLETION SCHEDULE

Name_____ **School** _____

Keep this schedule in a place where it is seen often.

Assignment	Date Due	Date Completed	Comments
1. Understand Judging Criteria			
2. Understand Scientific Method			
3. Preview Sample Program			
4. Review Project Idea and Question			
5. Identify a Problem			
6. Review of Literature			
7. State Hypothesis			
8. Project Proposal Written			
9. Locate Information			
10. Collect and Organize Data			
11. Keep a Journal			
12. Analyze and Interpret Results			
13. Research Report Written			
14. Construct Graphs, Tables and Diagrams			
15. Write Abstract			
16. Write Title Page, Table of Contents and References			
17. Build Project Display			
18. Develop Oral Presentation			
19. Present Project			
20. Evaluation of Project			
21. Revise Project			
22. Enter Project in Science Fairs at Local, State and/or National Levels			
23. Write Article to Share with Others			

GA1325

GUIDELINES FOR A SCIENCE FAIR DISPLAY

The following includes ideas on how a science fair project should be displayed. A typical science fair display looks like this:

The display board should be durable and made out of triple wall, cardboard, tagboard, Masonite, pressed wood or other self-supporting material. If three pieces need to be joined, connect them with inexpensive hinges or tape. The sides should measure 22" (55 cm) wide and 60" (150 cm) high, the back 30" (75 cm) wide and 60" (150 cm) high. Space is limited so adhere to these dimensions. Please notify me if your youngster's project requires special things like a computer, running water or electrical outlets. The display should have the following elements:

- Title
- Abstract
- Experimental design
- Background information including problem and hypothesis
- Results including tables and graphs of data
- Conclusion(s)
- Technical report
- Logbook
- Equipment, samples or other items from project activity

Help your child transport the project to and from school on time. The displays will be set up for _____ school day(s). Students will need to set up their displays in the _____ of the school between _____ and _____ . The displays are to be taken down between _____ and _____ .

Thank you for your help in this unique Science Fair Mentorship Program. Please join us and enjoy the rewards of the students' dedicated efforts.

GA1325

GUIDELINES FOR AN ORAL PRESENTATION TO JUDGES

In the oral presentation, you tell the judges what you have done in your study. Prepare well ahead of time. Careful preparation builds confidence and puts you at ease. Your talk should be three to eight minutes long and cover only the important points. You will need to communicate clearly. In most cases, you do NOT need to memorize your speech, but you should have neat note cards with an outline of your talk and important points you want to discuss. Write note cards so they are easy to follow. Number each card. Highlight key words and ideas with a marker. Be sure that your display is well-organized and presents accurate information about your study.

During your presentation, use both talking (verbal) and nontalking (nonverbal) behaviors. Talking behaviors deal with pace, pause, pitch, volume and clarity such as knowing what various scientific terms mean and pronouncing them correctly. Nontalking behaviors include posture, gestures, facial expressions such as eye contact which means you look into the judges' eyes as much as possible. Keep good eye contact, have good posture, use natural gestures and avoid unusual mannerisms.

Before you give your talk, take a deep breath. Then tell the judges how you came up with the idea for your project. Know your study well. Use the information on your display board, research paper, diary/logbook and various science materials as guides. Use a pointer. Tell the judges what you learned about what others found out about your topic. Include information on the steps you followed, the results, both positive and negative, and what may have caused these results. Come to the point. Explain what future studies should be done on the topic.

When you finish your talk, ask the judges if they have any questions. If so, answer the questions honestly and in a straightforward manner. Pause. Think. If you do not understand the question, ask the judge to repeat the question or ask it in a different way. Repeat the judge's question before you answer it. If you don't know the answer, say so. Again, be honest and straightforward. Relax. Thank the judges for judging your project. Your presentation to the judges will be a pleasant one if you follow these tips:

1. **PREPARE WELL**

2. **CREATE HIGH-QUALITY DISPLAY BOARD AND NOTE CARDS**

3. **KNOW SUBJECT AND TERMS**

4. **COMMUNICATE CLEARLY**

5. **EYE CONTACT, GESTURES, VOICE, POISE**

6. **COME TO THE POINT**

7. **ANSWER QUESTIONS HONESTLY**

GA1325

SAMPLE

SCIENCE FAIRS WITH STYLE PRESS RELEASE

SAMPLE PRESS RELEASE
(Use school letterhead.)

Contact: (Type your name and phone number here.)

Science Fairs with Style Day
Set for (Fill in date here.)

For immediate release.

_____ grade teacher in (city) (type date) at (type name of school) today announced that (type number of students) will display the results of their science fair projects at the (type name of local science day) on (type day of week and date) at (type location). The projects may be viewed by the public from (give times). The awards ceremony will be held at (give time) in (give room or auditorium).

The director of this year's Science Fair (give name and affiliation [school, grades and subjects taught]) said, "quote (a very positive statement and encourage others to attend)."

Superior winning students from (give name of science day) will attend (give name of District Science Day) at (name of location) on (date), where the students will qualify to attend State Science Day at (give name of location) on (date).

Extension: To improve your press release, you may list more details on additional pages such as names of students, special awards planned, a request for recruiting judges or any other pertinent information. Use a similar press release immediately after your event to summarize the names of students who participated, especially those who will attend other science fairs.

NOTES:

SCIENCE FAIR MENTORSHIP PROGRAM EVALUATION FORM

For each of the paired items listed below, place an X on the line that best represents your feelings about the Science Fair Mentorship Program.

Example: The Science Fair Mentorship Program was

Hot	X							Cold
	(1)	(2)	(3)	(4)	(5)	(6)	(7)	

1. **Interesting**	(1)	(2)	(3)	(4)	(5)	(6)	(7)	**Boring**
2. **Important**	(1)	(2)	(3)	(4)	(5)	(6)	(7)	**Useless**
3. **Informative**	(1)	(2)	(3)	(4)	(5)	(6)	(7)	**Worthless**
4. **Complete**	(1)	(2)	(3)	(4)	(5)	(6)	(7)	**Incomplete**
5. **Mixed Up**	(7)	(6)	(5)	(4)	(3)	(2)	(1)	**Smooth**
6. **A Downer**	(7)	(6)	(5)	(4)	(3)	(2)	(1)	**An Upper**
7. **Selfish**	(7)	(6)	(5)	(4)	(3)	(2)	(1)	**Unselfish**
8. **Enough Time**	(1)	(2)	(3)	(4)	(5)	(6)	(7)	**Not Enough Time**
9. **Light**	(1)	(2)	(3)	(4)	(5)	(6)	(7)	**Dark**
10. **Negative**	(7)	(6)	(5)	(4)	(3)	(2)	(1)	**Positive**
11. **High**	(1)	(2)	(3)	(4)	(5)	(6)	(7)	**Low**
12. **Bad**	(7)	(6)	(5)	(4)	(3)	(2)	(1)	**Good**
13. **Liked**	(1)	(2)	(3)	(4)	(5)	(6)	(7)	**Disliked**
14. **Black**	(7)	(6)	(5)	(4)	(3)	(2)	(1)	**White**
15. **Fast**	(1)	(2)	(3)	(4)	(5)	(6)	(7)	**Slow**

On the other side of this page, list responses to the following: (1) Things I like(d) best about the Science Fair Mentorship Program; (2) Things I like(d) least about the Science Fair Mentorship Program and (3) Suggestions for improvement of the Science Fair Mentorship Program. **Note:** Please return this form as soon as possible to the Director of the Science Fair Mentorship Program or place in the Return Box on the day of the Science Fair. Thank you.

ACTIVITY NO.	KEY	ACTIVITY	REFER TO PAGE(S)	DATE COMPLETED
J3 (T)	OC	Using a computer, prepare a spread sheet that has the names, addresses, telephone numbers of key media contacts and their affiliations.	194, 207	

TIPS FOR THE TEACHER
Data Base for Names of Key Members of the Media

NAME	ADDRESS	PHONE NO.	AFFILIATION	COMMENTS

NOTES:

GA1325

ACTIVITY NO.	KEY	ACTIVITY	REFER TO PAGE(S)	DATE COMPLETED
J4 ⓣ	OC	Invite a member of the media to class to discuss the components of high-quality visual, oral and written science fair projects.	193-194, 204, 208	

TIPS FOR THE TEACHER

Invite a Member of the Media to Class

After distribution of Science Fairs with Style Members of the Media Packet, invite an experienced member of the media to class to discuss effective techniques in preparing written reports, visual displays and oral preparations of science fair activity. Review Guidelines for an Oral Presentation to Judges (p. 204), Student's Guide on How to Write a Science Fair Report (pp. 86-87), Guidelines for a Science Fair Display (p. 203) and Criteria for Judging Science Fair Projects (p. 200). If possible, videotape the media member's presentation. Show the tape to other students as they prepare for the Science Fair.

NOTES:

GA1325

ACTIVITY NO.	KEY	ACTIVITY	REFER TO PAGE(S)	DATE COMPLETED
J5 ⓉT	OC	Publicize the Science Fair.	188, 205, 209	

TIPS FOR THE TEACHER
Publicizing the Science Fair

The following ideas may be used by you and your students to publicize your science fair. First, require your students, as part of a language arts lesson, to write press releases for school and local newspapers and for radio and television spots. Be sure students focus on *what* the event is (science fair), *who* is holding the event, *when* the event is to be held and *where* the event will take place. Second, in a computer science class, have students create banners to publicize the Science Fair. Display the banners in school and, with permission, in local businesses. Third, as part of an art lesson, have students create posters. Display posters in schools, local stores and businesses. Fourth, in art class, have students design a program for the science fair with special artwork on its cover. Fifth, have students design special invitations to be sent to parents, friends, relatives, mentors, judges, members of the media and personnel from local businesses. Sixth, encourage members of the local media to cover the Science Fair and report its results on local television, radio and in newspapers. Seventh, take photographs and/or make a videotape of the science fair experience. Use the photos and videotapes to recruit students for future science fairs by showing students examples of previous displays and projects. Publicize future science fair activity to all who participate in the science fair experience.

NOTES:

GA1325

ACTIVITY NO.	KEY	ACTIVITY	REFER TO PAGE(S)	DATE COMPLETED
J6 ⓉT	OC	If your school has an outdoor marque, place a "Welcome to Science Fairs with Style Day" message noting date and time of Science Fair.	208, 210	

TIPS FOR THE TEACHER
School Marque

Your marque may look like this:

WELCOME TO SCIENCE FAIRS WITH STYLE DAY

February 22, 1992

9:00 a.m.—1:00 p.m.

NOTES:

GA1325

ACTIVITY NO.	KEY	ACTIVITY	REFER TO PAGE(S)	DATE COMPLETED
J7 (T)	OC	Work with principal, teachers and support personnel to finalize plans for Science Fair.	11, 211	

TIPS FOR THE TEACHER

Working Together: Operation Science Fair Breakdown

Make copies of page 11, The Yearly Science Fairs with Style Interdisciplinary Web. At a staff meeting, distribute the copies to all who attend. Ask the principal, teachers and support personnel to hold a ten-minute "Operation Science Fair Breakdown" period during a school day prior to the day of the Science Fair. An all-school wide announcement about the Science Fair could be made followed by individual class discussions related to the Science Fair and its activities. Announce the date of the Science Fair and names of some of its participants with titles of topics. Encourage teachers of *all* subjects to integrate some phase of science fair activity into their teaching on this day.

NOTES:

GA1325

ACTIVITY NO.	KEY	ACTIVITY	REFER TO PAGE(S)	DATE COMPLETED
J8 (T)	OC	Organize and conduct a school-wide contest to select a cover design for the science fair program.	193, 212, 213	

TIPS FOR THE TEACHER

Program Cover Design Contest

In an effort to publicize the Science Fair, announce a school-wide contest that encourages students to submit art ideas for a catchy, eye-appealing cover for the science fair program. Include high-impact media such as scientific designs, computer-generated logos and characters, bumper stickers and T-shirt sayings. One such cover may look like this:

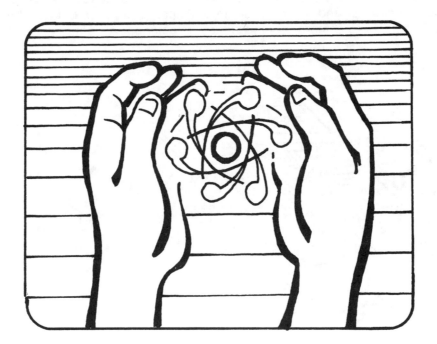

NOTES:

GA1325

ACTIVITY NO.	KEY	ACTIVITY	REFER TO PAGE(S)	DATE COMPLETED
J9 (T)	OC	Contact school district publicity director. Select winner of cover design for program. Plan, lay out, type and make sufficient copies of the program. Present award to student for the best cover design.	212-213	

TIPS FOR THE TEACHER
Final Program and Cover Design Winner

Award science-related computer program, videotape and/or audiotape to the winner of the cover design contest. An award-winning cover may look like this:

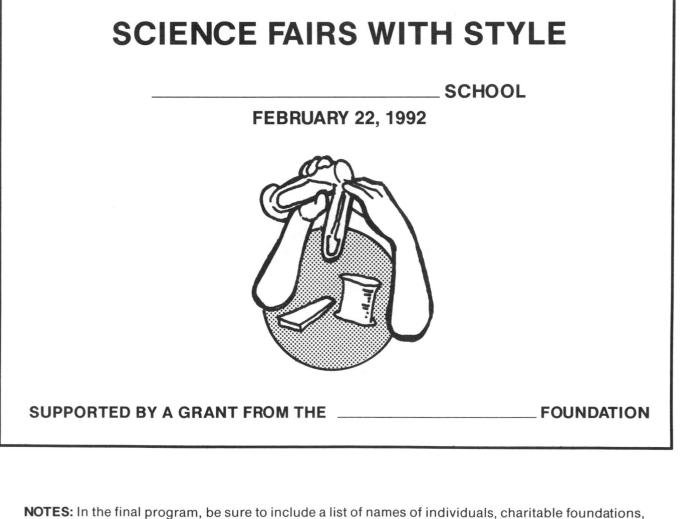

SCIENCE FAIRS WITH STYLE

_____ SCHOOL

FEBRUARY 22, 1992

SUPPORTED BY A GRANT FROM THE _____ **FOUNDATION**

NOTES: In the final program, be sure to include a list of names of individuals, charitable foundations, corporations, agencies and businesses who have contributed support for your program.

GA1325

ACTIVITY NO.	KEY	ACTIVITY	REFER TO PAGE(S)	DATE COMPLETED
J10 Ⓣ	OC	Contact school district media director. Ask director to arrange for videotaping and photographing of Science Fair from beginning to end.	214, 302-307	

TIPS FOR THE TEACHER

Photographs and Videotapes

Contact the school district media director *early* in the school year. Plan the day on which the Science Fair will be held. Encourage the media director to make arrangements for videotaping students for next year's Science Fair. Use also as support for writing a grant proposal (pp. 302-307) to obtain funding for next year's Science Fair.

School District Media Director Biographical Information

Name _____

Building _____

Room Number _____

Address _____

Telephone _____

Hours _____

NOTES:

GA1325

ACTIVITY NO.	KEY	ACTIVITY	REFER TO PAGE(S)	DATE COMPLETED
J11 (T)	OC	With cafeteria personnel, arrange refreshments for judges, mentors, contributors, exhibitors, parents, et al., who assisted in the science fair experience.	32, 215, 250	

TIPS FOR THE TEACHER
Refreshments

Early in January, recontact food personnel to arrange for refreshments at the Science Fair. Perhaps students in home economics classes could be involved in making goodies for the Science Fair. Ask the teacher of home economics for recommendations on what nutritious refreshments could be served. If refreshments are not available at school, perhaps parents may help. Here is a sample letter for that purpose.

Date _____

Dear Parents:

The Science Fair is fast approaching. We are excited about the accomplishments of our students. The Science Fair will be held on _____ , 19 _____ , in the _____ from _____ to _____ . All displays will be set up the day before the Science Fair. Students should report to the _____ at _____ on the day of the Science Fair. Judging will take place at _____ , awards given at _____ and exhibits removed by _____ .

We are having a hospitality room for all who attend the Science Fair. If you can help in any way, please note your involvement on the form below and return it to us by _____ .

We wish to extend our sincere thanks to you for your assistance and for your child's involvement in the program. We expect many superior projects to be displayed on _____ . We look forward to seeing you then. Thank you.

Sincerely,

_____

Name _____   Phone _____
Please check the items below that you could bring for the hospitality room:
_____ Paper napkins   _____ Two dozen cookies   _____ Cups for cold beverages
_____ One can of fruit punch _____ Cups for hot beverages   _____ Other:_____

ACTIVITY NO.	KEY	ACTIVITY	REFER TO PAGE(S)	DATE COMPLETED
J12 (T)	OC	Design a floor plan that shows the placement of booths to insure adequate facilities such as electrical, water and computers. Make transparency of floor plan. Display on overhead so all can identify the locations of various projects.	216, 238, 247	

TIPS FOR THE TEACHER

Floor Plan and Maps

When the number of science fair projects is known, design a floor plan that will be used in setting up the Science Fair. Make individual maps of the floor plan to be displayed at various strategic locations. Make a transparency of the floor plan for placement on the overhead projector near the exhibit room. A floor plan may look like this:

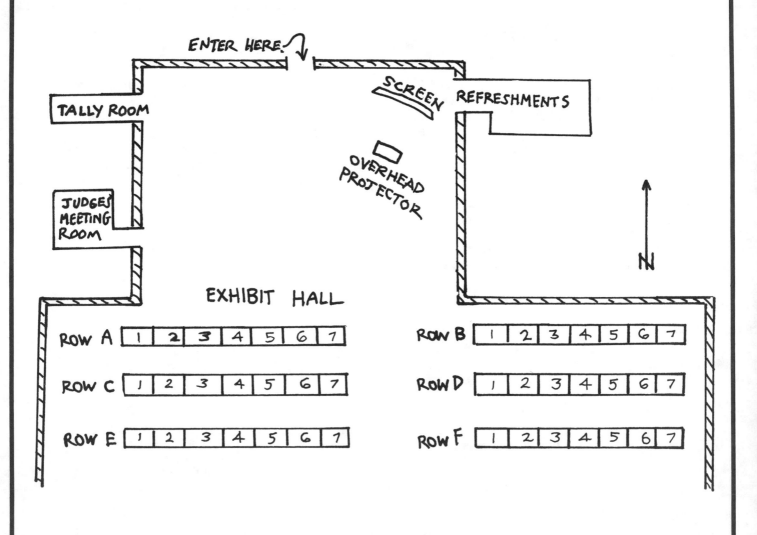

ACTIVITY NO.	KEY	ACTIVITY	REFER TO PAGE(S)	DATE COMPLETED
J13 (T)	OC	Acquire ribbons, certificates and other awards for various presentations.	172, 217, 264-265	

TIPS FOR THE TEACHER
Science Fair Awards and Certificates

Many Science Fair Directors present students with ribbons (first place—blue ribbon for superior, etc.) of various colors as awards based on the number of points awarded by the judges (see page 172). These ribbons are often presented to students on the day of the Science Fair. To avoid competition, others prefer that *all* students receive a Certificate of Participation on the day of the Science Fair. A Certificate of Award may be presented later at an all-school assembly. You may choose any method or a combination thereof. Ribbons, certificates and awards such as plaques may be purchased from a variety of companies. There are many things to consider when you order awards. You want a large quantity of high-quality, personalized awards delivered on time. Look for *wholesale* prices and cash discounts. One such internationally known and highly reputable wholesale company that provides both is listed below. Write for further information and a free catalog from:

Sylvan Studio
Box 59
Sylvania, OH 43560
(419) 882-3423
1-800-877-4758 (Toll Free)
(419) 882-8182 FAX

Name of Commercial Supplier in Your Area: _____

Address:_____
            Street   City   State   Zip

Phone Number: _____

NOTES:

GA1325

SAMPLE

AWARDS AND CERTIFICATES

The Certificate of Participation shown below may be given to each student on the day of the Science Fair if levels of performance are *not* specified. This eliminates various levels of competition. The Certificate of Award shown below may be given to each student later on a Day of Recognition at an all-school assembly. Enlarge to desired size, have printed on preferred paper or order similar certificates from the source listed on page 217.

Certificate of Participation

this is to certify that

_____

is hereby awarded this certificate for

Active and Cooperative Participation in

_____

for the year___

_____

CERTIFICATE OF AWARD

This is to certify that

_____

has been awarded this certificate for

_____

Given this ____ day of _____ 19__

_____   _____

These ribbons of various colors may be given to students on the day of the Science Fair if levels of Science Fair performance are specified. The color of ribbon given to students is dependent upon the number of points awarded by the judges. See page 172 for five such levels.

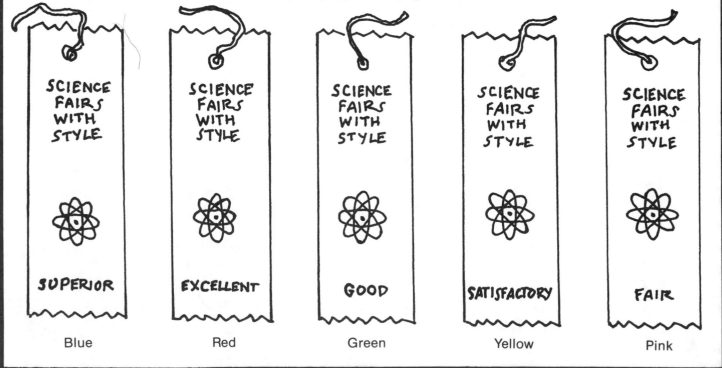

Blue	Red	Green	Yellow	Pink

ACTIVITY NO.	KEY	ACTIVITY	REFER TO PAGE(S)	DATE COMPLETED
J14 (T)	OC	Plan final schedule for science fair activity including setup, judging, viewing and awards presentation.	171, 219, 238, 245	

TIPS FOR THE TEACHER
Final Schedules

Whether you hold your Science Fair during the week or on Saturday, you will need to plan a final schedule for actual setup, judging, viewing of projects by others and the awards presentation. Here are two possible schedules, one for during the week, the other for Saturday.

Sample Weekday Schedule		**Sample Saturday Schedule**	
9:00-11:00	Project setup	7:30-9:00	Project setup
12:00-12:30	Judges' luncheon and briefing	9:00-9:30	Judges' breakfast and briefing
12:45-3:00	Judging of projects	9:30-11:30	Judging of projects
3:15-4:30	Project visitation	11:30-12:15	Project visitation
4:45-5:30	Awards ceremony	12:15-1:00	Awards ceremony

You may want to adjust these time allotments based on the number of projects and availability of judges. Be sure to assign the Science Project Indentification and Exhibit Numbers (p. 238) to each project. This ID-Exhibit number should be written on the abstract forms sent to the judges one week *before* the day of the Science Fair.

NOTES:

GA1325

ACTIVITY NO.	KEY	ACTIVITY	REFER TO PAGE(S)	DATE COMPLETED
J15 Ⓣ	OC	Invite parents, members of the PTA, Mother's Club, commercial distributors and professional groups to attend the Science Fair.	23, 220	

TIPS FOR THE TEACHER

An Invitation to Attend the Science Fair

Date _____

Dear _____ :

    This school year we have been involved in a unique Science Fair Mentorship Program for students. As avid teachers of science, our major goal was to afford students an opportunity to conduct a scientific research study under the guidance of a mentor in the community, a person knowledgeable in a subject matter area. We feel that we have reached our goal as some students have worked with physicians, veterinarians and engineers in the community. The time has now come to show you the results of the students' efforts.

    Our annual Science Fair will be held on _____ , _____ , at _____ . You are cordially invited to join us to view the accomplishments of these students, all of which are the result of a *total* community effort to help students become the best students they could be.

    If you have any questions about our activity, please feel free to contact us at _____ or _____ . Until then we hope that you will join us on _____ , 19 _____ , from _____ to _____ .

Sincerely,

Please join us!

NOTES:

GA1325

ACTIVITY NO.	KEY	ACTIVITY	REFER TO PAGE(S)	DATE COMPLETED
J16 (T)	OC	Invite mentors and other resource personnel to the Science Fair.	137, 150 221	

TIPS FOR THE TEACHER
An Invitation to Mentors and Resource Personnel

Date _____

Dear _____ :

This year we have been involved in a unique Science Fair Mentorship Program in which students worked with a mentor and/or resource person in the community to develop a high-quality science fair project. We are grateful to you for your efforts in helping us reach our major goal as some students worked with physicians, veterinarians and engineers. The time has come to show you the results of the students' efforts at our local Science Fair.

Our annual Science Fair will be held on _____, _____, at _____. You are cordially invited to join us to view the accomplishments of these students, all of which are the result of a *total* community effort to help students become the best students they could be.

If you have any questions about our activity, please feel free to contact us at _____ or _____ . Until then we hope that you will join us on _____, 19 _____ , from _____ to _____ .

Sincerely,

Please join us!

NOTES:

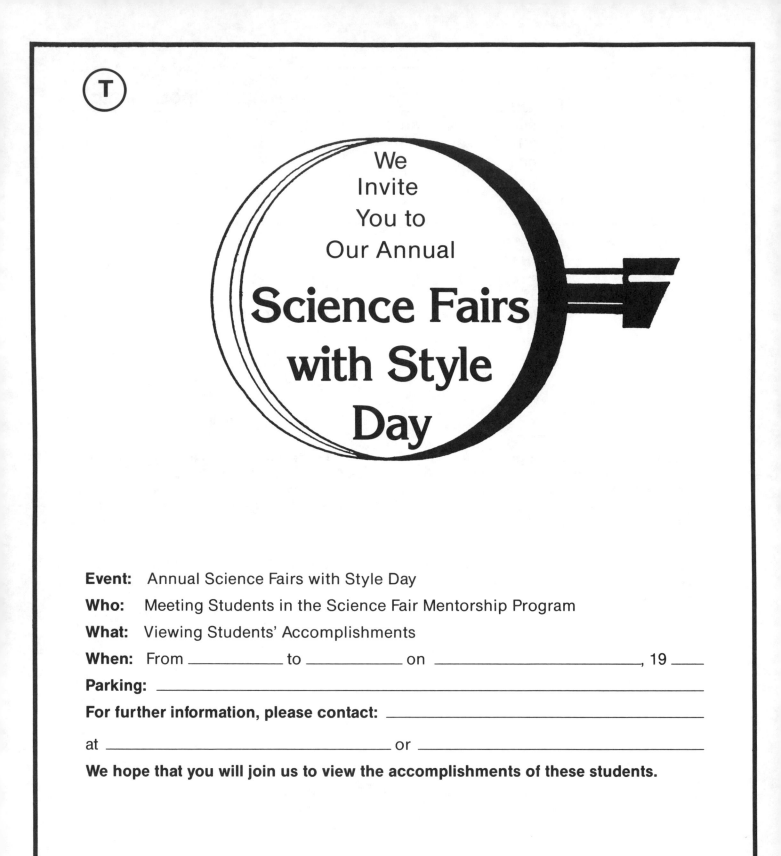

Event: Annual Science Fairs with Style Day

Who: Meeting Students in the Science Fair Mentorship Program

What: Viewing Students' Accomplishments

When: From _____ to _____ on _____, 19 _____

Parking: _____

For further information, please contact: _____

at _____ or _____

We hope that you will join us to view the accomplishments of these students.

GA1325

ACTIVITY NO.	KEY	ACTIVITY	REFER TO PAGE(S)	DATE COMPLETED
J17 (T)	IC	Have students design and send a press release (time, place, date, types of projects) to members of the media.	209, 223,	

TIPS FOR THE TEACHER

Student Written Press Release

Using their own writing skills and materials, have students write and send a press release announcing the Science Fair to various members of the media. Here is a possible format for such a press release.

Contact: (Type your name, address and phone number here.)

Science Fair set for _____.
(date)

For immediate release.

City _____ _____ _____ School today
(date) (school)

announced that _____ will display their science fair research
(numbers of students)

projects at the local Science Fair on _____ at _____.
(day) (location)

The projects may be viewed by the public from _____ to _____. An awards
(time) (time)

ceremony will be held at _____ in _____
(time) (room)

Members of the Science Fair Committee cordially invite members of the public to attend this program and bring their friends to view the results of these students' efforts.

ANNOUNCING!

NOTES:

GA1325

ACTIVITY NO.	KEY	ACTIVITY	REFER TO PAGE(S)	DATE COMPLETED
J18 (T)	IC	Have students complete final data collection, review of notes on readings, interviews and observations and draw conclusions from their study.	87, 154, 224	

TIPS FOR THE TEACHER

Drawing Conclusions

In preparation for writing the final paper, have students analyze all data from their trials and formulate their conclusions. When writing conclusions, encourage students to write about what they really learned from their trials and tests while doing their experiments. To begin writing, have students restate their hypotheses or questions. Encourage them to look for patterns or trends as a result of their research study. Students should be made aware that the conclusion does *not* necessarily have to support the original hypothesis which in the beginning of the study gave the student some direction. The student, however, may have identified an entirely different conclusion or experiment. Some hypotheses will show a conclusive direction, others will disprove the original hypothesis, still others will be inconclusive because of a possible weakness in the design. It is important that students understand that a wrong hypothesis yields new knowledge. In the *discussion phase* of the paper, students should state how this knowledge applies to their everyday lives. They should also make recommendations for future research on the topic. It should be emphasized that the discussion (card M, page 87) is separate from the conclusions (card L, page 87) and results (card K, page 87).

NOTES:

GA1325

ACTIVITY NO.	KEY	ACTIVITY	REFER TO PAGE(S)	DATE COMPLETED
J19 (T)	IC	Have students write and type their final science fair papers. Include sixteen components of a science fair paper from title page through appendices.	86-87, 180, 225	

TIPS FOR THE TEACHER
Final Written Science Fair Paper

The final Science Fair written paper should include the sixteen major sections found on pages 86 and 87 or a variation thereof for younger students. Make a transparency of each card. Place one card at a time on the overhead to review what constitutes a written science fair paper. Encourage students to include each section in their final written paper. Have students turn their papers in to you for final approval before presentation at the Science Fair. Review these tips with the students before they write their final science fair papers.

Pitfalls (P) to Avoid and Wise (W) Things to Do

1. (P) Writing to impress, rather than to inform.
   (W) Keep language simple. Know the audience. Clarity comes from simple, concise (not wordy) writing.

2. (P) Building up drama rather than telling it like it is.
   (W) Present results in a well-written summary.

3. (P) Including too much data to impress the reader.
   (W) Trim all nonessential data from the main text. Put extra data in the appendix.

4. (P) Confusing results, conclusions and discussion.
   (W) Do: Separate results, conclusions and discussion from each other. Know the characteristics of each.

5. (P) Incorrect grammar and spelling.
   (W) Use correct grammar and spelling as it reflects credibility of the writer.

6. (P) Sloppiness, smudge marks, erasures.
   (W) Stress neatness as it reflects organizational skills and attention to detail.

7. (P) Handwritten or poorly typed paper.
   (W) Use word processor or data base software to write the final paper. Put fresh ribbon in the printer.

Reference Books: (1) Day, Robert A. (1979). *How to Write and Publish a Scientific Paper.* Philadelphia: 1st Press. (2) Barrass, Robert (1978). *Scientists Must Write.* New York: Chapman and Hall, Methuen, Inc., (3) Strunk, William H., and White, E.B. (1979). *The Elements of Style.* New York: The MacMillan Co.

NOTES:

GA1325

ACTIVITY NO.	KEY	ACTIVITY	REFER TO PAGE(S)	DATE COMPLETED
J20 ⓣ	IC	Have students construct the backdrop displays for their projects.	112, 226-227	

TIPS FOR THE TEACHER
Building the Backdrop Display

The backdrop display is an important part of any scientific research presentation. Give each student a punched copy of page 227. Explain how the display should catch the attention of the viewers so they will want to look more closely at the display and learn what has been done in the study. Have student study the illustration carefully. Note how a typical display includes the following: (1) a title, (2) an abstract, (3) an experimental design, (4) some background information which includes the problem and hypothesis, (5) the results which include tables and graphs of data, (6) conclusion, (7) a diary/logbook and (8) some equipment, samples or other items from the experiment. Review steps followed when making a backdrop display. These steps include (1) obtain approval of science project from the teacher; (2) think about the display; (3) on paper, make a sketch of the display and its contents; (4) select materials for the display, including a photograph of yourself; (5) construct the backdrop for the display; (6) select appropriate colors and do the lettering; (7) assemble the display; (8) evaluate the display by asking questions such as "Is the display neat and attractive?" "Does the display tell the viewers what was done in the project?" and (9) acquire a carry-all container such as a box in which nonattachable materials can be carried. Students should then begin to build the actual backdrop displays.

NOTES:

GA1325

SAMPLE

BACKDROP DISPLAY FOR A SCIENCE FAIR PROJECT

GA1325

ACTIVITY NO.	KEY	ACTIVITY	REFER TO PAGE(S)	DATE COMPLETED
J21 (T)	IC	Have students make an audio and/or videotape presentation on their science fair projects.	193, 204, 228-229	

TIPS FOR THE TEACHER
Record Practice Oral Presentations

An effective way to prepare students for giving oral presentations of their research is to have them make audio or videotapes of their products. Seek the assistance of teachers who teach basic communication classes or someone well versed in such work such as a member of the media (p. 193). After the oral presentations are recorded, have the students review and critique their efforts. Provide constructive feedback on their presentations which may include tips such as standing in front of a mirror to show eye contact, enthusiasm and gestures. Encourage students to give their presentations to their friends, parents, brothers and sisters. Give each student a punched copy of pages 204 and 227 for inclusion in their three-ring binders. Review Guidelines for an Oral Presentation to Judges (p. 204, p. 229) before the Science Fair.

NOTES:

GA1325

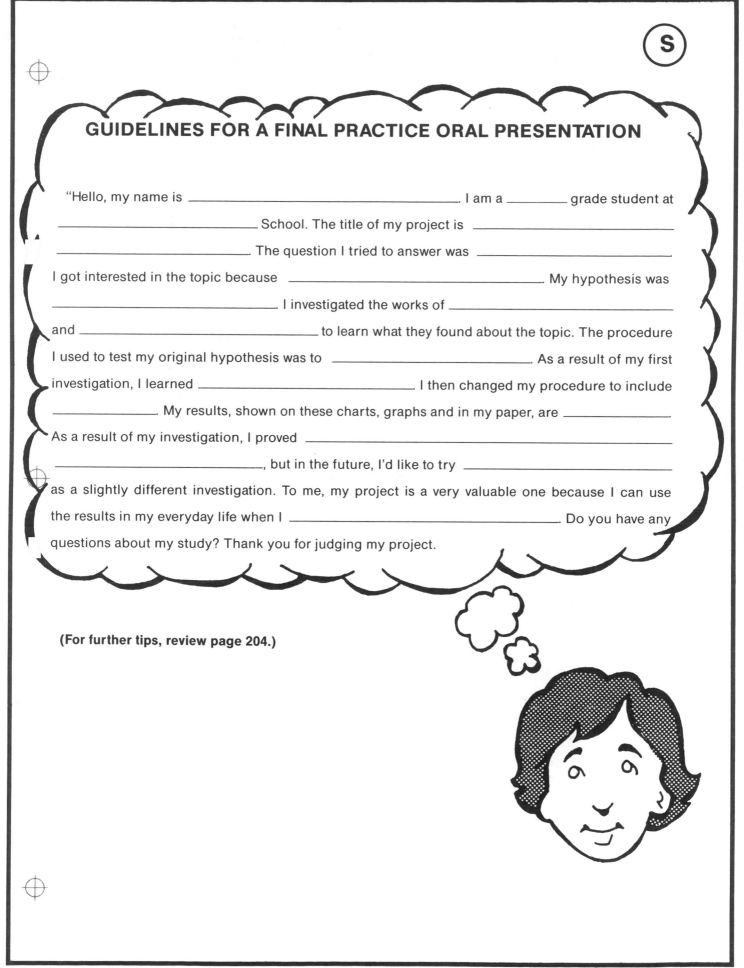

GUIDELINES FOR A FINAL PRACTICE ORAL PRESENTATION

"Hello, my name is _____. I am a _____ grade student at

_____ School. The title of my project is _____

_____ The question I tried to answer was _____

I got interested in the topic because _____. My hypothesis was

_____ I investigated the works of _____

and _____ to learn what they found about the topic. The procedure

I used to test my original hypothesis was to _____. As a result of my first

investigation, I learned _____. I then changed my procedure to include

_____. My results, shown on these charts, graphs and in my paper, are _____

As a result of my investigation, I proved _____

_____, but in the future, I'd like to try _____

as a slightly different investigation. To me, my project is a very valuable one because I can use

the results in my everyday life when I _____. Do you have any

questions about my study? Thank you for judging my project.

(For further tips, review page 204.)

GA1325

ACTIVITY NO.	KEY	ACTIVITY	REFER TO PAGE(S)	DATE COMPLETED
J22 (T)	IC	Have students give science fair presentations in class and to other classes (speech, English, math). Include students from other grade levels. Encourage all to attend the Science Fair and become involved in science fair projects.	229-230	

TIPS FOR THE TEACHER
Give Presentations to Members of Various Classes

In addition to having students make in-class presentations of their science fair projects, have them present to other classes, especially to students from different grade levels. Students often enjoy presenting their work to older or younger students. This is also an excellent recruitment tool for next year's Science Fair.

NOTES:

GA1325

ACTIVITY NO.	KEY	ACTIVITY	REFER TO PAGE(S)	DATE COMPLETED
J23 (T)	IC	Review judging sheets in class. Have students write abstracts to be sent to judges. Also fill in name, grade level, title and ID-Exhibit number on the abstract forms. Send abstracts to judges.	171, 219, 231, 238	

TIPS FOR THE TEACHER

Write, Then Send Abstracts to Judges

Review page 172, Criteria for Judging Science Fair Projects, with the students. Discuss each criterion item on which the student will be judged. Note item B "Abstract is interesting and helpful." Have students fill in the appropriate information. Then write an abstract for the judge using the suggested format and guidelines below.

SAMPLE ABSTRACT FORM

Project Title _____

Name _____

School _____

Grade _____

Teacher _____

Room _____

ID-Exhibit Number _____

ABSTRACT GUIDELINES

An abstract presents information about a study in a brief but complete form. Each student should prepare a 100 to 150-word abstract on a separate sheet of paper and insert this in the final written paper immediately following the table of contents. A copy of the abstract should be made and sent to the judges for review one week *before* the Science Fair takes place.

The abstract should be a specific, concise summary of the contents of the paper. Included in the abstract are (1) the purpose of the investigation, e.g., what was set out to be proved or disproved; (2) a description of the procedure of how the study was done, e.g., key points and general plan of the study; (3) the results, e.g., a brief statement of what was found and (4) the conclusions from the study, e.g., a statement or what was proved or disproved by the study. The abstract should be written in third-person singular and in past tense. See page 171 for a sample student written abstract entitled "The Effects of a Missing Ingredient in Chocolate Chip Cookies."

NOTES:

ACTIVITY NO.	KEY	ACTIVITY	REFER TO PAGE(S)	DATE COMPLETED
J24 (T)	IC	Have students complete an entry form that includes name, project title, ID-Exhibit number and signatures for student, parent and mentor (if applicable).	179, 232	

TIPS FOR THE TEACHER

Student Entry Form

Review page 179. Design a similar entry form that reflects your situation. Make copies of the Student Entry Form available for students to complete. Emphasize that appropriate signatures must be obtained before the project can be entered in the Science Fair.

STUDENT ENTRY FORM

Name: _____ Date: _____

Teacher: _____ Grade: _____

Project Title: _____

Project Description (be brief): _____

Project Hypothesis: _____

Project Area (Circle one.):

Animal (Zoology)	Plants (Botany)	Energy	Weather	Geology
Human Biology	Chemistry	Physics	Mathematics	Behavioral Science
General Science	Oceanography	Astronomy	Health Science	Environmental
Computers	Other_____			Science

Project Type (Check one.):

_____ **Experimental:** Forming a hypothesis (question) about something the student doesn't know the answer to, doing an actual scientific experiment, making observations, collecting data and reaching conclusions.
(OPTIONAL)

_____ **Scientific Investigations:** Science in a show and tell format. The student knows what is going to happen when he or she begins investigation. Includes models, mock-ups, kits, collections, hobbies, art projects, book reports, posters and library research studies.

Will your project require electricity? _____ Yes _____ No
Will your project require running water? _____ Yes _____ No
Will your project require a computer? _____ Yes _____ No

Your project should include the following items: (1) Exhibit that can stand by itself, (2) Research paper with bibliography, (3) Abstract (one-page summary, with bibliography), (4) Materials necessary for the exhibit, (5) Oral presentation (3 to 5 minutes) and (6) Diary/Logbook of daily work.

Return this form to your teacher by _____

Student's signature _____ Date_____

Teacher's signature _____ Date_____

Mentor's signature _____ Date_____

Parents only: My child, _____, has permission to participate in the Science Fair.

Signed_____ Date_____

GA1325

F I S F M = February
Implementation
Science
Fair
Month

THE SCIENCE FAIR TEACHER COMMUNICATES BY CONDUCTING A SUCCESSFUL SCIENCE FAIR

233

ACTIVITY NO.	KEY	ACTIVITY	REFER TO PAGE(S)	DATE COMPLETED
F1 Ⓣ	OC	Develop final schedule for judges. Assign two judges per six projects.	174, 234, 236	

TIPS FOR THE TEACHER

Final Schedule for Judges: Assign Projects to Judges

JUDGE # 1: _____ **JUDGE # 2:** _____
NUMBER OF PROJECTS ___6___

NUMBER	NAME OF STUDENT	ID-EXHIBIT NO.	GRADE LEVEL	TITLE
1				
2				
3				
4				
5				
6				

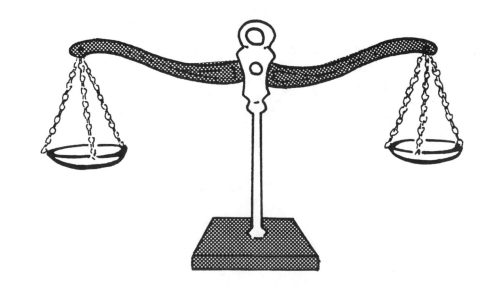

NOTES:

ACTIVITY NO.	KEY	ACTIVITY	REFER TO PAGE(S)	DATE COMPLETED
F2 (T)	OC	Distribute letter to judges. Include abstracts and information on day, time and location of Science Fair. Review criteria used in the judging process.	174, 235	

TIPS FOR THE TEACHER

Final Science Fair Day Letter to Judges

Date _____

Dear Science Fair Judge:

The long-awaited Science Fair is here. Thank you for your willingness to participate in this event as a judge. Final briefing of judges and assignment of teams will take place on _____ at _____ . The judges' meeting will begin promptly at _____ . Judges' packets are to be picked up between _____ and _____ . If an emergency occurs prior to the day, please try to get a substitute or contact me at _____ .

Enclosed are abstracts of the projects you are to judge. Judging sheets are found in your packet. Each judging team has no more than six projects. Also, enclosed in the packet is a copy of About the Judging Experience and the criteria by which the students are to be evaluated. Familiarize yourself with the interpretations of the judging criteria and the contents of the abstracts. We hope these will assist you in your preparation for judging.

A room has been secured for deliberations and discussion. Refreshments will be available in or near this room. A schedule for the day is enclosed. If this is your first time judging, please give yourself ample time to become accustomed to the Science Fair. Please feel free to contact one of the hosts who will direct you to where the projects are set up, the tally room and the meeting room for judges.

Thank you for your unique contribution to the success of the Science Fair. If you have questions, please call me at home _____ or at school _____ . Have a great day on _____ , _____ , 19 ____ .

See you then.

Sincerely,

NOTES:

GA1325

ACTIVITY NO.	KEY	ACTIVITY	REFER TO PAGE(S)	DATE COMPLETED
F3 (T)	OC	Prepare a folder for each judge. Include name tag, judging charts, maps and a list of exhibits to be judged.	234, 236	

TIPS FOR THE TEACHER
Sample Folder for Judges

A two-pocket folder for judges is ideal. The folder may contain the following: (1) a letter of introduction; (2) list of students' names, grade levels, project numbers and titles; (3) copy of Criteria for Judging Science Fair Projects; (4) name tag; (5) map; (6) abstracts; (7) judging sheets; (8) pencil and pad; (9) a Science Fair Mentorship Program Evaluation Form; (10) a Next Year's Judge Volunteer Form and (11) a Certificate of Appreciation. A sample letter of introduction follows.

Dear Judge Number _____:

Welcome to the annual Science Fair. You are paired with _____, another judge whose number is _____ . You will be seated next to each other for the briefing session which begins one-half hour before judging. You and your partner are asked to judge the following six projects:

Number	Name of Student	ID-Exhibit #	Grade Level	Title
1				
2				
3				
4				
5				
6				

Ribbons, based on the following categories, will be awarded. *All* students will receive at least one ribbon. In addition, *all* students will receive a Certificate of Participation for their efforts.

Number of Points	Rating	Color of Ribbon
90–100	Superior	Blue
80–89	Excellent	Red
70–79	Good	Green
60–69	Satisfactory	Yellow
50–59	Fair	Pink

Use the enclosed Criteria for Judging Science Fair Projects sheets for each student. Fill in the number of points awarded in each category. Discuss point values with your partner. Turn the sheets into tally representatives. Also included in this folder are the following: your name tag, a map of exhibits, abstracts of six projects, a pencil and pad for notes, a Science Fair Mentorship Program Evaluation Form which we ask you to complete and return before you leave, a Next Year's Judge Volunteer Form which we ask you to complete before you leave and a Certificate of Appreciation from us as a small token of appreciation for your time and effort in judging the Science Fair. Thank you very much for your support.

Sincerely,

GA1325

ACTIVITY NO.	KEY	ACTIVITY	REFER TO PAGE(S)	DATE COMPLETED
F4 (T)	OC	Arrange for hospitality. Identify students and teachers who are willing to be hosts. Ask the teacher of home economics classes to possibly have students prepare food for the Science Fair.	32, 215, 237	

TIPS FOR THE TEACHER

Identify Hosts

Recruit teachers and mature students to act as hosts. Record their names on a chart like this:

NAME	SUBJECT OR GRADE LEVEL	RESPONSIBILITY
		Greet Judges
		Greet Parents
		Greet Community Members
		Greet Members of the Media
		Greet Mentors
		Greet Exhibitors
		Greet Students from Other Grade Levels
		Monitor Halls
		Monitor Refreshment Area

NOTES:

GA1325

ACTIVITY NO.	KEY	ACTIVITY	REFER TO PAGE(S)	DATE COMPLETED
F5 ⓣ	OC	Draw a map that shows the location of various displays. Assign ID-Exhibit numbers. Identify locations of electrical outlets, water sources, computer facilities, entrances and exits.	216, 238, 242	

TIPS FOR THE TEACHER

Assign Exhibit Numbers

Using a computer, make up a set of science fair project cards that look like the ones below. Have students affix ID-Exhibit numbers to their projects.

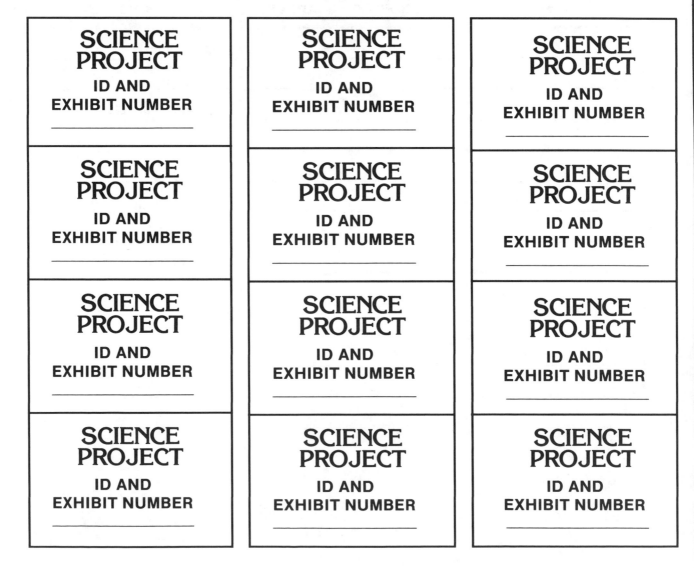

SCIENCE PROJECT
ID AND
EXHIBIT NUMBER
_____

SCIENCE PROJECT
ID AND
EXHIBIT NUMBER
_____

SCIENCE PROJECT
ID AND
EXHIBIT NUMBER
_____

SCIENCE PROJECT
ID AND
EXHIBIT NUMBER
_____

SCIENCE PROJECT
ID AND
EXHIBIT NUMBER
_____

SCIENCE PROJECT
ID AND
EXHIBIT NUMBER
_____

SCIENCE PROJECT
ID AND
EXHIBIT NUMBER
_____

SCIENCE PROJECT
ID AND
EXHIBIT NUMBER
_____

SCIENCE PROJECT
ID AND
EXHIBIT NUMBER
_____

SCIENCE PROJECT
ID AND
EXHIBIT NUMBER
_____

SCIENCE PROJECT
ID AND
EXHIBIT NUMBER
_____

SCIENCE PROJECT
ID AND
EXHIBIT NUMBER
_____

GA1325

SCIENCE PROJECT
INFORMATION FORM

Attach photograph of what your
display looks like here.

PROJECT TITLE _____

STUDENT _____

GRADE _____ **TEACHER** _____

SCHOOL _____

ROOM # _____ **ID-EXHIBIT #** _____

SCIENCE FAIR PROJECT DISPLAY
MAINTENANCE AGREEMENT

Project Title: _____

_____

ID-Exhibit #: _____

Student: _____

Grade: _____ Teacher: _____

School: _____ Room: _____

Because my project has special features, it is necessary for my display to be checked regularly and maintained if needed. Thus, my project needs to be checked every _____ days for the following things:

_____

_____

_____

The maintenance of my project will be done by _____

_____   _____
Student's signature   Date

_____   _____
Parent's signature   Date

_____   _____
Teacher's signature   Date

_____   _____
Mentor's signature   Date

GA1325

ACTIVITY NO.	KEY	ACTIVITY	REFER TO PAGE(S)	DATE COMPLETED
F6 ⓣ	OC	Set up tables and microphone the day before the Science Fair.	31, 112, 232, 241	

TIPS FOR THE TEACHER

Tables and Microphone Setup

There are many last-minute preparations to make several days prior to the Science Fair. Long-range planning is the key used to avoid last-minute delays. Review Building Request that was completed in September (p. 31) to verify that the rooms are available for the day of the Science Fair. Be sure that there is a large enough room to accommodate all student displays. Determine the number of tables that you will need. Submit a table request if needed. Arrange tables so accessibility to exits insures smooth traffic flow. Allow each student an equal amount of space. Review Guidelines for a Science Fair Display (p. 112) sent to parents as part of the parents' packet. Adhere to guidelines. Arrange displays so all students who need access to water, electrical outlets and computer facilities are accommodated. Remind students to bring *all* materials for their displays in a convenient carry-all box. Review Student Entry Forms (p. 232) for Science Fair. Set up microphone the day before. Use microphone to make announcements on set-up day and the day of the Science Fair. Primary teachers may choose to have their science fairs in their own classrooms for easy accessibilty to materials and supplies.

NOTES:

GA1325

ACTIVITY NO.	KEY	ACTIVITY	REFER TO PAGE(S)	DATE COMPLETED
F7 (T)	OC	Recruit a small committee of volunteers to tabulate and average the judges' final scores for each entrant.	219, 242	

TIPS FOR THE TEACHER

Tabulation Committee

Ask the mathematics teacher for recommendations of people to serve on the Tabulation Committee. Write their names on a chart like this:

NAME	SUBJECT OR GRADE LEVEL	EXPERTISE

RESPONSIBILITIES

Organize the Following Materials:
1. Ribbons and awards
2. Extra signed but blank certificates
3. Sharpened pencils
4. Pens (green, red, blue, yellow, pink and black ink)
5. Containers for separating judging sheets
6. Staplers
7. Paper clips
8. Ink pads and rubber stamps for ratings: Superior, Excellent, Good, Satisfactory and Fair.

Do the Following Things:
1. Calculate final ratings from judges' sheets.
2. Use red, green, blue, yellow and pink to mark sheets for easy identification of rating.
3. Stamp rating on student's certificate and/or determine appropriate ribbon:

Blue	Superior	90-100
Red	Excellent	80-89
Green	Good	70-79
Yellow	Satisfactory	60-69
Pink	Fair	50-59

4. Stamp all students' Certificates of Participation.
5. Organize certificates in the order in which they will be presented either at the Science Fair or at a large all-school assembly.

GA1325

ACTIVITY NO.	KEY	ACTIVITY	REFER TO PAGE(S)	DATE COMPLETED
F8 ⓣ	IC	Conduct classroom Science Fair.	232, 243	

TIPS FOR THE TEACHER

Classroom Science Fair

Having a science fair day in the classroom presents an excellent opportunity for a trial run before the final Science Fair. Have students complete all appropriate forms such as the Student Entry Form (p. 232), ID-Exhibit number form (p. 238), Science Fair Project Display Maintenance Agreement (p. 240) and the Student Vertebrate Animal Certificate (p. 69) if needed. The classroom Science Fair affords students an opportunity to polish their presentations to judges and avoid any last-minute glitches in their science fair setups. If possible, videotape all student presentations for later review.

NOTES:

GA1325

ACTIVITY NO.	KEY	ACTIVITY	REFER TO PAGE(S)	DATE COMPLETED
F9 (T)	IC	Have students revise presentations based on results of classroom Science Fair.	229-230, 244	

TIPS FOR THE TEACHER

Revise Science Fair Presentations

After students have presented their science fair projects in the classroom, have them revise their presentations based on feedback given by the teacher, students and classroom judges. If presentations have been videotaped, have students review the videotapes to further polish their presentations.

NOTES:

GA1325

ACTIVITY NO.	KEY	ACTIVITY	REFER TO PAGE(S)	DATE COMPLETED
F10 Ⓣ	IC	Present final schedule for Science Fair to students. This includes times for setup, judging, viewing and awards presentation.	219, 245	

TIPS FOR THE TEACHER

Final Schedule for Science Fair Day

Whether your Science Fair is held during the week or on Saturday, a final schedule for actual setup, judging, reviewing of projects by others and the awards presentation should be done well in advance. Sample schedules may look like this:

Sample Weekday Schedule	
9:00-11:00	Project Setup
12:00-12:30	Judges' luncheon and briefing
12:45-3:00	Judging of projects
3:15-4:30	Project visitation
4:45-5:30	Awards ceremony

Sample Saturday Schedule	
7:30-9:00	Project Setup
9:00-9:30	Judges' breakfast and briefing
9:30-11:30	Judging of projects
11:30-12:15	Project visitation
12:15-1:00	Awards ceremony

These time allotments may vary based on the number of projects and availability of judges. Assign a science fair ID-Exhibit number to each project. Have students write these numbers on their abstracts before sending them to judges for review.

NOTES:

GA1325

ACTIVITY NO.	KEY	ACTIVITY	REFER TO PAGE(S)	DATE COMPLETED
F11 ⊤	IC	Distribute Final Checklist for the Student.	227, 246, 249	

TIPS FOR THE TEACHER
Final Checklist for the Student

DATE COMPLETED	TASK TO BE COMPLETED
	Student Entry Form
	Science Project ID-Exhibit Number on Abstract
	Science Fair Project Maintenance Display Agreement Form
	Student Vertebrate Animal Certificate
	Science Fair Project Based on Scientific Method
	Abstract Is Written and Sent to Judges
	Science Fair Project Display Set Up
	Science Fair Diary, Log or Journal Is Visible
	Research Report Typed and Visible
	Electrical Outlets/Water/Computers Checked
	Practice Oral Presentation
	Reviewed Criteria for Judging
	Dressed Appropriately
	Oral Presentation Done at the Classroom Science Fair
	Parents' and Family Members' Invitations Written and Sent
	Oral Presentation Done at Science Fair
	Science Fair Evaluation Form Completed
	Project Revised for Presentation at Other Science Fairs
	Thank-You Notes Written and Sent
	Article Written and Shared

NOTES:

ACTIVITY NO.	KEY	ACTIVITY	REFER TO PAGE(S)	DATE COMPLETED
F12 (T)	IC	Post a list of students, their ID-Exhibit numbers and a map in both the classroom and exhibit rooms. Review the location of each project with the student.	216, 247	

TIPS FOR THE TEACHER

Location of Projects

A sample list may look like the one below. Review the map that shows where each project is located with the students so students are familiar with the locations of their particular science fair projects.

NUMBER	SCIENCE PROJECT ID-EXHIBIT #	ROW II	GRADE LEVEL	TITLE
1				
2				
3				
4				

NOTES:

GA1325

ACTIVITY NO.	KEY	ACTIVITY	REFER TO PAGE(S)	DATE COMPLETED
F13 ⓣ	IC	Have students set up projects during class time on the day prior to the Science Fair.	216, 248	

TIPS FOR THE TEACHER

Project Setups

Check to see if rooms are available for setups the day before the Science Fair. Review ID-Exhibit numbers with students. Set up overhead projector with transparency that features a map that shows the locations of various projects. Check electrical, water and computer facilities. Use microphone to alert students of project setups and the location of each.

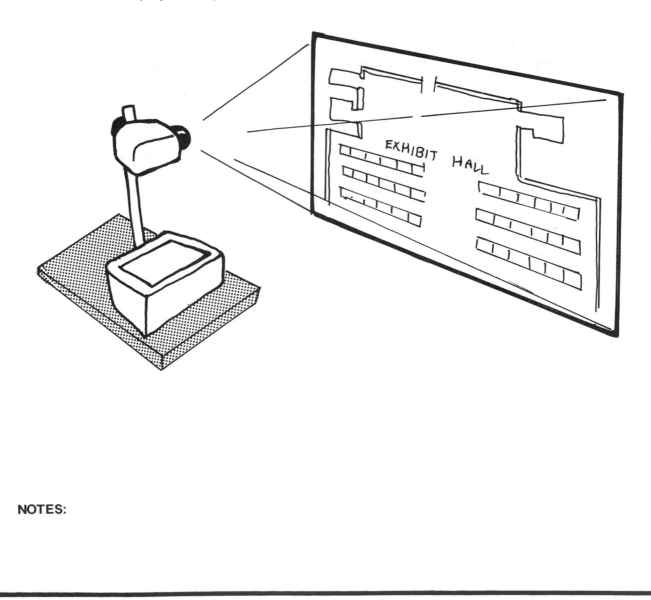

EXHIBIT HALL

NOTES:

GA1325

ACTIVITY NO.	KEY	ACTIVITY	REFER TO PAGE(S)	DATE COMPLETED
F14 (T)	IC	Remind students to dress appropriately for the Science Fair.	246, 249	

TIPS FOR THE TEACHER

Dress Appropriately

Discuss with students appropriate dress for the Science Fair. Emphasize that people are often affected by the way one looks, talks and acts. Thus, appropriate dress and manners are important. Students should be reminded that they are to wear safety glasses if an actual demonstration is done as part of the oral presentation of their science fair projects to the judges. Review other safety procedures related to each science fair project.

NOTES:

ACTIVITY NO.	KEY	ACTIVITY	REFER TO PAGE(S)	DATE COMPLETED
F15 (T)	IC	Hold Science Fair. Have re-freshments available for all who attend. Relax.	32, 215, 250	

TIPS FOR THE TEACHER
Hold Science Fair

Do a last-minute check to see that students, hosts, judges and tabulators are ready and at appropriate locations. Relax. If the Science Fair is well planned, it will run smoothly. Review procedures and criteria for judging at meeting for judges before actual judging begins. Encourage judges to judge a project that they are *not* assigned to judge for practice. Smile, relax and put your best foot forward as the long-awaited day has arrived.

NOTES:

GA1325

ACTIVITY NO.	KEY	ACTIVITY	REFER TO PAGE(S)	DATE COMPLETED
F16 Ⓣ	IC	Have Director of Media Services make a videotape of the Science Fair to be used as a recruitment tool for next year's Science Fair Mentorship Program.	34, 37, 251	

TIPS FOR THE TEACHER
Videotape Science Fair

Ask the Director of Media Services to make a videotape of all aspects of the Science Fair, such as student presentations to judges and interviews with key personnel. The videotape may be used to publicize the Science Fair and to recruit future science fair students into the Science Fair Mentorship Program.

Name of Director of Media Services _____

Address _____

Telephone _____

Room Number _____

Hours _____

NOTES:

GA1325

ACTIVITY NO.	KEY	ACTIVITY	REFER TO PAGE(S)	DATE COMPLETED
F17 (T)	IC	Have Director of Media Services take photographs of exhibits for permanent file of science fair project ideas.	251, 252, 271	

TIPS FOR THE TEACHER
Photographs of Exhibits

In addition to videotaping the Science Fair, ask the Director of Media Services to take photographs of all projects exhibited at the Science Fair. These photographs may be used in many ways: (1) a permanent file of science fair project ideas; (2) publicity (newspapers, brochures) with parental permission; (3) attach to admission applications for advanced schooling; (4) permanent record of student activity; (5) gifts for students, parents and other family members; (6) placement in school yearbook or annual and (7) support for further grant proposal activity. If the school has a Student Photography Club, encourage *students* to also take photographs of their science fair projects for school use.

Name of Director of Media Services _____

Address _____

Telephone _____

Room Number _____

Hours _____

NOTES:

GA1325

ACTIVITY NO.	KEY	ACTIVITY	REFER TO PAGE(S)	DATE COMPLETED
F18 (T)	IC	Encourage student hosts to greet all people who attend the Science Fair including students from other grade levels who come to view the science fair projects.	237, 253	

TIPS FOR THE TEACHER
Student Hosts

Students, as hosts, are capable of performing many duties at the Science Fair. Encourage them to dress their best and smile a lot as they greet judges, parents, community members, mentors, students and members of the media. Choose mature, capable students to perform these duties. If possible, have another teacher organize and supervise the group of student hosts for the Science Fair.

NOTES:

GA1325

ACTIVITY NO.	KEY	ACTIVITY	REFER TO PAGE(S)	DATE COMPLETED
F19 (T)	IC	Greet the judges one-half hour before the Science Fair. Present folders to judges. Review numbers of projects and judging criteria. Have judges give completed judging sheets to Tabulation Committee for averaging and ranking.	175, 219, 254	

TIPS FOR THE TEACHER

Judges' Decisions Are Final

In the briefing meeting with judges, review pairings of judges and the number of projects to be judged. Have judges reread the abstracts sent to them previously before judging the students' projects. Review judging criteria and judging sheets. Instruct judges to give final results to Tabulation Committee for averaging and ranking. Request that judges complete the Science Fair Mentorship Program Evaluation Form and the Next Year's Judge Volunteer Form after the judging experience is over.

Extension: Judges may want to do a trial run by judging a project *not* assigned to them before judging their assigned projects.

NOTES:

GA1325

ACTIVITY NO.	KEY	ACTIVITY	REFER TO PAGE(S)	DATE COMPLETED
F20 Ⓣ	IC	Have only students with projects and respective judges in the science fair exhibit room when judging is taking place.	173, 255	

TIPS FOR THE TEACHER

Please: Only Students and Judges

To avoid interruptions and confusion, it is recommended that only students, with their projects, and their respective judges be in the exhibit room while projects are being judged. Others may visit the hospitality room until judging has been completed. Later, the public may view the projects, converse with the students and take appropriate photographs of the science fair activity.

NOTES:

GA1325

ACTIVITY NO.	KEY	ACTIVITY	REFER TO PAGE(S)	DATE COMPLETED
F21 **(T)**	IC	Using a computer, have the Tabulation Committee tally the judges' scores and rank order student scores.	172, 256	

TIPS FOR THE TEACHER

Tabulate Scores

Encourage tabulators to use a computer to enter student scores given by judges. Tabulators should double check the final scores and ratings from the judges. The judging sheets can be coded by using blue, red, green, yellow and pink markers. Tabulators can stamp the ratings on student certificates and/or determine appropriate ribbon for each. They can also prepare a Certificate of Participation or ribbon for each student and organize these in the order in which they will be presented either at the Science Fair or at an all-school assembly. Tabulators, working in pairs, should double check each score given to them by the judges to avoid inaccurate ratings.

NOTES:

GA1325

ACTIVITY NO.	KEY	ACTIVITY	REFER TO PAGE(S)	DATE COMPLETED
F22 Ⓣ	IC	Give out awards and certificates based on the final ratings given by judges.	218, 257	

TIPS FOR THE TEACHER
Awards Ceremony

Individual awards such as ribbons may be awarded to students at the Science Fair. Certificates of Participation should be given to *all* students who have participated in the Science Fair. In some cases, individual award certificates may be presented to students at an all-school assemby to give students further recognition for their science fair activity. Competition should be de-emphasized, although projects may be rated Superior, Excellent, Good, Satisfactory and Fair based on the previously determined criteria such as 100 points. This procedure guarantees feedback to students on the quality of their projects, feedback that can be used to further refine the students' projects for entrance into other science fairs.

NOTES:

GA1325

ACTIVITY NO.	KEY	ACTIVITY	REFER TO PAGE(S)	DATE COMPLETED
F23 Ⓣ	IC	Have judges complete Next Year's Judge Volunteer Form. Insert data into computer data base as a record of judges for next year's science fair.	175, 258	

TIPS FOR THE TEACHER

Complete Next Year's Judge Volunteer Form

After judges turn in the completed judging sheets to the tabulators, have them complete a copy of Next Year's Judge Volunteer Form on page 175. This information, when entered into a computer, becomes a data base that contains names of judges for next year's Science Fair. Be sure judges complete the form before they leave the Science Fair. In some cases, duplicate carbon-based forms are used: one copy has your name, address and phone number, given to the judge; the other has pertinent information about the judge and is retained by the Director of the Science Fair for future use.

NOTES:

ACTIVITY NO.	KEY	ACTIVITY	REFER TO PAGE(S)	DATE COMPLETED
F24 (T)	IC	Have available ample copies of final evaluation surveys for judges, media, students, principal, teacher volunteers, parents and mentors to complete. Include provisions for return of surveys. Thank all people who attended the Science Fair.	259, 261	

TIPS FOR THE TEACHER

Final Evaluation Surveys

Have ample copies of page 261, Student Science Fair Project Evaluation Survey, available at strategic locations for all participants to complete. Have baskets or boxes entitled "Return Surveys Here" with an accompanying thank-you sign near the exits. Encourage people to complete the evaluation surveys immediately after the Science Fair. If taken home, place a return due date on the form so results can be tabulated easily in March. Appropriate decisions about next year's Science Fair can then be made based on feedback gathered at this year's Science Fair.

NOTES:

SCIENCE FAIR MENTORSHIP PROGRAM EVALUATION FORM

Circle role and/or occupation of person completing this form.
1. Parent   3. Mentor   5. Student Visitor   7. Community Member
2. Judge   4. Teacher   6. Student Presenter   8. Member of Media

For each of the paired items listed below, place an X on the line that best represents your feelings about the Science Fair Mentorship Program.

Example: The Science Fair Mentorship Program was

Hot $\underline{\text{X}}$ _____ _____ _____ _____ _____ _____ Cold
      (1)   (2)   (3)   (4)   (5)   (6)   (7)

#	Left	(1)	(2)	(3)	(4)	(5)	(6)	(7)	Right
1.	**Interesting**	(1)	(2)	(3)	(4)	(5)	(6)	(7)	**Boring**
2.	**Important**	(1)	(2)	(3)	(4)	(5)	(6)	(7)	**Useless**
3.	**Informative**	(1)	(2)	(3)	(4)	(5)	(6)	(7)	**Worthless**
4.	**Complete**	(1)	(2)	(3)	(4)	(5)	(6)	(7)	**Incomplete**
5.	**Mixed Up**	(7)	(6)	(5)	(4)	(3)	(2)	(1)	**Smooth**
6.	**A Downer**	(7)	(6)	(5)	(4)	(3)	(2)	(1)	**An Upper**
7.	**Selfish**	(7)	(6)	(5)	(4)	(3)	(2)	(1)	**Unselfish**
8.	**Enough Time**	(1)	(2)	(3)	(4)	(5)	(6)	(7)	**Not Enough Time**
9.	**Light**	(1)	(2)	(3)	(4)	(5)	(6)	(7)	**Dark**
10.	**Negative**	(7)	(6)	(5)	(4)	(3)	(2)	(1)	**Positive**
11.	**High**	(1)	(2)	(3)	(4)	(5)	(6)	(7)	**Low**
12.	**Bad**	(7)	(6)	(5)	(4)	(3)	(2)	(1)	**Good**
13.	**Liked**	(1)	(2)	(3)	(4)	(5)	(6)	(7)	**Disliked**
14.	**Black**	(7)	(6)	(5)	(4)	(3)	(2)	(1)	**White**
15.	**Fast**	(1)	(2)	(3)	(4)	(5)	(6)	(7)	**Slow**

On the other side of this page, list responses to the following: (1) Things I like(d) best about the Science Fair Mentorship Program, (2) Things I like(d) least about the Science Fair Mentorship Program and (3) Suggestions for improvement of the Science Fair Mentorship Program. **Note:** Please return this form as soon as possible to the Director of the Science Fair Mentorship Program or place in the Return Box on the day of the Science Fair. Thank you.

STUDENT SCIENCE FAIR PROJECT EVALUATION SURVEY

(S)

From doing my project, I learned _____

_____

The most challenging part of my project was _____

_____

_____

The things I enjoyed the most about my project were _____

_____

_____

I probably could have made my project better by _____

_____

The judges' comments about my project were _____

_____

_____

Some other comments I heard about my project were _____

_____

_____

The people, like my mentor and parents, who helped me with my project were _____

_____

_____

They helped me to _____

Things I wish I could do now that my project is over are _____

_____

I think that someday I'd like or not like (choose one) to be a scientist because _____

_____

GA1325

ACTIVITY NO.	KEY	ACTIVITY	REFER TO PAGE(S)	DATE COMPLETED
F25 (T)	OC	Post thank-you announcement on school marque immediately following Science Fair.	262	

TIPS FOR THE TEACHER

Thank You

If your school has a marque, show your appreciation to all those who participated by placing an announcement like this on the marque. Thank-you notices should also be placed in newspapers, on electronic bulletin boards and in communications from the school to parents and other members of the public.

NOTES:

M E T F = March
Evaluation
Teacher
Focus

THE SCIENCE FAIR TEACHER COMMUNICATES METHODS OF PROGRAM EVALUATION

263

GA1325

ACTIVITY NO.	KEY	ACTIVITY	REFER TO PAGE(S)	DATE COMPLETED
M1 (T)	OC	At an all-school assembly, give an award certificate to *all* students who participated in the Science Fair.	217-218, 264-265	

TIPS FOR THE TEACHER
Certificates of Participation

During the science fair experience, each student will have received a Certificate of Participation and/or a ribbon based on previously determined criteria. After the Science Fair, each student should receive an individual Certificate of Award for his/her efforts. These may be stamped with an appropriate color that corresponds to the color of the ribbon and given at an all-school assembly. Of utmost importance is that each student receives a Certificate of Award for participation in the science fair experience. Encourage students to place these certificates in a portfolio for later use such as for attachments to various applications for jobs or advanced schooling. See page 218 for samples of both certificates. Here are some others that you may want to consider.

CONGRATULATIONS!

You did super work on your science fair project!

Science Investigator: _____

_____

Comments: _____

_____

_____

_____ _____
Principal   Teacher

_____
Date

KEEP UP THE SUPER WORK!

SENIOR SCIENTIST

_____
Name

has been declared a
Senior Scientist
for outstanding scientific efforts in
the Science Fair Mentorship Program.

_____
Date

_____
Teacher's Signature

_____
Principal's Signature

NOTES:

GA1325

Certificate of Award
CONGRATULATIONS!

SCIENCE FAIRS WITH STYLE

This is to certify that _____ has been awarded this certificate for excellent work on his/her science fair project. Given this _____ day of 19 _____ .

Comments: _____
_____
_____

_____   _____
Principal   Teacher

_____
Date

Keep up the excellent work!

GA1325

ACTIVITY NO.	KEY	ACTIVITY	REFER TO PAGE(S)	DATE COMPLETED
M2 (T)	OC	Write thank-you notes to judges, teacher volunteers, parents, mentors, members of the media and all who participated in the science fair experience.	246, 266, 274	

TIPS FOR THE TEACHER

Thank-You Notes and Letters

Thank you for your contribution to the Science Fair Mentorship Program!

Dear _____ :

This school year we were involved in a unique Science Fair Mentorship Program for students. Because of your efforts we were able to reach our goal of having students conduct scientific research and present the results of their research at our annual Science Fair on _____ .

On behalf of all who were involved in the program, we wish to thank you for your assistance. Your participation has made this experience a truly rewarding one for all who chose to participate. The relationship between our students, school and community is a viable one and has been strengthened further because of your efforts.

Thank you for your support.

Sincerely,

GA1325

ACTIVITY NO.	KEY	ACTIVITY	REFER TO PAGE(S)	DATE COMPLETED
M3 ⓣ	OC	Collect and tally results of final evaluation surveys from principal, students, judges, teachers, volunteers and media representatives.	261, 267	

TIPS FOR THE TEACHER
Tally Results

Results from the evelation surveys can be tallied with the use of the computer according to subpopulation. Lower numerical values indicate a more favorable response on the surveys. See page 260 for sample survey. Answers to open-ended responses can be grouped into various subcategories for analysis. Some of these subcategories may include evaluations of facilities, judging procedures and publicity.

NOTES:

GA1325

ACTIVITY NO.	KEY	ACTIVITY	REFER TO PAGE(S)	DATE COMPLETED
M4 (T)	OC	Publicize results of science fair activity in school and local newspapers.	205, 264-265, 268	

TIPS FOR THE TEACHER

Publicize Results: Include Names of Volunteers

Encourage members of the media to publicize the efforts made by all those who contributed to the Science Fair. *All* who participated in the Science Fair in any way should receive recognition for their efforts. These include students, parents, teachers, mentors, judges, members of the media and the general public. Student accomplishments should also be publicized in an effort to promote further student recognition for their efforts.

NOTES:

GA1325

ACTIVITY NO.	KEY	ACTIVITY	REFER TO PAGE(S)	DATE COMPLETED
M5 (T)	OC	Develop a computerized master data base of science fair topics for next year's science fair program.	89-90, 269	

TIPS FOR THE TEACHER
Develop Data Base of Science Fair Topics

Pages 89 and 90 feature forty-two topics that students could examine as possible science fair projects. At the conclusion of the Science Fair, enter the titles of student projects into a computerized data base of projects. Add and delete projects to and from the data base as new projects are identified or old ones are revised or deleted. Tap data base for next year's science fair topics.

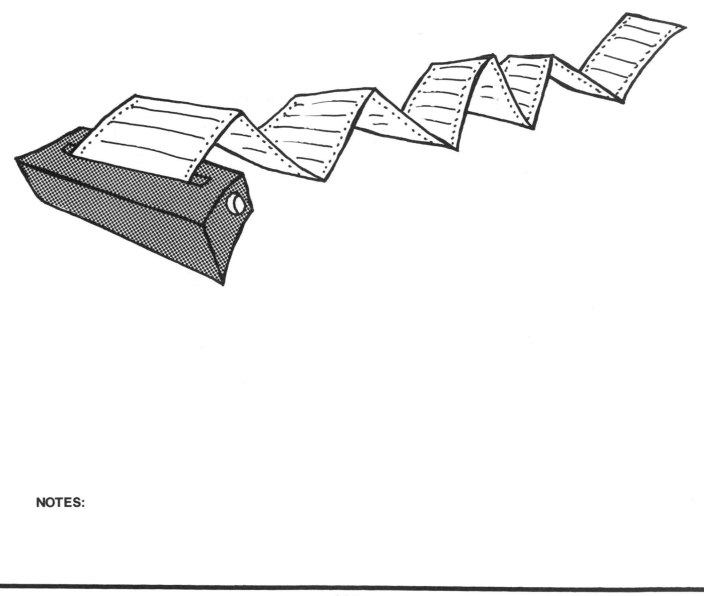

NOTES:

GA1325

ACTIVITY NO.	KEY	ACTIVITY	REFER TO PAGE(S)	DATE COMPLETED
M6 (T)	OC	Develop a photo album of pictures of science fair projects. Taken by the Director of Media Services, these photographs can be used as a source of ideas for next year's science fair.	252, 270	

TIPS FOR THE TEACHER

Photographs Yield More Ideas

At the conclusion of the Science Fair, contact the Director of Media Services. Ask for photographs taken of science fair projects. Place photos in a photo album. Have students review album to obtain ideas for next year's science fair activity.

NOTES:

GA1325

ACTIVITY NO.	KEY	ACTIVITY	REFER TO PAGE(S)	DATE COMPLETED
M7 (T)	OC	Present a summary of the results from the final evaluation surveys to all who participated in the Science Fair Mentorship Program.	261, 267, 271	

TIPS FOR THE TEACHER

Results

Overall results may be tallied and given to the principal as evidence to support next year's program. Results for each subpopulation, e.g., parents, can be sent directly to members of these groups. Include responses to both Lickert and open-ended sections of the evaluation survey. By making the results of the Science Fair known, further support for the program will be generated.

NOTES:

GA1325

ACTIVITY NO.	KEY	ACTIVITY	REFER TO PAGE(S)	DATE COMPLETED
M8 (T)	IC	Meet with parents and students to revise projects based on judges' comments.	272, 275	

TIPS FOR THE TEACHER

Revise Projects

Students may wish to enter their science fair projects in one or more local, state and national science fair programs. With individual parents and students, review the judge's final ratings and written comments. Study the comments made on each of the twenty items on the sheet Criteria for Judging Science Fair Projects. Have the students revise their projects based on feedback given by the judges and other knowledgeable people who reviewed their projects. Encourage the students to enter their revised projects in other science fair programs such as those found on page 273.

NOTES:

GA1325

ACTIVITY NO.	KEY	ACTIVITY	REFER TO PAGE(S)	DATE COMPLETED
M9 (T)	IC	Encourage students to enter their revised projects in district, state and national science fair events.	272-273	

TIPS FOR THE TEACHER

Enter Other Science Fair Programs

In addition to local and state science fair programs, students may consider entering their science fair projects in these national programs. Write for further information from these sources.

International Science and Engineering Fair (ISEF) Science Service 1719 N. Street, N.W. Washington, D.C. 20036	Junior Science and Humanities Symposium Academy of Applied Science 98 Washington Street Concord, NH 03301
Space Science Student Involvement Program National Science Teachers Association Division of Space, Science and Technology 5110 Roanoke Place, Suite 101 College Park, MD 20740	Westinghouse Science Talent Search 1719 N. Street, N.W. Washington, D.C. 20036
Science Olympiad 5955 Little Pine Land Rochester, MI 48064	JETS Inc. c/o United Engineering Center 345 E. 47th Street New York, NY 10017
Younger Scholars Awards Division of General Programs National Endowment for the Humanities 1100 Pennsylvania Avenue, N.W. Washington, D.C. 20506	American Chemical Society Education Division 1155 16th Street, N.W. Washington, D.C. 20036

NOTES:

GA1325

ACTIVITY NO.	KEY	ACTIVITY	REFER TO PAGE(S)	DATE COMPLETED
M10 (T)	IC	Have students write thank-you notes to judges, media representatives, parents, mentors and teacher volunteers who assisted them in the Science Fair Mentorship Program.	246, 266, 274	

TIPS FOR THE TEACHER

Student Thank-You Notes and Letters

Writing thank-you notes and letters need not be a long and tedious task. Computers are helpful in this exercise. Meet with teachers who work with computers and/or teach art and communications. Ask for their ideas on how to get started. As part of a writing exercise, have students design and write thank-you letters to all people who have helped them with their science fair activities. (Review card N Acknowledgements on page 87 or consult the Acknowledgements section of student papers for names of people who helped with the projects.) Encourage students to be creative in their designs and be short and to the point in their writing. Here are a few samples.

Something to SHOUT about! THANK YOU!

HERE'S SMILING AT YOU!

MANY THANKS!

NOTES:

GA1325

A P R T F = April
Reflections
Teacher
Focus

THE SCIENCE FAIR TEACHER COMMUNICATES WITH THE SELF BY REFLECTIONS

Going in Ness, Going out Ness, Ever There Ness

275

GA1325

ACTIVITY NO.	KEY	ACTIVITY	REFER TO PAGE(S)	DATE COMPLETED
AP1 (T)	OC	Plan to write and submit an article for publication in a national science education publication that describes your science fair program so others may benefit from what you have done.	276-282	

TIPS FOR THE TEACHER

Plan to Write and Submit an Article for Publication

There are many avenues available to teachers that provide an opportunity to share the results of their science fair programs with others so others may benefit from successful science fair experiences. Writing an article for publication is one such way to share ideas with others. *Writer's Market* published by F and W Publications, 1507 Dana Avenue, Cincinnati, Ohio 45207 lists over 4000 places where free-lance writers can sell their works. Numerous science education journals actively solicit articles from teachers. Four such journals are *Science and Children*, *Science Scope*, *The Science Teacher* and *Science Activities*. The first three journals are published by the National Science Teachers Association, 1742 Connecticut Avenue, N.W., Washington, D.C. 20009-1171, the latter one by Heldref Publications, 4000 Ablemarle Street, N.W., Washington, D.C., 20016. Read and follow the writing guidelines (see pages 277-280). A sample published article written about a successful program is found on pages 280 and 281. Another published article on science fair tips for parents appears on pages 109-111.

NOTES:

GA1325

Writing for *Science and Children* ⓣ

AUDIENCE. *Science and Children*, a journal devoted to preschool through middle school science teaching, publishes articles of many kinds: descriptions of innovative projects and programs, hands-on activities, informational and think pieces, reports of research in science education, and helpful hints. *S&C's* audience and authors are people like you teachers and teacher educators, principals, librarians, resource persons, supervisors, and parents. If you have something to share with others, *S&C's* staff may be able to help you put your ideas into print.

IDEAS & TOPICS. We like variety. Interesting, innovative ideas help us help teachers bring good science into the classroom. Our files fill quickly with scientific method approaches, school projects, cabbage juice chemistry, and dramatic play simulations. And though many of these pieces are worthy of print, good appropriate manuscripts on physics and geology are always hard to find. Ideas that employ interdisciplinary teaching are also desirable, as well as an occasional commentary on recent issues in science education. But the manuscripts most likely to be seriously considered are those that are about what you know best, that require only simple inexpensive materials, and that reflect something new or contain a new twist to an old idea.

WRITING ELEMENTS. Select a subject that you know well and limit your message. (We favor manuscripts that do their work in 1,500 words or fewer.) Keep in mind that you're dealing with a busy, diverse audience, so make your writing to the point, logical, concise, simple, and grammatically correct. Cite sources to which you are indebted in the text and provide complete bibliographical information about them at the end of your article. We would also appreciate a list of readily available resources that would be helpful for teachers and for their students. The resources might include filmstrips and kits as well as books and articles. If you are not familiar with *S&C*, begin by looking through a few issues to acquaint yourself with our approach.

DETAILS, DETAILS! Please send a cover letter that includes your name, home and work addresses and telephone numbers. Indicate one mailing address. Keep resumes, or other personal, informational sheets separate from the manuscript. Make sure to indicate all authors. Please double-space your article and use one side of the page only. Each manuscript should have a title, and pages should be numbered. Give all measurements in metric. Send the original and two copies. The two copies will be sent out for blind review, so please do not include any data that will identify you (name, address, etc.) on those two copies. Include two copies of all illustrations for the reviewers. If your manuscript is word processed, try to use a letter-quality printer, and send a disk if you can for IBM or compatible computers. **Neither manuscripts nor disks will be returned, so you should keep copies for yourself.**

ILLUSTRATIONS. Put any tables and charts on separate pieces of paper, but make sure to indicate where they should be inserted in the text. Drawings or diagrams can be rough as long as they're clear and well labeled. If possible, include black-and-white photographs printed on glossy paper, or negatives and contact sheets. Please number photos and provide photo credits and full photo captions on a separate sheet of paper. Never risk ruining a photograph by writing something on the back. Use "post-it" notes to number photos. If you have a cover-quality slide that is relevant to your article, we'd like to see it. Since a cover slide will be enlarged many times, the image must be very crisp and the slide itself unmarred. All negatives, photographs, and artwork will be returned.

ACKNOWLEDGEMENT & SELECTION. Within approximately 60 days of the date we receive your manuscript, we will send you an acknowledgement letter and copyright transfer form. The editor will then assign the manuscript to two reviewers, who will assess it for technical accuracy and appropriateness for *S&C*. After the manuscript has been returned from the reviewers it will go into the pending files, from which manuscripts are chosen for use in *S&C*. Manuscripts may stay in the pending files for extended periods, up to two years. Manuscripts are selected based on appropriateness of subject matter, uniqueness of ideas, accessibility, and our ability to obtain good illustrations. The percentage of unsolicited manuscripts chosen for publication is approximately 25 percent. If the waiting period becomes too long for you, you may withdraw your manuscript from consideration for publication at any time. Simply call or drop us a note.

When an article has been selected and scheduled, the staff edits it to conform to the journal's standards, style, and space requirements. At that time you will be sent a copy of the edited manuscript for review. Sometimes a reviewer may make recommendations for revision. If a revision is recommended, you will be sent a letter with appropriate comments to guide you.

COPYRIGHT. All material appearing in *S&C* is copyrighted by NSTA, so all persons submitting manuscripts are required to sign a copyright transfer. All manuscripts submitted to *S&C* must be original. **If your manuscript has been previously published, or is under consideration elsewhere, *S&C* will not consider it for publication.** NSTA is a nonprofit organization and does not pay contributors for their material. Authors receive complimentary copies of the issue in which their article appears.

Send submissions to:
Editor, *Science and Children*
National Science Teachers Association
1742 Connecticut Avenue, NW
Washington, DC 20009-1171

(T)

From the Editor

Science Scope wants you!

How many times have you read about an activity in *Science Scope* and thought to yourself, "I've got a similar activity that the kids just love!" Well, this is your invitation to write for *Science Scope*.

Each of NSTA's journals relies on manuscripts submitted by educators like yourself. If you find *Science Scope* useful, it's because one of your colleagues took the time to share an activity with us. Wouldn't **you** like to be part of the *Science Scope* team?

What we're looking for from you

Science Scope publishes activity-oriented articles that are appropriate for the middle level science classroom. In every issue of *Science Scope*, we try to include a variety of articles on biology, chemistry, physics, Earth science, process activities, interdisciplinary activities, and computer applications to science education. We are asking for articles in all of these areas, but we especially need articles in the areas of biology, chemistry, and computer applications.

There are other ways to contribute to *Science Scope*. Submit your quick and easy teaching ideas to the "Potpourri" section, or tap into your collection of life-saving hints for the "New Teacher Feature." You can also submit a "Bulletin Board" idea, or review a book on science for "Instructional Reviews."

What happens to your manuscript

When you send your manuscript to us, we pass it on to two reviewers from our Review and Advisory Boards, most of whom are middle level classroom teachers like yourself. They read your manuscript and let us know if it is appropriate for the middle level science teacher, if it is clear and understandable, if there are any safety concerns, and how the activity might be adapted for students of varying ability. Then the editors decide, based on the reviewers' recommendations, whether the article is appropriate for *Science Scope*, needs revision, or should be sent back to the author.

If your article is accepted for publication, you will eventually receive a copy of *Science Scope* starring **you**! It is quite a thrill to see your name in print. It also impresses your administration, and your students will love reading about an activity they did in class.

What do you do now?

Think of your best activities. Ask yourself, "What works with my students?" "What do I most enjoy teaching?" "What activities do visiting, former students always seem to remember?" Then sit down and put your ideas on paper. We don't need Shakespearean prose. What we *do* need are ideas clearly presented and completely described. We all have a tendency to omit important details when we are writing about something that we know very well, so allow a trusted colleague to read your article. He or she can help you "fill in the holes" before you send in the article. Don't worry about the finishing touches, we will work with you to make your article the best that it can be.

Science Scope needs you!

Since we moved to eight issues per year, we need 70 to 80 full-length articles and 25 to 30 "Potpourri" articles each year. So, please consider sharing one of your excellent ideas with your colleagues. It's useful, it's fun, and, once you start writing articles, you won't be able to stop! ◪

Write for The Science Teacher

Manuscript guidelines for feature articles.

Each month, from September through May, *The Science Teacher* finds its way into the hands of tens of thousands of secondary classroom teachers, principals, supervisors, and librarians. Why not share with them what you know about innovations in science teaching, developments in science, and classroom projects and experiments by writing a feature article?

Sitting down to write

You are writing for an audience whose reading time is limited and who may not be familiar with specialized subjects. To best serve readers, write clearly and concisely, organize your material logically, and use an active voice and a conversational tone. Avoid abstract and very technical language; define all specialized terms. A *TST* feature article is not a dissertation or a research report. Write about your firsthand experiences or your unique area of expertise. Stress classroom applicability. *TST*'s editors will keep these points in mind when editing your article for publication.

We cannot consider your manuscript if it is being considered by other publishers or if it has been published already. Also, you must guarantee the originality of your work. Give proper credit for any other author's ideas that you use or build on.

Manuscript mechanics. Your manuscript should not exceed 1500 words. Longer manuscripts will be considered for review at the Editor's discretion. Very long manuscripts will be returned for revision without being reviewed. On the title page, give each author's name, current position, mailing address, and daytime phone number. Do not put your name(s) on any other page of the manuscript.

Metric. Use only the SI (metric) system of weights and measures.

Photographs and illustrations. Feel free to submit photographs of students working in the classroom or lab, a setup for an experiment, equipment you construct, or phenomena you observe. Students in lab must be shown following all appropriate safety guidelines, including wearing goggles. Their faces should be visible, but they should not be looking directly into the camera. Compose your shots to leave space around your subjects so that the editors can crop for publication.

Photos should be black-and-white glossy prints, 5x7 or larger, with excellent focus, fine grain, and good contrast. (Color prints and slides can sometimes be used also.) Tape an identifying label to the back of each photo. Do not write on the back of photos, ink stamp them, or paper clip labels to them. On a separate sheet of paper, type a description and the photographer's credit for each photo.

Submit only rough sketches for figures and diagrams, unless you have a professional artist available. Type captions on a separate sheet of paper, along with any credit lines. Photographs, illustrations, and sketches are returned only upon request.

Reference and resource lists. Because most articles recount firsthand experiences, references are seldom necessary. If you must use them, cite only your direct sources, and use the author-date reference style in the text. Bibliographies and resource lists should be alphabetical and limited to current, readily available items. Use the following style:

For books: Jones, J.A. *A New View of Science,* 3rd ed. Chicago: Crown Publishing, 1983.

For articles in periodicals: Jones, J.A., and W.J. Smith. (1983) "Outlook in Chemistry." *New Journal of Chemistry,* 42(3):593-606.

Check the accuracy of your items carefully. *TST* cannot check or supply information for you.

Submitting a manuscript

You may submit your manuscript either on paper or electronically. Manuscripts on paper must be double-spaced, on one side of standard white paper. Submit the original and two copies of everything, including figures, photos, and tables, to *TST*'s Editor, Dr. Juliana Texley, Box 215, New Baltimore, MI 48047. And, submit one copy of everything to the Managing Editor, at NSTA Headquarters, 1742 Connecticut Ave. NW, Washington, DC. 20009. (Indicate that you have sent copies to the Editor.)

Electronic manuscripts may be submitted either on disk or via one of NSTA's electronic bulletin boards at (202) 328-5853 or 265-4496. Contact *TST* before submitting electronically.

All authors submit manuscripts on a contributed basis only.

Getting acknowledged

The Editor will acknowledge your manuscript within a few weeks of receiving it, without obligation for publication. Peer reviewers and the Editor consider all manuscripts and make recommendations for revision, acceptance, or rejection. The Editor will notify the corresponding author of the decision, normally within 3 months.

Rejected feature manuscripts are sometimes considered for publication in shortened form as Idea Bank items. Manuscripts needing revision are either sent back, or revised by the Editor and then sent back to the author for approval.

Being accepted

TST currently has a backlog of accepted manuscripts in some science disciplines, for example, science education theory. Because it is a *TST* policy to try to offer an article from each science discipline in each issue, accepted manuscripts in backlogged disciplines will wait considerably longer for publication than will manuscripts in disciplines without backlogs, such as computers, physics, and earth science. Waits in backlogged disciplines can be as long as several years. Waits in other disciplines can be several months.

Coming up for publication

You will be alerted when your accepted manuscript has been scheduled into an issue. Next, all manuscripts are edited with the tone, style, space, and content needs of *TST* in mind. The editorial staff will send you proofs of the edited manuscript for approval shortly before publication.

Maintaining tone

The final title of the published article, subheads, captions, photographs and illustrations, and other elements that attract attention to the article and contribute to the tone and appearance of the journal are the Editor's prerogative.

Research for gifted students: cultivating a national resource

Piyush Swami, John F. Schaff, and Jerome E. DeBruin

"There are a lot of kids so turned off by sleazy academic programs designed for the very average student that they are willing to try anything—except school." This harsh indictment of schooling by one gifted student underscores an urgent need to properly challenge our gifted and talented students.[1] Dorothy Sisk, director of the Office of Gifted and Talented of the U.S. Department of Health, Education and Welfare, reported recently that "national statistics on educational programs for gifted and talented students reveal the shocking neglect of these students." [3] According to these statistics, only about 12 percent of the gifted and talented youngsters in this country are being adequately served through educational programs.

---

[1] *On Being Gifted,* written by student participants in the National Student Symposium on the Education of the Gifted and Talented (Mark L. Krueger, project director; sponsored by The American Association for Gifted Children). Walker and Company, New York, N.Y. 1978, p. 91.

Piyush Swami, science consultant with the Ohio Department of Education, is also a visiting professor at The Ohio State University, teaching elementary science methods. He has helped to develop two science instructional television series for elementary schools. (Address: Ohio Dept. of Education, Columbus, OH 43215.)

John F. Schaff, professor and associate dean in the College of Education, University of Toledo, studied science education in Europe and Russia in 1974 as a member of the National Science Education Delegation. He has taught at several universities as well as in high school.

Jerome E. DeBruin, professor of elementary science education, also at the University of Toledo, has developed several specialized education courses for elementary science teachers, and has written widely. (Address: Department of Science Education, University of Toledo, Toledo, OH 43606.)

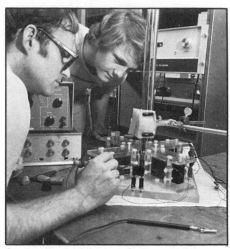

Student and advisor perform contactless measurement tests on solids.

We are convinced that gifted and talented youngsters are one of our nation's irreplaceable resources—further, that such young people should be familiar with the methods of science whether or not they will later choose this as their vocation. Hence, we designed and implemented a scientific research program for gifted and talented high school students in northwest Ohio, obtaining support from the Student Science Teaching Program of the National Science Foundation. The decision to stress research reflects our belief that the American enterprise system thrives on creative advancement in science and technology, though of late national commitment to basic research has unfortunately been waning. [2, 4]

Uncommon opportunities

The program, called Student Science Research Program, began in summer 1977 and continues through this school year.[2] Its major purpose is to give talented high school students the opportunity to engage in a concentrated research experience outside school, working either on a research team, or under the direct supervision of a practicing scientist. We arranged for students to use one of three facilities: the Owens-Illinois Technical Center (an industrial research center), the Medical College of Ohio at Toledo, or The University of Toledo. Student participants enroll in The University of Toledo, and are eligible to receive six quarter-hours of undergraduate credit, with tuition paid by our project.

---

[2] We hope to continue the program in future summers.

More specific goals of the program include:

• Motivating students toward a research career in science;

• Expanding students' background and understanding of scientific research, including its philosophy and objectives;

• Providing students with a challenging and worthwhile science experience not normally available in high school or undergraduate classes;

• Providing students an opportunity to work with scientists actively engaged in research;

• Providing students the chance to become familiar with a variety of research topics, problems, and experiences;

• Providing students an opportunity to write research reports as well as articles for possible publication, and to prepare oral reports of their results.

The entire program is composed of three parts: (a) a concentrated eight-week summer research experience; (b) seminar sessions held twice weekly during the summer; and (c) five biweekly sessions in the fall which focus on the writing of a research report. Over 65 students, selected from high schools in the Toledo, Ohio area, have participated in the program over the past two years.

During the eight-week summer phase, each student investigates a research problem under the direction of a volunteer research advisor at either the technical center, medical college, or university. An extensive array of special equipment and opportunities for study in all areas of the physical, medical, engineering, and life sciences are available at these facilities. Research advisors agree to expose students to as many basic research skills and techniques as possible. Each student generally conducts research daily during the week throughout the summer session. Students are required to keep daily logs of their research activity, in addition to any record books requested by the advisor; project directors review the logs biweekly and discuss them with students.

Seminar sessions for the entire group of students are conducted twice weekly throughout the summer. These 90-minute meetings provide a forum in which students may share research experiences—through discussion, through observing the facilities of their fellow students, and through engaging in a variety of tasks designed to teach them about the nature of scientific research, both in industrial and academic settings. The sessions may consist of individual student presentations,

GA1325

large-group presentations by research specialists, or small-group discussions to encourage interchange of ideas.

We feel that the chance for students to meet informally, both with other students and with many different research scientists is enormously important. Topics considered during the seminar sessions include:

1. Procedures and techniques used when conducting a literature search on a research problem, using library resources at the three locations. Focus is on conducting computer searches, and using various abstracts, indexes, reviews, and condensates;

2. Reviewing and abstracting research articles and reports;

3. Analyzing different types of research studies;

4. Developing research designs and procedures, and estimating the cost of such activities;

5. Analyzing research facilities and personnel requirements;

6. Writing brief research reports and abstracts;

7. Developing and preparing research articles for publication;

8. Preparing oral presentations describing research studies and results;

9. Studying careers in scientific research;

10. Considering the future of scientific research.

Scientists as communicators

With the start of school in the fall, student research comes to an end, and group sessions shift from emphasizing basic laboratory research to a series of in-depth activities on writing research reports, abstracts, and articles for possible publication. At the end of the fall sessions, all participants are required to submit a final report of their study in the form of a research paper to the project directors. A draft copy of each research paper is also examined and critiqued by the appropriate research advisor during its preparation. Research advisors and students also consider the possibility of jointly publishing research results.

In addition to writing reports, participants organize and prepare an oral presentation of their results for possible presentation at the Junior Science Humanities Symposium, Ohio Academy of Science, as well as other professional scientific meetings. Peer group practice sessions, using videotaped

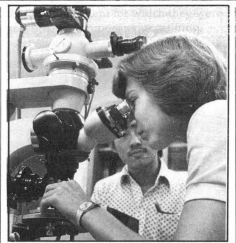

Student conducts coal analysis by spectrofluorescence measurements.

"run-throughs" of student speeches, assist students and research advisors in analyzing and critiquing.

Five sessions are held from September through December at two-week intervals. They are scheduled for two hours during the late afternoon or early evening to accommodate school and work schedules of students and research advisors.

Students receive two letter grades for participating in the program. One grade, given by the research advisor, evaluates the student's progress in scientific research during the summer phase. It is based on the student's scientific attitude, curiosity, inventiveness, initiative, and work habits. The second grade, determined by a member of the project staff responsible for the fall sessions, evaluates student progress in preparing the oral presentation, written research report, article, or paper.

Program assessment

The program has spurred noteworthy accomplishments. For example: three students have jointly published their research results in scientific journals with their research advisors; eight of twelve papers presented at the local Junior Science Humanities Symposium in 1978 were given by members of the program [1]; and several students presented the results of their research to faculty seminars at the Medical College and the university College of Pharmacy. In addition, 14 first-year students continued their research experiences under their same advisors for a second year on special arrangements; these students shared their first-year experience with incoming students and later became seminar leaders.

Several second-year students elected to gain additional university credit for their continued research experience by paying their own tuition costs; others were hired by their advisors on special grants to continue their research activities. We hope to expand the second-year program in the future by organizing separate research seminars for those students.

Students have grown noticeably as a result of the program. The summer and fall seminar sessions, with their free exchange of ideas between students from a variety of schools, have helped to increase student self-confidence and an appreciation for the abilities of their peers. In addition, the seminars provided opportunities for students to gather information about different colleges and about scientific careers. Several social gatherings were also held to help "break the ice."

Interest in the program has increased during its short duration. The number of scientists at the three cooperating institutions offering to serve as research advisors has increased steadily. Faculty members of the university speech and educational media and technology departments have also joined the project staff to assist students in preparing written and oral reports during the fall sessions. Several students have involved their high school science and English teachers in the critique of their reports and manuscripts. Recently, a medical doctor from a nearby community established a fund to support four students from his community in the program each summer.

In the future, we hope to attract greater numbers of gifted minority students to the program. For low-income families particularly, we will seek funds to reimburse the student for loss of summer employment income.

We have been tremendously encouraged by student and community response thus far, and we intend to pursue our efforts to insure that our students' "gifts" are not squandered. ∎

References

1. DeBruin, Jerome E., Stephen Barber, and John F. Schaff. "Research, 'Rite, and Rap: Getting Gifted Students Involved in Scientific Research." *Science Activities* 14(6): 10–13; November–December 1977.
2. Gwynne, Peter. "A Growing R + D Gap." *Newsweek* XCII (1):89; July 3, 1978.
3. Sisk, Dorothy. "Gifted: Their Discovery and Nurturance." *Journal of Creative Behavior* 12(1):i; 1978.
4. Walsh, John. "Historian of Science States Case for Catching Up on Basic Research." *Science* 199:1188–90; March 17, 1978.

GA1325

(T)

WRITE FOR *SCIENCE ACTIVITIES*

GUIDELINES FOR CONTRIBUTORS:

Manuscripts should be submitted to the managing editor in double-spaced typescript throughout, including footnotes and bibliography at the end of the text, with generous margins to allow for copyediting. *Science Activities* prefers the University of Chicago *A Manual of Style,* 13th ed., for all matters of style, including reference form. Each manuscript should be submitted in duplicate—the original and one copy. The author's name, institutional affiliation (if any), and preferred mailing address should be listed on a separate title page.

Contributors are encouraged to submit photographs, drawings, and diagrams. They must be black and white, with captions keyed and typed in order, double-spaced, on a separate page. Originals must be furnished if a manuscript is accepted for publication. Reviewers will be expecting articles to include

- grade levels of targeted students;
- curriculum areas for which the article is appropriate;
- hands-on activity for the classroom, and its rationale;
- materials list;
- safety provisions;
- currency of topic;
- follow-up activities (areas to investigate, writing exercises, etc.);
- bibliography and/or resource list useful to other teachers;
- author reference list.

When a manuscript is published, each author receives two complimentary copies of the appropriate issue and permission to reproduce additional copies of the article.

NOTES: See pages 109-111 for a published article in *Science Activities* that gives tips for parents on how to help their child with a science fair project.

ACTIVITY NO.	KEY	ACTIVITY	REFER TO PAGE(S)	DATE COMPLETED
AP2 (T)	OC	Read article "Teach, Reflect and Write" for tips on how to write and then get your article published. Then write and submit your article for publication.	283-296	

TIPS FOR THE TEACHER

Writing an Article for Publication

Read the following article carefully for tips on how to publish an article. Then sit down, write and submit your article for publication so others may benefit from your successes. Here are some further tips.

TIPS ON MANUSCRIPT PREPARATION

If possible, use a computer to prepare your manuscript for publication. Use a word processor or data base software to create information cards. Use your software to rearrange the cards. Keep a backup copy. Write your article and check with a spelling checker. When writing your article, begin the first paragraph well below the title and byline. Indent the first line of each paragraph three or five spaces. Double space all manuscripts. Leave a minimum of a 1″ margin on the left, ¾″ on the right. The title on page one should be halfway down the page. Start 1″ from the top on the other pages. Leave a 1″ margin at the bottom. Type the same number of lines on each page. Keep the character count the same on each line.

Make your typescript as neat as possible. Use a good, dark computer or typewriter ribbon, white bond paper, at least twenty-pound weight. Number each page in the upper right corner. Print your last name below the number. Print the title or a tagline in the upper left corner. Send a stamped, self-addressed envelope (SASE) with your article. Send the article nonfolded or flat. The SASE should be slightly smaller so it fits in the outside envelope without folding.

Enclose a brief cover letter. If photos or other graphics are included, list these on a separate page. Do not insert photos in text. Include captions with photos and graphics. It is permissible to use *30* or *End* to designate the end of your article.

GA1325

Jerry DeBruin, Ph.D.
College of Education and Allied Professions
The University of Toledo
Toledo, OH 43606
(419) 537-2689
(419) 537-2488

3000 Words

First Time Rights

TEACH, REFLECT AND WRITE

by

Jerry DeBruin

Science and Children arrives at my office regularly and on time. As I read the journal, I spot an article entitled "Writing for Science and Children" in which the editors seek articles that are interesting, innovative and help teachers bring good science into the classroom. Being a science educator, writer and teacher of writing, I am interested in the prospect of writing such articles. I reflect on the many occasions when teachers, graduate assistants and colleagues have indicated how they wanted to use their professional skills to publish in professional journals but lacked the knowledge and information on how to break into the publishing field.

GA1325

These people often read widely and feel strongly that they could publish many of the articles they read. Upon closer examination, they confide, "I just don't know how to go about doing it." Their dilemma is a common one, their motives legitimate. They would like to see their ideas in print and eventually become established science writers. The following includes some practical tips on how you can publish your work in journals for those interested in science education.

Writing Starts with Ideas

A successful writer first becomes aware of, and then collects, ideas to write about. Fortunately, ideas are found everywhere. Look closely at yourself and what you do in your everyday life. Science educators are most successful when they write about practical ideas and activities that involve students. These ideas come from everyday teaching events and include favorite teaching units and activities. In addition, science educators who write often combine experiences from their teaching with ideas related to their personal lives. One science teacher recently wrote an article on how a teacher can be both a successful teacher and single parent.

Keep a Record of Your Ideas

Successful writers jot down ideas immediately when they come to mind. Keep a small writing pad on your person, desk at school and nightstand near your bed at home. Scientists tell us that the best time for ideas to surface is when we are in a state of near sleep. At this time, the mind is in a mind state called "Alpha" level which features the brain pulsating waves at 8-12 cycles per second. In fact

GA1325

you may already have experienced your most creative ideas while in this state. If so, be sure to have your pad handy and write the ideas down before you fall asleep. Don't rely on your memory to retrieve these ideas the next morning. Do it at the time the idea surfaces whether it be during "Alpha" level or during normal waking hours. Whatever the time or situation, it is important to jot down ideas as soon as possible, or they may slip into the realm of deep subconsciousness forever.

Keep a Daily Diary

Keeping a daily diary helps you jot down ideas. This practice gives you a permanent record of your everyday activities. In addition, a diary allows you to read past entries. You see how ideas begin, how they are related to each other and how patterns of ideas unfold over time. An added advantage is that a diary actually helps you become a more effective science educator. By writing, ideas will flow naturally and become crystallized in your own mind and in the minds of your students. Your writing skills also improve. You learn to write concise, cogent statements which are needed when you write for publication. For one university science educator, the task of writing recommendations for student teachers soon became easier. In short, the practice gained when you keep a daily diary leads to improved writing performance, which in turn may result in the production of more acceptable manuscripts for science education journals.

GA1325

Visit the Library

Your school, public, and university libraries are vast storehouses of information for you to tap. Seek help from librarians who are often willing to help you brainstorm ideas for writing. They will also help you locate sources of information on your topic. When you write about a difficult science topic, your school librarian can usually find a book written for youngsters that uses simple words to explain difficult concepts on an elementary level. This helps you, the writer, clarify ideas in your own mind and sharpens your writing skills in the process.

Spend time in the library. Learn how the Dewey Decimal and Library of Congress classification systems work. Look under the term "Writing-Authorship." Find the *Writer's Market*, *Directory of Publishing Opportunities*, *America's Education Press*, and the *Magazine Index*. These references list thousands of both paying and non-paying potential markets for your manuscripts. Look for related volumes such as *Arts and Crafts* and the *Photographer's Market* which list hundreds of places, in addition to education markets, where you can submit your related works. Various indexes including *Education Index* list educational periodicals that are possible markets. Most importantly, get to know the markets that specialize in science topics.

After you examine books and indexes, visit the Central Serials Record. Find out what science periodicals and journals the library carries. Then go to the

GA1325

periodical section and look for current issues of the *Writer's Digest* and *The Writer*. These are monthly publications that contain information and tips on how to write and where to submit your manuscript for possible publication.

In addition to books and periodicals, become familiar with recent technological advances in the library. Does the library have a computer network that enables you to acquire books from other libraries? Does the library have a microfilm and microfiche service? Does the library have a computer retrieval search service such as CD-ROM that prints out a list of bibliographical citations of works related to your topic? Two such services are CompuServe and The Source. Become familiar with the service called *The Education Resources Information Center* (ERIC). This network has 16 national clearinghouses of information, one of which is the ERIC Clearing House for Science, Mathematics, and Environmental Education located at Ohio State University. ERIC CD-ROM features post 1981 citations.

Many teachers send their favorite curriculum ideas and activities to ERIC for possible publication. You can do the same by sending your manuscript to the Acquisitions Coordinator at ERIC/SMEAC, Ohio State University, 1200 Chambers Road, Columbus, Ohio 43212.

When you use the ERIC guides, be sure to examine two particular guides, Research in Education (RIE) and Current Index to Journals in Education (CIJE).

RIE is a semi-annual index to education research reports, programs and other documents of educational significance. Curriculum ideas are listed by title in RIE. CIJE is a monthly, semi-annual, and annual index to articles in education from more than 700 major journals. Printout bibliographies with or without annotations can be obtained from the original publishers, University Microfilms International, 300 N. Zeeb Road, Ann Arbor, Michigan 48106, or from your library by using CD-ROM.

Check with your librarian on whether the library is a depository for government documents, which means that government documents are sent to your library regularly. You will not find these publications listed in the main card catalog but rather in a separate system by itself. Learn how to use the system. Government documents are very useful because they supply a wealth of information on science topics and issues. An added bonus is that you can use the ideas *free*. Remember, however, to cite the source of your ideas when you write your article.

Analyze Periodicals

Before you begin to write, examine a number of publications for which you feel your idea is appropriate. Carefully examine back issues of the publication to insure that a similar article has not been published recently. Note the geographical dis-

GA1325

tribution and circulation for each periodical. Find out for whom the publications are written. Men? Women? Children? Teachers? Calculate the average number of words per article and note whether photographs, illustrations and diagrams are used in each. Every bit of information that you can gather about a periodical helps.

You will want to look at the types of articles in each publication. Some may be "how to" articles, others may be personal essays, news features, narratives or research-type articles. Still others may give the results of a survey, feature an interview with an important personality or have a touch of nostalgia. This will help you decide the type of article you want to write.

Select a single article from a past issue of the periodical. Analyze the article. Does the lead paragraph capture your attention? Are long and/or short sentences used? Does the writing flow smoothly? Does the conclusion restate the central idea? In short, the more you know about the journal and the types of articles it features, the greater your chance of having a manuscript accepted by that publication.

Write a Query Letter

After you have examined an available copy of the periodical, write a query letter to its editor. Ask for a copy of the writer's guidelines, a free copy of the publication and a list of themes, if any, that the publication will address in the future. Give the editor your ideas for an article and the approximate number of words. Be sure to define your idea precisely. Make it interesting. Sell the editor on your idea.

GA1325

Tell why your idea appeals to readers and why you feel you have the qualifications for writing the article. State the availability of photographs, sketches or diagrams. Above all, keep your query letter brief. Always include a self-addressed, stamped envelope (SASE) for the editor's reply.

Write the Article

Write your article after you have received writer's guidelines and the "go ahead" from the editor. Your first task is to clearly define the topic. Then pinpoint the audience for whom you want to write the article. Most science teachers write for other science teachers or for youngsters or parents who are interested in science. You can easily do the same. Be sure to decide on your purpose for writing the article. Do you want to share some of your teaching ideas with other teachers? To inform teachers and parents of recent developments in science? To share a bit of science humor? Do you want to write a story for youngsters? Whatever the reason, clearly state your purpose. You can usually do this when you complete the following sentence: "In this article, I want to tell the reader . . . ."

Before you begin the actual writing of your article, ask yourself specific questions that deal directly with the topic. Make a list of these questions. Do research on the topic. Gather background information that answers the questions. Write this information on note cards or enter it into a computer. Arrange your note cards in the order or enter the topics into a computer in the order that you want the article written. For example, the article may be written in a chronological time sequence from early ages to the present, a space sequence from city, county, state, to nation, by a major to minor topics sequence, from simple to complex issues, and topics listed in sequence or from most important to least important.

Whatever sequence you follow, be sure to develop an outline of topics that matches the order and flow of the article that you desire. Keep in mind, however, that note cards or a computer can always help you resequence the topics to develop a more logical outline which will give your article a smooth flow. Then the rest is up to you. Go ahead, write your article.

Mechanics of Writing

When you write, remember to write in a straightforward, direct manner. Write the *lead* paragraph so it captures the reader's attention and supplies the central idea of the article. Provide plenty of examples that are based on well-researched ideas. Conclude your article by restating the central idea.

Emphasize nouns and verbs when you write. Put yourself in the place of the reader. Evaluate your writing from a reader's point of view. Use one complete thought per sentence. Use transition sentences between paragraphs. Restate your thesis.

Then rewrite until your writing flows smoothly and accurately conveys your message to the reader.

You must rewrite in order to write effectively. You can help yourself rewrite when you read silently what you have written. Make notes on sections that are not clear. Read your manuscript aloud into a tape recorder. Replay the tape. Listen to your own words. Do they convey the message that you want to convey? If not, use more precise words. Transcribe the tape. Photos, sketches and diagrams can also be used to amplify what you say. These media help you both write and rewrite because you can describe exactly what happens in each situation. Rewriting makes the manuscript clearer, helps the reader further understand what you have to say, and enhances your chances of getting your manuscript published.

Have Others Read Your Writing

Solicit help from other people who can give you a different perspective on your writing. People can do for you what students in classes on writing do when they critique each other's manuscripts. You will want to have at least two unbiased people critique your manuscript. Select readers who know something about the topic. Have them identify the major point(s) of the article and describe the feelings your writing has evoked in them. Be sure to listen carefully to individuals who give you feedback. They may give an entirely new slant to your article or supply ideas for future articles.

GA1325

Recruit people in your school who can help. An English teacher can check sentence structure, spelling and grammar. Your librarian can help locate bibliographical sources. Your students can do trial runs of your activities to clear up fuzzy directions and inaccurate information. The media specialist can take photographs that will enhance your article. Photographs are especially helpful when you rewrite your article. Describe the action portrayed in the photographs. Things look different through the camera lens when compared to what you see with your own eyes. Rewrite again until your words accurately describe the action in each instance. After you revise your manuscript several times, put it aside for a few days. Then read the entire manuscript once again in one sitting. Rewrite until your ideas become even more clear before you prepare to submit your article for actual publication.

Preparation for Submission

Reread the writer's guidelines that you received from the editor before you type the final copy of your manuscript. Follow the guidelines exactly. Make your manuscript as neat as possible. Leave ample margins. Use a good, dark black typewriter or computer ribbon and clean 20-pound bond paper. Computer submissions on discs are often acceptable. Corrections should be clean. There should be no strike-overs or crossed-out words. The appearance of your manuscript is your initial introduction to the editor. Put your best copy forward. Make at least four clean copies of your article. Keep one for youself. Submit three copies to the editor.

GA1325

Before you submit your article, review the name and address of the editor, usually listed on one of the first pages in the publication. Send your manuscript in triplicate, along with a self-addressed, stamped return card to the editor.

Mail your manuscript flat. Include a self-addressed, stamped envelope (SASE) of sufficient size for a return. Include a brief cover letter. Thank the editor for sending the writer's guidelines, the free copy of the periodical and list of themes. Refresh the editor's mind by saying that your manuscript is in response to the editor's initial "go ahead" to write and submit the article. If photographs are included, number each one on the reverse side with a grease pencil. List the numbers on each photograph and a description of each on a separate page. Do not insert photos between pages in the manuscript. Double check that you have included all the pages of your manuscript in the correct order. Slip the manuscript under the flap of the return envelope, place both of these in the larger envelope, seal and mail.

Acceptance/Rejection of Article

Waiting for a reply to your submission can take as little as one week or longer than six months. Be patient; editors are very busy people. If you haven't heard from the editor within two or three months, write a follow-up letter. Inquire whether the editor has received and taken action on your manuscript. Include a self-addressed, stamped envelope (SASE). Eventually, an answer will come. If your

GA1325

manuscript is accepted, your dilemma in learning how to get published will be solved. Momentum will be generated. It will be up to you to keep it going.

If your manuscript is rejected, read carefully the reasons why it was rejected. It's quite possible that your manuscript did not fit within the current thematic structure of the journal; therefore, you may want to submit it to another publication. Sometimes a journal will accept your article if you make revisions suggested by the editor. If this occurs, you need to decide if the suggested revisions meet the intent of the article. If so, follow the editor's suggestions and resubmit the article. If not, submit the article to another publication. Eventually, your article will be published. You will then begin to reap the profits from your labors.

When your article is published, you may receive calls and/or letters inviting you to speak at various meetings or conduct in-service sessions regarding the content of your article. After a few of these experiences, editors of various publications may ask you to submit articles to their publications. Increased momentum is gained. Then you, like so many others, will reach the goal of becoming a published teacher-writer in a science education journal.

ACTIVITY NO.	KEY	ACTIVITY	REFER TO PAGE(S)	DATE COMPLETED
AP3 (T)	IC	Assist students in writing articles for publication that describe their science fair experiences.	297-300	

TIPS FOR THE TEACHER

Student-Published Works

Students, along with their mentors, frequently publish the results of their science fair investigations. An excellent publication for student writers of scientific papers and articles is *BASE* published by:

Alin Foundation Press
1 Alin Plaza
2017 Dwight
Berkeley, CA 94704-2062

BASE is for young authors and is distributed worldwide to stimulate fruitful communications between students and scientists everywhere. *BASE* is recommended for every junior high and high school science teacher and library. A sample student-mentor published article is found on pages 298-300.

NOTES:

RELATIONSHIP BETWEEN LOCUS OF CONTROL AND ALCOHOL AND DRUG-RELATED BEHAVIORS IN TEENAGERS[1]

WILLIAM F. COX, JR.
University of Toledo

JOYCE A. LUHRS
Lake High School

Seventh, ninth, tenth and twelfth graders, classified as internal or external according to Rotter's Locus of Control Scale, indicated whether or not and why they engaged in alcohol consumption or marijuana smoking behaviours. Overall, a higher proportion of externals than internals drank but the two groups did not generally differ in marijuana smoking behaviors, both findings unsupportive of the "control by addiction" hypothesis. Developmentally different trends among internals and externals for the two types of behaviours suggested an interactive effect between peer culture influences and the locus of control variable. Both groups were otherwise generally similar in their reasons for engaging in the behaviors, in their desire not to stop, and in their increased opinions of themselves.

The amount of control that individuals believe they have over their own fate (locus of control) seems to be an important determinant of human behavior. The perception that events are largely contingent upon personal actions is indicative of a belief in internal control. Conversely, if the individual perceives that events are more a function of surrounding, rather than personal forces, this is indicative of a belief in external control (Rotter, 1966).

Differences among individuals who score at various points on the locus of control continuum are represented in the following characteristics (Lefcourt, 1976): the degree to which individuals perceive themselves as externally controlled pawns versus responsible actors (p. 50), the degree of yielding or resistance to external pressures (pp. 45, 65), differences in reasons for yielding to externally oriented pressures (p. 48), and the willingness to risk social rejection for maintaining "proper" behavior (p. 49). From attributes such as these, one would predict that internals are less controlled by others and thus lead a more "internally fulfilling" life. Externals, on the other hand, would supposedly be more apt to lead an "others directed" life.

Regrettably, the complexity of motivations for human behaviors often dilutes predictions made from any single personality dimension. For instance, cigarette smoking and alcohol abusive habits, as hygienically detrimental behaviors, would assumedly be engaged in more by externals than internals. While this apparently is the case for smoking behaviors (Hjelle and Clouser, 1970), it is not so clearly the case for alcohol related behaviours. Indeed, Goss and Morosko (1970) found that alcoholics tend to score in a more internally controlled direction, assumedly because the alcohol provides a means for the individual to experience greater personal control over internal feelings. The effect that substance-induced control over feelings has on locus of control measures is similarly used to explain the finding that hospitalized drug addicts scored more internally than did university students (Palmer, 1971).

On the topic of substance abuse, drug and alcohol problems are considered to be a "spreading menace" in the United States and are closely related to increased problems in our school systems ("Alcohol and Marijuana", 1975). The present study investigated marijuana and alcohol abusive behaviors in junior and senior high school students with the intent of interpreting the results with and clarifying the nature of the locus of control variable.

If peer pressure (typically a powerful force at these age levels) is the prime motivating factor, then more externals than internals should engage in both of these abusive behaviors. However, if control of emotions, etc., is the prime force, then the reverse should occur, *i.e.*, internals will outnumber externals, assuming, of course, that both groups had similar feelings about the value of these two substances (*i.e.*, marijuana and alcohol).

---

[1] Research was conducted under the direction of the first author for the second author's project in the Junior Science Humanities Symposium, University of Toledo, February, 1978.

298

METHOD

SUBJECTS

Subjects were 280 students in the 7th, 9th, 10th and 12th grades at Lake local schools. Most of the students were from middle-class homes in the Walbridge and Millbury, Ohio locale.

INSTRUMENTS

Rotter's (1966) I-E scale was administered concurrently with a 20-item Drug and Alcohol Survey. Basically, the survey required students to indicate whether or not they had tried smoking "pot" and drinking alcoholic beverages, whether or not they still do it and, if so, their reason for continuing, their opinions of self since smoking "pot" and/or drinking, and their desire to stop.

PROCEDURE

Both questionnaires were distributed in randomly selected homerooms at the 10th and 12th grade levels and to randomly selected science classes at the 7th and 9th grade levels. Students were allowed one week to complete and return the instruments.

RESULTS

Students characterized as internals and students characterized as externals were differentiated in their responses to the Drug and Alcohol Survey. Generally, the pattern of responses for internals and for externals regarding pot smoking was different from the pattern of responses for the two groups regarding drinking alcohol. Specifically, with all grades combined, internals and externals responded similarly in pot smoking behavior ($p > 0.05$) but differed in their drinking behavior, $\chi^2(1) = 5.63$, $p < 0.05$, with a larger proportion of externals (37/102) than internals (39/170) reporting that they drank (see Table 1).

Differences between the two groups also occurred in developmental trends. For pot smoking, a significant difference, $\chi^2(1) = 23.69$, $p < 0.05$, between externals who smoked (12/54) and internals who smoked (1/32) occurred at the lowest grade level (7th), washing out at all other grades with the incidence of smoking increasing from 15% in the 7th grade to 32% in the 12th grade. An increase by grade level also occurred regarding the incidence of drinking (from 17% to 52%) but the proportion of externals (14/20) who drank and the

TABLE 1: NUMBER OF INTERNALS AND EXTERNALS WHO DO AND DON'T ENGAGE IN SMOKING AND DRINKING BEHAVIORS

Grade	Control	Smoke Pot Do	Smoke Pot Don't	Drink Alcohol Do	Drink Alcohol Don't
7	Internal	1	31	3	28
	External	12	42	12	41
9	Internal	16	40	14	42
	External	9	28	10	26
10	Internal	4	19	5	17
	External	6	19	4	19
12	Internal	9	24	13	19
	External	8	12	14	6
Total	Internal	36	138	39	131
	External	29	77	37	65

proportion of internals (13/32) who drank differed significantly, $\chi^2(1) = 4.26$, $p < 0.05$, only at the highest (12th) grade level.

Otherwise, internals and externals did not differ, either in the percentage of those who tried but stopped smoking or drinking, or in the reasons (*e.g.*, friends, curiosity, control of behavior, escape from problems) for smoking or drinking, or opinions of self since smoking or drinking. In fact, internals and externals were similar in their increased opinions of self since smoking or drinking and in their expressed desire not to stop smoking or drinking. (Analysis by grade level was not computed owing to the numerous occasions of low or zero cell frequencies.)

DISCUSSION

(T)

Obviously, at these age levels, internals and externals do not behave similarly in regard to both smoking pot and drinking alcohol; the groups differed overall in drinking but not smoking, and they exhibited different developmental trends.

Regarding pot smoking, the occurrence of differences at the 7th grade level only and the increasingly higher percentage of smokers by grade level suggest that both groups increasingly engage in the behavior but that internals hold out a little longer, in a developmental sense. At some point, internals apparently decide that it is to their benefit to smoke pot. Perhaps this changeover occurs where the balance swings from adherence to parental standards to adherence to peer culture standards. This adherence to peer standards would not be inconsistent with internal directedness if the individual views himself as having a voice in establishing these standards. Further, the absence of a predicted (Berzins and Ross, 1973; Goss and Morosko, 1970) higher incidence of pot smoking by internals than externals (based on the facilitation of personal control) could thus be explained if both groups are responding to the highly probable peer culture versus parental standards dynamic.

Similarly, the prediction that more internals than externals would drink was not founded. Indeed, the two instances of significant differences (12th grade and all grades combined) indicated a higher incidence of externals who drank than internals. While drinking may also convey the same unifying effect for the peer culture (in opposition to adult values), the effect evidently occurs at different grade levels (*i.e.*, at later rather than earlier grades) than for pot smoking. The nature of this differential effect seems plausible given society's ready acceptance of drinking contrasted with its legalistic nonacceptance of drug-related behaviors typically associated with today's youth culture. Further, to expect to find more internals than externals drinking at this age range, on the basis of control by addiction, is probably premature, given the improbability of extended addiction by the present population.

The assumption that the peer culture-parental standards dynamic has an interactive effect with the locus of control variable is certainly open to investigation. Based on this study, one might hypothesize that the magnitude of differences between peer culture and parental standards influences not only the onset but also the convergence or divergence of behaviors in internally and externally controlled teenagers.

Concluding, the authors are concerned, from a rehabilitation point of view, that those who engaged in alcohol and pot smoking behaviors generally did not want to stop and that their opinions of themselves had increased—both attitudes suggestive of increased feelings of control associated with the use of consciousness-altering substances.

ACKNOWLEDGMENTS

The authors wish to thank Karen Guthrie for assistance in data analysis, Lynne Hudson for helpful suggestions, and Sheila Hackler for typing the manuscript.

REFERENCES

Anon., 1975: Alcohol and marijuana—Spreading menace among teenagers. *U.S. News and World Report* (November 24). Pp. 28-30.

Berzins, J. I.; Ross, W. F., 1973: Locus of control among opiate addicts. *Journal of Consulting and Clinical Psychology, 40*: 84-91.

Goss, A.; Morosko, T. E., 1970: Relation between a dimension of internal-external control and the MMPI with an alcoholic population. *Journal of Consulting and Clinical Psychology, 34*: 189-92.

Hjelle, L. A.; Clouser, R., 1970: Internal-external control of reinforcement in smoking behavior. *Psychological Reports, 26*: 562.

Lefcourt, H. M., 1976: *Locus of Control: Current Trends in Theory and Research.* Wiley, New York.

Palmer, R. D., 1971: Parental perception and perceived locus of control in psychopathology. *Journal of Personality, 3*: 420-31.

Rotter, J. B., 1966: Generalized expectancies for internal versus external control of reinforcement. *Psychological Monographs, 80* (Whole No. 609).

Reprints of this paper are available from Dr William F. Cox, Department of Educational Psychology, University of Toledo, Toledo, Ohio 43606, U.S.A.

Reprinted from *The Journal of Social Behavior and Personality*, 6(2): 191-194, 1978. Copyright © 1978 by the Society for Personality Research, Inc. Used with permission.

GA1325

ACTIVITY NO.	KEY	ACTIVITY	REFER TO PAGE(S)	DATE COMPLETED
AP4 (T)	OC	Develop a computerized data base that features the names and addresses of students who pursue advanced schooling and the awards they received as a result of science fair activity. Use this data for support in writing a grant proposal for funding of a science fair program.	239, 247, 301	

TIPS FOR THE TEACHER

Supporting Data for Grant Proposal Activity

Keeping long-term, accurate, up-to-date records of student accomplishments as a result of science fair activity can lead to the funding of grant proposals that support future science fair programs. A spread sheet of student accomplishments may look like this:

Name of Student	First SF Exp.	ES Grad.	JHI Grad.	HS Grad.	Scholarship	Awards	Degree	College	Employment
Curie, Michelle	1985	1986	1988	1992	Academic $2000	Blue— State Sci. Fair			

Using a survey, gather data from participants who participated in past science fair programs. Elicit reactions from students on how well the science fair program helped them develop the following skills for use in later life: public speaking skills, research skills, writing skills, organizational skills, family involvement, community involvement and self-fulfillment. Tally the results of the survey and use to support the need section in a grant proposal to continue the Science Fair Mentorship Program.

NOTES:

GA1325

ACTIVITY NO.	KEY	ACTIVITY	REFER TO PAGE(S)	DATE COMPLETED
AP5 ⓣ	OC	Write and submit a grant proposal to obtain funding for next year's Science Fair Mentorship Program.	23-24, 302-307	

TIPS FOR THE TEACHER
Grant Proposal Writing

Grant proposals can be written to obtain funding for science fair programs. Go to the library. Examine a copy of a book that lists city, state and national charitable foundations. Write a letter to those foundations that specialize in funding projects for education. In the letter, briefly outline the nature of your Science Fair Mentorship Program. Explain why you request support from the foundation to run the program. Request a copy of the guidelines for writing a grant proposal and an application from the foundation. Follow the guidelines exactly when you write the proposal. Present data to support the need for funding your proposal. Obtain appropriate signatures from school personnel. Submit the proposal to the foundation. If funded, send a thank-you note and carry out the project with zest. Keep accurate records for use in writing a final report to the foundation. If not funded, submit another request to a different foundation. Hard work pays off. Eventually you will succeed. Students will benefit from your efforts.

SAMPLE LETTER TO A FOUNDATION

Date _____

Dear _____ :

During the next school year, we plan to involve our students in a unique Science Fair Mentorship Program. As avid teachers of science, our major goal in the program is to provide students an opportunity to conduct a scientific research study under the careful guidance of a mentor in the community, a person knowledgeable in a subject area such as a physician, veterinarian or engineer.

In order to reach our goal of having a successful Science Fair Mentorship Program, we need your support. As a result of a pilot project this year, we learned that funds are needed for specialized science equipment, such as thermometers and other scientific materials to help our students in their studies. Thus, the purpose of our request is to obtain funding to cover the cost of these materials.

Please send a copy of the grant proposal guidelines and an application used when writing a grant proposal to your foundation. Thank you for your consideration.

Sincerely,

NOTES: A copy of a funded proposal for a Science Fair Mentorship Program is found on pages 303-307. Modify this proposal to meet your situation. When writing your proposal, follow the guidelines obtained from a charitable foundation in your area exactly. Good luck. Students will be the beneficiaries of your efforts.

GA1325

PROPOSAL FOR GRANT-TO-TEACHERS

(T)

Date: _____29 May 1989_____

To develop a Science Fair Mentorship Program that will encourage fifth-grade students to become involved in hands-on science fair projects.
(Describe your project very briefly. For example, "Develop a course in human relations for ninth graders.")

Amount: ___$3000.00___

Name: Mr., Mrs., Miss ____Dr. Jerry DeBruin____   Year of Birth: __1941__

School: Stranahan Elementary School, Toledo, Ohio 43615   District: Sylvania School District
School Address: 3840 Holland-Sylvania Road, Toledo, Ohio 43615
Home Address: 7321 Gwenn Court, Sylvania, Ohio 43560
Telephone Numbers and Area Codes: School 419-885-7927   Home 419-885-2932

Higher Education: Includes credits toward incomplete advanced degrees

Institution	School or Department	Years From	To	Degree	Major Subject	Minor Subject
U. of Illinois	El. Ed.	1969	1972	Ph.D.	El. Ed.	Science Ed.
U. of Illinois	El. Ed.	1968	1969	M.Ed.	El. Ed.	Science Ed.
U. of Wisconsin	El. Ed.	1962	1966	B.S.	El. Ed.	Phys. Ed.

Years of Classroom Teaching Experience:

Elementary and Secondary Teaching Experience Under Contract:
From __1966__   To __1968__

(Has taught all grade levels in some capacity as graduate student and professor)
Other pertinent experience: The University of Toledo—1972 to Present—Professor, Elementary Science Education

Ohio certification _____ Provisional _____ Professional _____ Permanent: Year Issued:
___x___ Intensive Science Provisional: 1985

Details of the Proposal

On these pages, please use this outline as a guide in explaining your proposal to the foundation.

  I. Full description of the project and its purpose
  II. Your special qualifications for carrying out the project
  III. The results anticipated from the project
  IV. Proposed means for evaluating the project
  V. Proposed methods for reporting the results of the project
    A. To the foundation
    B. To the educational community
  VI. Dates the project will begin and end
  VII. Estimates of expenses (List or describe items included.)
    A. Professional time
    B. Nonprofessional personnel services
    C. Necessary supplies not normally supplied by the school
    D. Necessary travel, accommodations, registrations, etc.
    E. Other (specify)
    F. Total

VIII. A statement why you believe this project should be supported by the foundation
  IX. The application should not exceed the form and, if necessary, two pages
   X. Additional comments if desired

I. Full description of the project and its purpose
    The purpose of this project is to develop a Science Fair Mentorship Program that encourages fifth-grade students to do hands-on science fair projects. The goal of the project is to maximize student potential by using methods of pure scientific research and original data collection. The objective of identifying students who have an interest in science and providing them with enrichment experience will be reached.

    The primary objective of the project is to involve students in hands-on science fair projects under the guidance of experienced mentors. By matching fifth-grade students with mentors (undergraduate students) from the University of Toledo, medical personnel (researchers) at the Medical College of Ohio and retired personnel (skill trades people from local businesses), youngsters will be involved in a planned course of action over a period of six months. With the use of contracts, students will have the opportunity to seek assistance from their teachers, university undergraduate students, medical researchers and retired personnel as they work on science fair projects of their choice. This plan will be developed so that each student will receive individualized attention from teachers, undergraduate education majors, medical researchers and retired people when developing their science fair projects. The program is tailored so students can independently collect scientific information about a science topic and then develop science process skills that extend well beyond those experienced in regular classroom activity.

    A vast majority of students often lack the guidance and supplies needed to conduct scientific research and the know-how to visually display the results of their work. Instructional materials and experiences designed to motivate students in science will be designed to expose youngsters to scientific methods through practical hands-on research. This creates the necessity for organized planning, providing opportunities to consult with experts in various fields of science, channeling interest in science as a career, showcasing scientific talent by involvement in a school science fair, entrance into other area competitions and guiding each student in the selection of a project that lies within his/her range of ability. In the future it is hoped that these students will continue to conduct research and enter their results in the Junior Science Humanities Symposium.

    The quality of science teaching will be increased at each of three levels: classroom teachers at Stranahan School, preservice elementary education students at the University of Toledo and researchers at the Medical College of Ohio. Retired personnel will also gain a sense of accomplishment as they help students build materials and visual displays to show the results of the students' research. Ultimately, the quality of science education will be upgraded with the creation of a model that can be replicated in other schools across the nation.

II. Your special qualifications for carrying out the project
     Dr. Jerry DeBruin
     *Professor of Elementary Science Education, 17 years
     *Director of two NSF grants for teachers, 2 years
     *Northwest Ohio Jennings Outstanding Educator Award, 1986
     *University of Toledo Outstanding Educator Award, 1986
     *University of Toledo Outstanding Teacher Award, 1984
     *Leader of University of Toledo Exemplary Science Education Program. National Science Teachers
       Association Award for one of seven top science education programs in the United States, 1986.
     *Author of 23 books for teachers, parents and youngsters and over 170 educational publications

III. The results anticipated from the project
      The primary anticipated result of this Science Fair Mentorship Program is to develop and carry out a successful science fair and increase the involvement of students in doing hands-on science fair projects at Stranahan Elementary School. Academic excellence and scientific literacy will be achieved as students have opportunities to operate at higher intellectual levels beyond those experienced in a regular classroom setting.

GA1325

All youngsters will have access to experienced mentors and ample supplies that promote scientific investigation. Learning disabled students, through participation in hands-on science research, will receive recognition and acclaim which should further increase their desire to achieve excellence. Gifted science students will also receive recognition and commendations for their efforts. Exposure to experts acting as mentors, will increase personal self-esteem, peer relationships and the self-concepts of students involved in the project.

Significant integration of academic disciplines such as science, mathematics, language arts, social studies, communication skills, art and industrial arts in the presentation of a project will be an additional anticipated result of this project. By working with retired personnel skilled in building trades, students will gain practical experience in building materials and developing a proper visual display of their research results.

A well-conceived plan for planning, developing, organizing, presenting and evaluating a science project suitable for entry into a science fair is expected to evolve. This experience provides students with an opportunity to compete and excel at a local school science fair and in area science fair competitions. In addition to the students, the school system will benefit as a result of the students' effort. The project will be exemplary in that it will contribute to a greater public appreciation of educational opportunities offered in the school system. (See *Bulletin*, Vol. 18, No. 1, April 1990.)

IV. Proposed means for evaluating the project
   —Increased interest in and numbers of science fair projects
   —Increased numbers of science fair entrants in science fairs
   —Successful development and implementation of a local science fair
   —Objective and subjective forms completed by students, teachers, mentors, retired personnel, media representatives, medical researchers, parents and administrators involved in the project
   —Greater community involvement
   —Greater parental involvement

V. Proposed methods for reporting the results of the project
   A. The foundation will be appraised of the results of all aspects of the project in writing via direct mail within two months after conclusion of the project.
   B. The results of this project will be submitted to editors of publications related to the school system, University of Toledo, Medical College of Ohio and organizations for retired personnel. The science fair will be publicized via intensive media coverage. Articles will also be submitted to various educational and medical journals in addition to those appropriate for retired people.

VI. Dates the project will begin and end
   Begin date: 1 October 1989
   End date: 31 March 1990
   These dates reflect student involvement at both the local school and university levels. University students will enroll in a two-quarter sequence of classes, fall and winter quarters, from September 1989 through March 1990. Thus, undergraduate education majors at the University of Toledo will act as mentors for the fifth-grade students for the duration of the project. In addition, the undergraduate teacher education students will be involved with classroom teachers in the actual setup and implementation of the science fair itself. By the end of this experience, these future teachers should be competent in the implementation of their own science fairs when they become full-time teachers.

VII. Estimates of expenses (List or describe items included.)
   A. Professional time

No
Remuneration

   1. Project Director: Dr. Jerry DeBruin
   Coordinates University of Toledo students with fifth-grade students in conjunction with university classes. Attends mentor sessions and science fair. Responsible for overall budgetary concerns such as dissemination of funds for various supplies and activities.

GA1325

$500	2. Teachers (3) Fifth Grade (Ruth Flaskamp, Carolyn Boellner, Karen Sigler) Coordinate science projects at Stranahan School, science fair, disseminate materials, collate packets, write letters and memos, make initial presentations, assist students with projects, send mail, answer questions, disseminate supplies, write evaluation forms and final report.
No Remuneration	3. Coordinator at Medical College of Ohio: Dr. Frank Saul Coordinates meetings of medical college researchers with fifth-grade students and university mentors. Three meetings for duration of the project.
$500	4. Building Trades Specialist: Mr. Zeny Pytlinski, et al. (retired) Assists students in the construction of appropriate science fair materials and displays. The building of ancillary equipment for science fair projects is also included as part of these duties.
No Remuneration	5. Medical College of Ohio Researchers (5) Coordinator, Dr. Frank Saul, will identify five researchers who will meet with the fifth-grade students and their university mentors on three separate occasions to provide expertise in the development of science fair projects.
No Remuneration	6. University of Toledo Mentors (Project is considered part of university course requirements.)

B. Nonprofessional personnel services

$125	1. Secretary Typing and duplication of letters, announcements, invitations, materials for judges and news releases.

C. Necessary equipment/supplies

$1775	1. Materials for visual displays. Triple wall, plastic strips, stencils, latex-based paint, construction paper, poster board. 2. Packets of materials for science fair judges and refreshments. 3. Awards for science fair participants. 4. Resource materials and reference books on science fair projects. 5. Film for the development of a slide presentation and scrapbook; videotapes, cassette tapes and slide trays; tapes for reviewing practice science fair presentations; and slides for a permanent record of science fair projects will be needed. 6. Medical College of Ohio mentor. Supplies and laboratory materials for mentors will be issued upon request. These materials will replace supplies used as a result of the project. 7. Certificates of Appreciation for University of Toledo students, Medical College personnel and retirees for placement in personal and professional files.

D. Travel, accommodations, registrations

$100	1. Local travel to acquire science supplies and attend meetings with mentors from the Medical College of Ohio, University of Toledo and experienced teachers who run successful science fairs.

Total
$3000.00

GA1325

VIII. A statement why you believe this project should be supported by the foundation

With financial assistance from the foundation, this original and innovative Science Fair Mentorship Program will feature the development of science fair projects and will significantly improve the quality of science education in the district in the following ways: First, a successful science fair experience will be planned and carried out by classroom teachers and university undergraduate students acting as a team. Second, students will benefit from the expertise and experience of their teachers, undergraduate university teacher education students, medical researchers and retired personnel. Third, the program will develop in students a strong sense of pride and will promote a positive image of the school in the eyes of members of the community. Fourth, by acting as mentors, university undergraduate teacher education students will gain knowledge of science concepts and how youngsters learn science. In addition, the university students will learn how to set up and carry out a successful science fair. Fifth, the program will provide an opportunity for retired people to share their vast experience and expertise with students. In the process, the experience will reinforce in retired personnel a sense of pride in their continued contributions to society. Sixth, researchers at the Medical College of Ohio will gain an appreciation of how students learn science. The experience will impress upon the researchers the critical role they play as role models in attracting students to the field of science. All personnel involved in the program will understand fully that a science fair winner is proof of academic excellence, scholastic effort and creativity. The mentors should gain a sense of pride in knowing that behind every science fair participant is a mentor whose dedication has helped some person become the best person he/she could be. In conclusion, funding of this proposal will promote the major mission of education "to foster the development of young people to the maximum possible extent through improving the quality of teaching in secular elementary and secondary schools."

X. Additional comments

Thank you for the opportunity to present to you a program that will help people become the best people they can be. Your efforts will be graciously appreciated. I look forward to continued growth as a result of this program.

Superintendent's Endorsement

I have examined this proposal and approve it as a worthwhile project for this school system.
The applicant in my judgment is well-qualified to carry out the project.
The estimates of expenses appear to be realistic for the successful completion of the project.

(Additional comments)

After reviewing this proposal, I find it to be of value to the Sylvania City Schools and to Stranahan Elementary School. The persons listed are highly qualified to carry out the grant and the budgetary arrangements appear to be adequate and realistic. In addition, as I understand the proposal, the activities are to be carried out primarily outside the school day. The school district will provide the classroom space and any available science equipment that may be needed to conduct the various experiments.

I endorse the applicant's request for this Grant-to-Teachers in the amount of $ 3000.00

Robert W. Zimpfer	Robert W. Zimpfer
Signature of Superintendent	Type Name of Superintendent
6850 Monroe St., Sylvania, Ohio 43560	(419) 885-7900 May 15, 1989
Address	Telephone Date

GA1325

REFLECTIONS ON A SCIENCE FAIR MENTORSHIP PROGRAM

Levels of Participation in a Science Fair Mentorship Program

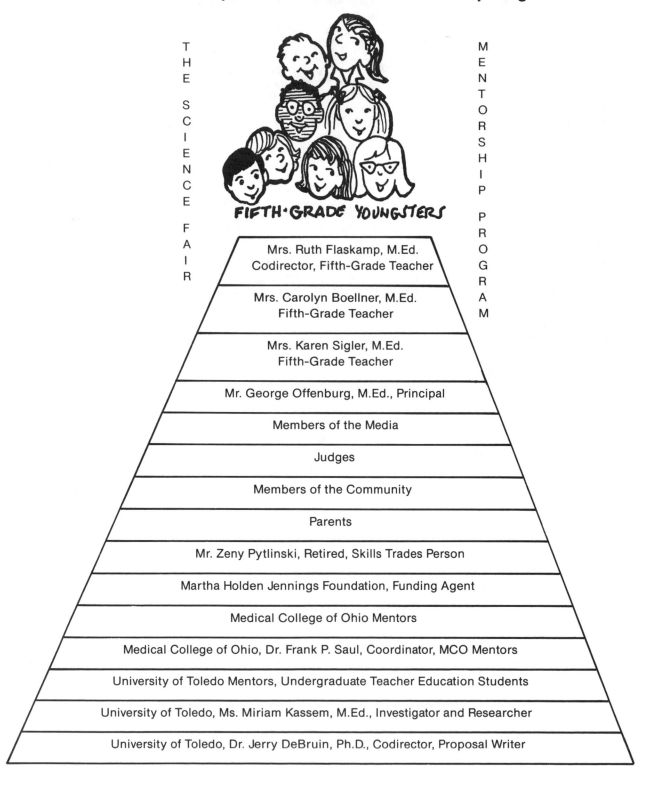

FIFTH-GRADE YOUNGSTERS

THE SCIENCE FAIR

MENTORSHIP PROGRAM

Mrs. Ruth Flaskamp, M.Ed.
Codirector, Fifth-Grade Teacher

Mrs. Carolyn Boellner, M.Ed.
Fifth-Grade Teacher

Mrs. Karen Sigler, M.Ed.
Fifth-Grade Teacher

Mr. George Offenburg, M.Ed., Principal

Members of the Media

Judges

Members of the Community

Parents

Mr. Zeny Pytlinski, Retired, Skills Trades Person

Martha Holden Jennings Foundation, Funding Agent

Medical College of Ohio Mentors

Medical College of Ohio, Dr. Frank P. Saul, Coordinator, MCO Mentors

University of Toledo Mentors, Undergraduate Teacher Education Students

University of Toledo, Ms. Miriam Kassem, M.Ed., Investigator and Researcher

University of Toledo, Dr. Jerry DeBruin, Ph.D., Codirector, Proposal Writer

TIPS ON HOW TO DEVELOP A SCIENCE FAIR MENTORSHIP PROGRAM

Dear Teachers and Parents:

The Science Fair Mentorship Program, shown on page 308, was funded with the proposal found on pages 303-307. You, as teachers and parents, can run a similar program with careful planning and organization. After personal reflection, the following tips are offered to those who want to develop a program of this nature:

1. Contact the principal of the school. Obtain the principal's support for the Science Fair Mentorship Program.

2. Contact fellow staff members and seek their support.

3. Contact support personnel such as librarians, secretaries, food service workers and maintenance personnel. Clear the date for the Science Fair with them early in the school year.

4. After you have received favorable commitments from the principal, fellow staff members and support personnel, survey parents to elicit their views on the feasibility of a Science Fair Mentorship Program. Parents need to have an opportunity to provide input into the program.

5. Involve all students at the particular grade level first; then later on involve students from other grade levels.

6. Introduce the program to the students. Brainstorm ideas for research topics. Take them through a practice science fair experience. Help students narrow down their topics.

7. Help students gather research materials for each individual topic.

8. Identify mentors from the community and match mentors with students by topic area.

9. Stress an interdisciplinary approach to science fair activity with the inclusion of mathematics, science, language arts, social studies, music, physical education and other disciplines into the study of science.

10. Gather books that have tips on how to run high-quality science fair programs and how to involve students in science fair activities.

11. Introduce and carry out the program with a feeling of excitement and adventure.

12. Keep a daily diary/log of science fair activity noting successful components of the program and aspects you would change in the future.

13. Tell others about your program by submitting an article for publication and/or presenting the results of your program at a local, state or national conference or meeting.

14. Relax and enjoy the satisfying feeling of helping students become the best students they can be.

Your friend,

Jerry DeBruin

Jerry DeBruin

GA1325

ACTIVITY NO.	KEY	ACTIVITY	REFER TO PAGE(S)	DATE COMPLETED
AP6 (T)	OC	Write and submit a proposal for presenting your Science Fair Mentorship Program at a local, state or national conference. Develop plans for presentation. Submit your proposal for acceptance. When presenting, include science fair students and their works as part of your presentation.	310-311	

TIPS FOR THE TEACHER

Presentation at Professional Conferences

Proposals for the presentation of the results of a successful Science Fair Mentorshop Program at a professional meeting can be written to gain further recognition for students' accomplishments. Many local, state, national and international organizations have yearly meetings at which teachers share their ideas with other teachers. Read announcements of upcoming events disseminated by organizations. Complete and submit a Program Proposal that describes your program. When accepted, present your science fair program to others at the professional meeting. If possible, include students as part of your presentation. The experience will be a rewarding one for all involved.

NOTES: A copy of a completed Program Proposal is found on page 311.

GA1325

PROGRAM PROPOSAL

Please type information as you wish it to appear in the convention program.

Presenters

1. Name Dr. Jerry DeBruin

   Dept. Elementary Education

   School/Inst. University of Toledo

   Work Address 2801 W. Brancroft St.

   City, St., Zip Toledo, OH 43606

   Work Phone (419) 537-2689

   Home Phone Phone (419) 885-2932

2. Name _____

   Dept. _____

   School/Inst. _____

   Work Address _____

   City, St., Zip _____

   Work Phone _____

   Home Phone _____

Additional presenters are listed on the reverse side.

Presider: Complete only if you wish to name the presider for your presentation.

Name _____ Dept. _____ School/Inst. _____

Work Add. _____ City _____ St. ____ Zip ____ Phone (____)_____

Session Data: (See reverse side for definitions.)

I. Type of Session
   ____ Hands-On Workshop (60 min.)
   ____ Demonstration (30 min.)
   _x_ Demonstration (60 min.)
   ____ Contributed Paper (15 min.)
   ____ Contributed Paper (30 min.)
   ____ Panel (60 min.)
   ____ Other _____

II. Subject Area
    Teacher Preparation

IV. Equipment Requirement
    ____ Overhead Projector
    _x_ Slide Projector
    ____ Other(s) Specify
        ½" VHS _____
    NSTA will provide only Apple and
    IBM computers.

III. Intended Audience
    ____ Preschool
    _x_ Elementary
    _x_ Middle/Jr. HS
    _x_ High School
    _x_ College
    ____ Supervision
    ____ General

V. How many participants can you accommodate at your session? ____ 30-50   _x_ 51-80

VI. Session Title: Science Fair Mentorship Program

Brief Description (25-word limit): This session focuses on the funding, planning, production, judging and evaluation of a unique Science Fair Mentorship Program. Take home a comprehensive science fair packet.

VII. Abstract (150-200 words—Use reverse side.)

VIII. Signature _____Jerry DeBruin_____ Date of Submission 22 June 1991

ABSTRACT

The goal of this session is to provide information on the planning, funding, implementation, judging and evaluation of a unique Science Fair Mentorship Program. In the program, students are afforded an opportunity to conduct a science research study of their choice under the careful guidance of a mentor, a person experienced in a topic area. Such mentors include researchers from a medical college and university, undergraduate teacher education students at a university and scientists from the community including physicians, veterinarians and engineers.

After an initial hands-on science fair activity, participants attending the session will view a slide presentation that features students on research location and a brief videotape of the culminating science fair event. Students who participated in past Science Fair Mentorship Programs will also share their experiences.

This session supports current research findings on the value of mentors and the role they play in the teaching of science and the promotion of science as a viable career choice. A comprehensive Science Fair Mentorship Program packet that provides tips on how to accomplish this task will be given to each participant who attends this session.

ACTIVITY NO.	KEY	ACTIVITY	REFER TO PAGE(S)	DATE COMPLETED
AP7 ⓣ	OC	Plan next year's Science Fair by visiting other classrooms to describe your program to potential participants. Invite your experienced science fair students to accompany you on your visits. Have them describe their experiences to future science fair participants.	2-7, 312	

TIPS FOR THE TEACHER

Student Recruiters

After the results of the Science Fair have been tabulated, begin to recruit students for next year's Science Fair Mentorship Program. Ask your principal for permission to show a short videotape of past science fair students and their projects at a year-end, all-school assembly. Place photos and science fair materials in a display case. Have a photo album of science fair photos readily available for future participants to examine. Encourage experienced science fair students to accompany you on visits to other classrooms to recruit additional students for next year's Science Fair Mentorship Program.

NOTES:

GA1325

ACTIVITY NO.	KEY	ACTIVITY	REFER TO PAGE(S)	DATE COMPLETED
AP8 (T)	OC	Publicize the date and entry deadline for the next year's Science Fair before the school year ends.	28-30, 313	

TIPS FOR THE TEACHER
Set the Date and Entry Deadline

Before the school year comes to a close, meet with the principal and other support personnel to set the date and entry deadline for next year's Science Fair. Place announcements in end-of-year correspondence to parents, students and members of the community.

NOTES:

GA1325

ACTIVITY NO.	KEY	ACTIVITY	REFER TO PAGE(S)	DATE COMPLETED
AP9 (T)	OC	Encourage students to continue their scientific investigations under the guidance of mentors in the community. Summer employment and hours of enjoyment are often the net result of a Science Fair Mentorship Program.	138-139, 314	

TIPS FOR THE TEACHER

Summer Science

As a result of the Science Fair Mentorship Program, many students may continue their studies of related work during the summer. Encourage them to continue their scientific investigations or look for new science fair projects over the summer. Older, experienced science fair students often gain summer employment because of working with mentors on a science fair project during the regular school year.

NOTES:

GA1325

ACTIVITY NO.	KEY	ACTIVITY	REFER TO PAGE(S)	DATE COMPLETED
AP10 (T)	OC	Relax. Give credit to those who have helped you receive the recognition that you richly deserve for planning and carrying out a successful Science Fair Mentorship Program.	315-317	

TIPS FOR THE TEACHER

Relax: Enjoy the Feeling of Accomplishment and Contentment

After the school year has ended, take time to relax and enjoy the feelings of satisfaction and accomplishment. Give special thanks to those who have helped you make the Science Fair Mentorship Program a successful one. Read the following verse carefully and think about what you have accomplished.

> There's no thrill in easy sailing,
>   When the sky is clear and blue;
> There's no joy in merely doing
>   Things which anyone can do.
>
> But there is some satisfaction
>   That is mighty sweet to take,
> When you've reached a destination
>   That you thought you couldn't make.
>
>   —Author Unknown

NOTES:

GA1325

TEAMING UP FOR THE SAKE OF RESEARCH

Anna Chan is very interested in Alzheimer's disease. She's met some patients, and she is learning a lot about their behavior and feelings. She knows that the illness effects the brain causing loss of memory, and she is simply interested in learning as much as she can about it.

Anna is one of 15 fifth grade students researching some very sophisticated scientific topics. Equally as challenging, some of her classmates are investigating lupus and leukemia, while others are studying the development and functions of the brain.

Getting Help From the Pros

These scientifically-minded students began their investigations last fall when they joined a mentorship program designed to get students involved in "hands-on" science fair projects. The students are fifth graders at Stranahan Elementary School in Sylvania, Ohio (west of Toledo). Their mentors are student teachers from The University of Toledo, medical personnel from The Medical College of Ohio and interested persons from the Sylvania community. Individualized attention from these adults keeps the students' interest high, allows them access to behind-the-scenes information and challenges them to do their very best.

The mentorship program was started by Dr. Jerry DeBruin, professor, elementary education, The University of Toledo, with a Grant-to-Teachers from the Martha Holden Jennings Foundation. Past successes at the high school and junior high school levels inspired him to design a mentorship experience for younger children, and fifth grade teacher Mrs. Ruth Flaskamp was eager to get her students involved.

Interested students were selected for the program from the school's three fifth grade classes on the basis of ability, commitment and parental support. Once on board, they chose a topic to study that was being researched at the medical college. Then they were matched with two mentors, student teachers from Dr. DeBruin's science methods class.

Students and mentors were required to spend at least one hour together each week, but often that stretched to two or three. The groups met wherever it was convenient — at home, the public library or the university. At times, students were even excused from class to meet their mentors during school hours.

Students in the science mentorship program get the feel of a real human brain.

Three visits to the medical college put the students and mentors in touch with practicing research physicians. The doctors spent several hours with the groups showing them the labs, helping with their literature search, critiquing their work and offering suggestions for their final projects.

"It's great to see a doctor from the medical college sitting down with a fifth grade youngster at a computer terminal doing a literature search," says Dr. DeBruin. "All these people working together in that cooperative spirit is really a sight to see."

Science On Display

The results of the students' research were showcased at a day-long science fair held in February. With the help of a retired community member, the students constructed large display boards to mount their work. Photographs, data and drawings detailed just how much they had learned.

"In addition to the technical information, the students learned that there's a lot more out there than just what is in the four walls of a fifth grade classroom," says Dr. DeBruin. "They've realized that the world of science is a very exciting world. Just being around their mentors has opened their eyes to what it is really all about."

HANDS-ON SCIENCE

"The ultimate goal of the program is to get them interested in science careers," says Mrs. Flaskamp, "but there's so much more being offered. They're getting a real life idea as to how important reading and writing is and just how much work is involved in doing research."

While the fifth graders undeniably learned much from the experience, Dr. DeBruin adds that the student teachers may have benefited the most of all.

"They learned how to set up a science fair, they gained confidence in their teaching skills and they realized what youngsters really are capable of doing," says Dr. DeBruin. "I'm very confident they can go out and do the same things when they become teachers."

FOR FURTHER INFORMATION CONTACT:

Dr. Jerry DeBruin
The University of Toledo
2801 W. Bancroft Street
Toledo, Ohio 43606

Mrs. Ruth Flaskamp
Stranahan Elementary
  School
3840 Holland-Sylvania Rd.
Sylvania, Ohio 43560

Students and mentors worked side-by-side for several months to put together hands-on displays for the science fair.

EPILOGUE

Science Fair Mentorship Program Receives Award

Each year the National Education Association's A+ Awards for Excellence in Education honor the real and creative contributions of association members who have participated in programs or projects to enhance learning opportunities for students.

The annual A+ Awards—first presented in 1988—are designed to demonstrate school employee commitment to educational excellence and to salute the creative reform efforts now under way in school districts across the nation. The award winners serve as national examples of the many grass roots programs that are producing demonstrable achievements. (*NEA NOW: A Weekly Newsletter*, January 29, 1990. Copyright © 1990. Used with permission of the National Education Association, 1201 16th Street, N.W., Washington, D.C. 20036.)

During American Education Week in November 1990, leaders of the Science Fair Mentorship Program (see page 308) featured in this book received one of six national NEA A+ Awards for Excellence in Education. Notification of the award was subsequently reported in the December 1990 issue of *Ladies Home Journal*. We are deeply honored to receive such an award and thank all who have worked so hard to make this dream become a reality.

REFLECTIONS

Thirty-Five Years Ago: A Reflection

In 1957 as Commanding Officer of the U.S. Army Office of Ordnance Research at Duke University, the idea of a high school level science symposium entered my mind. After initial efforts, the first symposium, the North Carolina Junior Science Symposium, was held in 1958. In a few short years this small scale, grass roots community project grew into a prominent national program called the National Junior Science and Humanities Symposium. Little did I know at that time that thirty-five years later a parallel grass roots program for younger students interested in science would be born.

Thirty Years Ago: A Reflection

I initiated and directed the planning for the first National Junior Science and Humanities Symposium held at the U.S. Military Academy, West Point, New York, in April 1963. This national grass roots program was attended by 153 high school students and alternates who gave formal presentations of their research results to an audience interested in science. The format of the first program was established and a grass roots program of high school students who often conducted scientific research with experienced mentors was in place. Little did I know at that time that thirty years later a parallel grass roots mentorship program for young fifth-grade students interested in science would be born.

Twenty Years Ago: A Reflection

After retiring from the Army, I became Special Assistant to the Vice President of Research and Engineering at the Owens-Illinois Corporate Headquarters in Toledo, Ohio. In keeping with past practice, I established a State of Ohio Junior Science and Humanities Symposium in 1964 followed by the Toledo Area Local Junior Science and Humanities Symposium in 1967. The promotion of scientific research by high school students with subsequent presentation of research results at the Symposium was paramount. New recruits were needed. It was then that I met Dr. Jerry DeBruin who twenty years later would lead a nationally recognized Science Fair Mentorship Program for young budding scientists that would act as a "feeder system" for my own Junior Science and Humanities Symposium.

A Final Reflection

It is 1991. Thirty-five years have passed since the idea of a National Junior Science and Humanities Symposium entered my mind. From the beginning of a grass roots program of one state symposium in 1958, I have seen the National Junior Science and Humanities Symposium grow into the current program of forty-six regional symposia and one national symposium. I now realize that a parallel grass roots program can be implemented at an earlier age and later act as a "feeder system" for my own symposia.

Twenty years have also passed since I first met Dr. Jerry DeBruin. Jerry has been Program and Program Evaluation Chairperson of the Toledo Area Junior Science and Humanities Symposium for twenty years and the Ohio Junior Science and Humanities Symposium for six years. Jerry also recruits students to become involved in scientific research. His Science Fair Mentorship Program which features fifth-grade youngsters conducting scientific research under the guidance of experienced mentors is nationally recognized. Aptly described in this book, I see Jerry's grass roots program evolving into a prominent national program. I look forward to having these young budding scientists presenting the results of their science research at the Local, State, Regional and National Junior Science and Humanities Symposia in the not-so-distant future. Teachers and parents together using the wealth of material in this book could result in no less happening.

George F. Leist

Colonel George F. Leist, U.S. Army (Ret.)
Founder, Junior Science and Humanities Symposium

BIBLIOGRAPHY
1970-1990

Akron-Summit County Public Library. (1983). *Science Fair Project Index, 1973-1980*. Metuchen, NJ: The Scarecrow Press, Inc.

Baal, Harold. (1989). *Where's the Book? Science Projects*. Lakefield, ON: Communication Planning Consultants.

Beller, Joel. (1984). *So You Want to Do a Science Project!* New York: Arco Publishing, Inc.

Barman, Natalie S., and Charles Barman. (1989). *Addison-Wesley Science Fair Guide for Teachers*. Menlo Park: Addison-Wesley.

Berenstain, Stan, and Jan Berenstain. (1977). *The Berenstain Bears Science Fair*. New York: Random House.

Bishop, Cynthia, and Deborah Crowe. (1986). *Science Fair Project Index, 1981-1984*. Metuchen, NJ: The Scarecrow Press, Inc.

Blume, Stephen C. (1990). *Science Fair Handbook: A Resource for Teachers, Principals and Science Fair Coordinators*. Columbus, OH: Merrill.

Bombaugh, Ruth J. (1990). *Science Fair Success*. Hillside, NJ: Enslow Publishers.

Bonnet, Robert L., and G. Daniel Keen. (1989). *Botany: 49 Science Fair Projects*. Blue Ridge Summit, PA: Tab Books, Inc.

_____. (1989). *Earth Science: 49 Science Fair Projects*. Blue Ridge Summit, PA: Tab Books, Inc.

_____. (1989). *Environmental Science: Science Fair Projects*. Blue Ridge Summit, PA: Tab Books, Inc.

Caratello, John, and Patty Caratello. (1989). *All About Science Fairs*. Huntington Beach, CA: Teacher Created Materials, Inc.

_____. (1989). *Problem-Solving Science Investigations*. Huntington Beach, CA: Teacher Created Materials, Inc.

Carter, Constance. (1988). *Science Fair Projects*. (Report No. SE 050318). Washington, D.C.: Library of Congress. (ERIC Document Reproduction Service No. ED 303 339).

Darrow, Edward E. (1985). *The Science Workbook of Student Research Projects in Food-Agriculture-Natural Resources*. Columbus, OH: The Ohio State University, College of Agriculture.

DeBruin, Jerry. *Cardboard Carpentry*. Carthage, IL: Good Apple, Inc. (Available from JED and Associates, P.O. Box 7143 RC, Toledo, OH 43615).

_____. (1986). *Creative Hands-On Science Experiences*. Carthage, IL: Good Apple, Inc.

_____. (1990). *Creative Hands-On Science Cards & Activities*. Carthage: IL: Good Apple, Inc.

_____. (1989). *School Yard-Backyard Cycles of Science*. Carthage, IL: Good Apple, Inc.

DeBruin, Jerry, and Don Murad. (1988). *Look to the Sky*. Carthage, IL: Good Apple, Inc.

DeBruin, Jerry. (1987). *Scientists Around the World*. Carthage, IL: Good Apple, Inc.

Edmund, Robert M. *Your Science Project*. Barrington, NJ: Edmund Scientific Company.

GA1325

Fredericks, Anthony D., and Isaac Asimov. (1990) *The Complete Science Fair Handbook.* Glenview, IL: Good Year Books.

Gardner, Robert. (1989). *More Ideas for Science Projects.* New York: Franklin Watts.

Hillsborough County Public Schools. (1989). *Great Investigations One Step at a Time: A Teacher's Guide to Science Fairs and Science Olympics.* Tampa, FL: Hillsborough County Public Schools.

Iritz, Maxine H. (1987). *Science Fair: Developing a Successful and Fun Project.* Blue Ridge Summit, PA: Tab Books, Inc.

Lyon, Laurie A. (1980). *Guidelines for High School Students on Conducting Research in the Sciences.* Durham, NC: Moore Publishing Company.

Mann, Joanne. (1984). *Science Day Guide.* Columbus, OH: The Ohio Academy of Science.

Markle, Sandra. (1990). *The Young Scientist's Guide to Successful Science Projects.* New York, NY: Lothrop, Lee and Shepard Books.

Moeschl, Richard. (1988). *Exploring the Sky: 100 Projects for Beginning Astronomers.* Chicago, IL: Chicago Review Press.

Moore, Anne L. (1978). *Science Fair Projects.* Washington, D.C.: Library of Congress, Science and Technology Division.

Moorman, Thomas. (1974). *How to Make Your Science Project Scientific.* New York: Atheneum.

National Science Teachers Association. (1988). *Science Fairs and Projects: Grades K-8.* Washington, D.C.: National Science Teachers Association.

_____. (1988). *Science Fairs and Projects: Grades 7-12.* Washington, D.C.: The National Science Teachers Association.

Saul, Wendy, and Alan Newman. (1986). *Science Fairs.* New York: Harper and Row Publishers.

Science Service. (1971). *Thousands of Science Projects.* Washington, D.C.: Science Service.

Stoffer, Janet Y. (1975). *Science Fair Project Index, 1960-1972.* Metuchen, NJ: The Scarecrow Press, Inc.

Stoltzfus, John C., and Morris N. Young. (1972). *The Complete Guide to Science Fair Competition.* New York: Hawthorn Books, Inc.

Thomas, David A. (1988). *Math Projects for Young Scientists.* New York: Franklin Watts.

Van DeMan, Barry. (1980). *Nuts and Bolts: A Matter of Fact Guide to Science Fair Projects.* Harwood Heights, IL: The Science Man Press.

Varnerin, Robert E. (1980). *Chemistry Projects and Science Fairs.* Washington, D.C.: Chemical Manufacturers Association.

Webster, David. (1974). *How to Do a Science Project.* New York: Franklin Watts.

Wels, Bryon G. (1976). *Science Fair Projects.* New York: Drake Publishers, Inc.

World Book Encyclopedia. (1970). *Science Projects.* Chicago: Field Enterprises Education Corporation.

GA1325

AN INDEX TO REPRODUCIBLE PAGES FOR STUDENTS

This index features pages that can be reproduced for student use. Choose the pages appropriate for your situation. The pages are identified by this symbol:

GA1325

AN INDEX TO REPRODUCIBLE PAGES FOR PARENTS

This index features pages that can be reproduced for parent use. Choose the pages appropriate for your situation. The pages are identified by this symbol:

GA1325

AN INDEX TO REPRODUCIBLE PAGES FOR COMMUNITY MEMBERS

This index features pages that can be reproduced for community members. Choose the pages appropriate for your situation. The pages are identified by this symbol: Ⓒ

AN INDEX TO REPRODUCIBLE PAGES FOR SCIENCE FAIR JUDGES

This index features pages that can be reproduced for the judges. Choose the pages appropriate for your situation. The pages are identified by this symbol:

GA1325

AN INDEX TO REPRODUCIBLE PAGES FOR MEMBERS OF THE MEDIA

This index features pages that can be reproduced for use by members of the media. Choose the pages appropriate for your situation. The pages are identified by this symbol:

GA1325

Dr. Jerry DeBruin

MEET THE AUTHOR

Jerry is a teacher at The University of Toledo. He is a member of the Department of Elementary and Early Childhood Education and his specialty is science, although he truly enjoys all facets of education and life. Jerry was born and raised on a farm in Kaukauna, Wisconsin, and it was there that he nurtured his interest in science, the world around him and life in general. He has taught all grade levels in some capacity or another and currently spends a great deal of his time in schools helping teachers and youngsters. In addition to being the author of twenty-three books (available in such prestigious places as the Smithsonian Institute in Washington, D.C., National Air and Space Museum, National Museum of Natural History—National Museum of Man, National Museum of American History) and over 180 educational publications, Jerry is the recipient of many awards. Some of these include the 1984 Outstanding Teacher of the Year Award at The University of Toledo, the 1986 Martha Holden Jennings Outstanding Educator Award and the National Science Teachers Association 1986 Search for Excellence in Science Education Program Award. Being a local, state, regional, national and international consultant in science education, Jerry's main interest in life is to help people grow in awareness, knowledge and understanding of feelings toward themselves and others. His work nurtures his interest.

Mr. Charles Ortenblad

MEET THE ARTIST

Charles Ortenblad, a native of Colorado, is a self-employed communications consultant and illustrator who lives in Tucson, Arizona. Following high school in Omaha, Nebraska, Charlie joined the Army Security Agency. After his service, he moved to New York City. From 1969 to 1976 Charlie was Vice President/Creative Director of TCA Corporate Communications Division of the Benton and Bowles Advertising Agency.
In 1980 Charles began to concentrate most of his communicative abilities in illustration and cartooning for advertising agencies and publishers. His works appear in this Good Apple book and other Good Apple books written by Sister Judy Bisignano.

GA1325